MODERN GOTHIC

This lively collection of essays aims to chart the survival of the Gothic strain – the dark, the forbidding, the alienated, the fantastic – in a spectrum of popular and 'high cultural' forms of representation.

Modern Gothic showcases a variety of international scholars and their approaches to this mutable and ever-contemporary tradition. It offers information on the politics of neo-Gothic 'petrification' in the novels of Iain Banks and John Banville; of the horrors of the pre-Oedipal father in *Blue Velvet*; the Gothic unconscious of feminist criticism and of postmodern 'feminine' horror fiction; the Gothic spaces in the works of Toni Morrison; insights into 1950s body snatching and alien invasion; the emerging postcolonial Gothic; Ramsay Campbell's debt to traditional forms and wide-ranging essays on the novels of Isak Dinesen, Stephen King and Angela Carter.

An illuminating trip through postwar Gothic literature and film, using feminist, socio-cultural, postmodern and post-psychoanalytic frameworks, *Modern Gothic* is essential reading for all those interested in the genre.

Victor Sage is a Reader and Allan Lloyd Smith is a Senior Lecturer in the School of English and American Studies at the University of East Anglia.

edited by Victor Sage & Allan Lloyd Smith

MODERN GOTHIC

A reader

MANCHESTER UNIVERSITY PRESS

MANCHESTER AND NEW YORK

distributed exclusively in the USA by St. Martin's Press

Published by Manchester University Press
Oxford Road, Manchester M13 9NR, UK
and Room 400, 175 Fifth Avenue,
New York, NY 10010, USA

Distributed exclusively in the USA
by St. Martin's Press, Inc.,
175 Fifth Avenue, New York, NY 10010, USA

British Library Cataloguing-in-Publication Data
Catalogue record available from the British Library

Library of Congress Cataloging-in-Publication Data
Modern gothic: a reader / edited by Victor Sage and Allan Lloyd Smith.
      p.   cm.
    ISBN 0–7190–4207–0 (alk. paper). — ISBN 0–7190–4208–9 (alk. paper)
    1. Horror tales, English—History and criticism.   2. Horror tales, American—History and criticism.   3. English fiction—20th century—History and criticism.   4. American fiction—20th century—History and criticism.   5. Gothic revival (Literature)   I. Sage, Victor, 1942–   .   II. Smith, Allan Lloyd.
PR888.T3M63   1996
823′.087309—dc20   95–44012
                                                                                                      CIP

ISBN 0 7190 4207 0 *hardback*
ISBN 0 7190 4208 9 *paperback*

First published in 1996
00 99 98 97 96   10 9 8 7 6 5 4 3 2 1

Typeset in Dante by
Graphicraft Typesetters Limited, Hong Kong
Printed in Great Britain
by Bell & Bain Ltd, Glasgow

CONTENTS

INTRODUCTION

This collection of essays attempts to interpret the unmistakable presence, through structural or verbal allusion, or wholesale rewriting, of the Gothic in some of the fictions of the postwar period. The emblem of a characteristic running allusion to the Gothic tradition might be the one that David Seed picks out in his piece 'Alien Invasions by Body Snatchers and Related Creatures': namely, that Jack Finney's original 1955 novel, *The Body Snatchers*, made into the famous movie by Don Siegel, *Invasion of the Body Snatchers*, is an echo of Robert Louis Stevenson's short story 'The Body Snatchers' of 1884. Stevenson's tale itself looks back to Edinburgh in the 1820s, when the 'resurrection men', as the people who exhumed bodies for the medical trade were sardonically christened by the population, were performing their ghastly trade. The 1956 cult movie we are all familiar with carries in its title and its central motif a specific intertextual link between a group of texts in the history of Science Fiction, the Cold War context, and the Old Gothic. The Old Gothic, however, as the backdating of Stevenson's own tale suggests, doesn't stand still as a point of reference: even in the eighteenth century, it was itself an anarchic, popular, and indeed 'camp' recycling of the past, long before Sir Walter Scott sought to transform and rationalise it into an official literary genre, the so-called 'historical romance'; and its reappearance in the Victorian period, we can now see, turns out to be only one of its reappearances: the Gothic is a resistant strain, palpably recurrent in the popular and the literary culture of the postwar period.

Evidently, the Gothic is not merely a literary convention or a set of motifs: it is a language, often an anti-historicising language, which provides writers with the critical means of transferring an idea of the otherness of the past into the present. By the flickering light of neo-Gothic narratives, we see modernity, as Liliane Weissberg puts it in her essay on Toni Morrison, invented with a 'backward glance'.

And equally these writers testify to the liveliness and the variety of contexts in which the compositional vocabulary (scenic and linguistic) of this tradition continues to manifest itself. Modern Gothic – usable without attachment to a particular object – is not simply an allusion to its own *literary* past, a remote eighteenth-century genre; it is immediately recognisable to the contemporary sensibility – its features, for example, instantly capable of parody – as a distinctive aesthetic shorthand, a code of iteration, which tends to imply a critical relation between the present and the past. The strength of this unstable and corrosive code, it seems, lies in its paradoxical ability to flaunt and camouflage itself at one and the same time. As these essays demonstrate, there is no point in thinking of the Gothic as 'pure'; it is an apparent genre-badge which, the moment it is worn by a text, becomes an imperceptible catalyst, a transforming agent for other codes: the uncanny, a form of Gothic or fantastic effect quite central to modern fictions of screen and novel, is not one code but a kind of gap between codes, a point at which representation itself appears to fail, displace, or diffuse itself.

So the writers in this collection locate the labyrinth of the Gothic in a fascinating variety of contexts: in both the lightnesses and the dark spaces of the feminist unconscious; the postmodernist analysis of desire; the postcolonial discourses of domination and subjection; the psychoanalytic master-narrative of the Oedipus complex; the cultural history of the McCarthy era; the political topography of the Irish, Scottish, and Afro-American heritages; the landscape of Liverpool; the Canadian road narrative; the political aesthetics of slave literature; the serials, sequels, and resurrecting villains of the contemporary horror movie.

But these Gothic black spots, lurking like the sites of past road accidents in so many different contemporary contexts, are not simply deconstructive aporias transformed into spatial metaphors; they form in themselves textual negotiations with history, and the corollary of this critical preoccupation with the Gothic's latest history of itself is a description of a present whose very presentness is diminished and vitiated by irruptive images of the past.

Thus, though it is often treated as the perfect paradigm for the traditional Gothic, even that master narrative of the past, the Oedipal story itself, exhibits the tell-tale symptoms of a blind spot, a leak in the Freudian metalanguage, a site of repression, when confronted by the selfconsciousness of modern Gothic. Laura Mulvey, for example, scrutinises the significance of the self-conscious Gothicism of David Lynch's *Blue Velvet* (1986), excavating the the repressed content of Freud's original Oedipus narrative, and figuring the allusion to the 'pre-Oedipal father' in Lynch's film as a conflict between Freudian and Proppian models of the iterative power of popular folk tale. Ros Ballaster brings Isak Dinesen's *Seven Gothic Tales* (1934) face to face with the recent history of feminist criticism and by using the text to criticise the critics, exposes an unconscious deflection of the political allegory of the text in the psychological bias of commentary on the Gothic. Helen Stoddart, adopting a more 'dialectical' and philosophical approach, provides us with an equally positive critical reading of Dinesen's fictions, demonstrating that Dinesen's Gothic retellings constitute a witty rejection of the 'gravity' of male Cartesianism in favour of a very bearable lightness of female being. While David Punter's examination of the readerly problems of reconstruction (and rememoration) of the past in the reflexive iterations of Stephen King's Gothic, the reversal of remembering and forgetting, ambiguously reveals a hairline crack in the real and in the Oedipal master-narrative itself that purports to stabilise our relation to the past, concluding that these fictions can only be read in terms of 'the depths to which the historically real . . . will go to avoid the possibility of that which . . . smacks of the primal scene'.

Beate Neumeier's analysis of desire in Angela Carter's *The Infernal Desire Machines of Dr Hoffman* (1972), sees Carter's novel as a parody of psychoanalytic attempts to 'pen desire in a cage', revealing the inseparability of the fantastic and its Freudian interpretations, while the metalanguage is, conversely, incorporated into the narrative text. Suzanne Becker examines the figure of the sexual woman in postmodern feminist Gothic, concentrating on the conflict between covert and overt plots of Canadian novelist Aritha Van Herk's 1985 road novel, *No Fixed Abode*, and isolating its alienated desire for incessant motion as a metaphor for the horror of imprisonment 'within the feminine'.

Judie Newman, Victor Sage, Giles Menegaldo, and Liliane Weissberg arrive at another version of the Gothic's narrative relation between present and past. Newman argues that the Gothic register in the languages of postcolonial fiction, and specifically in the transformations of an international criminal case, that of Charles Sohbraj, into fiction by Ruth Prawer Jabvala, provides Jabvala with a strategy for negotiating the familiar *impasse* of collusion between dominant and submissive discourses in the postcolonial novel. Victor Sage finds that allusions to the Gothic castle or decaying dark house present themselves as the ironic site of resistance to contemporary historical process in the masterplots of the Scottish and Irish writers Iain Banks and John Banville, linking it to a dialectic between a-historic 'petrifaction' and its Other, 'incarnation', in which characters are able to join their own histories. Giles Menegaldo also updates the topographical theme: he examines the discourse of 'setting' in the 'urban Gothic' of Ramsay Campbell's Liverpool, in which he finds a development from the Old Gothic sublime in the paranoid anthropomorphism of his monstrous metamorphoses of the trivial. While Liliane Weissberg traces the relation in *Beloved*, Toni Morrison's 1987 'ghost story about history', between the ghost story itself and the political pre-text of the oral slave narrative of Margaret Garner, showing how the one dehistoricises and disrupts the other.

The anxiety of influence is not a pattern for the authors and critics represented in this book – the Gothic, it seems, is a language that, by definition, belongs to no one; with its air of pastiche – only made, never born – it forms a ready-made language for the aesthetic and cultural politics of our times. The Gothic is a tradition of representation, evidently still in the making, whose psychological and cultural content – built of the permutation of a few simple elements – is as recognisable and conventionalised as the Renaissance Sonnet or the Blues, and yet which can seem as adequate a representation of the dominant tone of recent Western European or American cultural tradition as those forms are eloquent of love or misery in their own times. The Gothic is the perfect anonymous language for the peculiar unwillingness of the past to go away. Peter Hutchings extends the notion of the iterative structure of the Gothic's masterplots by reviewing some recent examples of seriality, sequel, resurrection, and return in recent horror movies and concludes that this structure creates an image of open-endedness in the present.

These essays show that the reflexive selfconsciousness of modern Gothic is part of a popular tradition which moves between airport racks, late-night cinemas, video shops, daylight family trips to the Odeon, and the literary shelves. And the vitality of this modern popular tradition suggests not a dead form of pastiche, in Fredric Jameson's sense of a museum of styles, a parody whose point has been lost, but a disturbing, sometimes offensive, essentially critical, form of open-endedness based on a deliberate foregrounding of reiteration. Reiteration is the modern form of haunting; reiteration of narrative manoeuvres and motifs, unholy reanimation of the deadness of the past that has the power to make something new.

The penchant amongst writers and film-makers for a Modern Gothic (witness the 1991 appearance of an anthology, *The Picador Book of the New Gothic*, edited by Patrick McGrath and Bradford Morrow, both of them publishing authors) appears to fit with several aspects of postmodernism. For these authors the appeal of the New Gothic is distinctly apocalyptic:

> We stand at the end of a century whose history has been stained perhaps like no other by the blacker urges of human nature. The prospect of apocalypse – through human science rather than divine intervention – has redefined the contemporary psyche. The consolation that Western souls once found in religion has faded; Faustus no longer faces a Mephistopheles from divinity's antithetic underworld, nor is Ambrosio doomed to Christianity's eternal hell. Now hell is decidedly on earth, located within the walls and chambers of our own minds.

The spirit of the essays below is not apocalyptic. Reiteration, not a vision of the end, is the form of their haunting; but there is one sense in which haunting is the form of reiteration too. Allan Lloyd Smith argues that there is a curious 'match' between the last half of the eighteenth century and the end of our own. He reminds us that the much-prophesied

4

end of the Enlightenment and the debates between Habermas and Lyotard have some relevance to the astonishing rise of this extravagant popular mode in the last thirty years from marginality to one of the central languages of the popular contemporary. The literary declension of terror is an inevitable response to the atrocity exhibition of the twentieth century, just as it was for the writers of the late eighteenth and early nineteenth centuries as they confronted the social, economic, and political instabilities of a new order, and the mayhem of a revolutionary period. But whereas early Gothic proposed a delightful excursion through the realms of imaginary horror, contemporary use of the Gothic register strikes a darker and more disturbing note. It is the horror now that is real, and the resolution that is fanciful. Hence the peculiar effect we sometimes find, akin to the dropping of a stone through a spider's web, when the actuality or realisation of the horrors of contemporary life strikes through the web of highlighted representation with an effect that may be comic, or grotesque, or uncannily chilling. But as this and several other of these pieces demonstrate, the continuity and variety of this popular evocation of horror is itself significant; the mode doesn't simply 'reflect' a modern condition by a form of inverted mimesis.

Nor is the Gothic simply synonymous with the the postmodern; it may play against it in some cases, for not only does the pastness of the past not disappear in a welter of imprisoning pastiche, but also, as many of the authors below seem to be urging in their very different ways, the conditions are always, endlessly right in the proliferating branches and spaces of the Modern Gothic, for the barbarous vitality of the Past, the Alien, or the Other to erupt, and threaten a familiar plot, an accepted environment; and such a repeated pattern allows us first to glimpse, and then to reflect critically upon, the changing processes at work in our imaginings, and even in our theories, of our own contemporaneity.

V. S.

A. L. S.

Allan Lloyd Smith

Postmodernism / Gothicism

There are some striking parallels between the features identified in discourses concerning postmodernism and those which are focused on the Gothic tradition. The first is perhaps to the intellectual credit of neither: it is that both areas are frequently contested as unacceptably vague and quite possibly even specious categorisations of tendencies or predilections – one can hardly call them traditions or practices – that are appealed to at the convenience of the critic or cultural commentator. Maurice Lévy's attack on incoherence in the use of the word 'Gothic' – which he would prefer to see restricted to a particular period (1764–1824) and to a specific cultural, aesthetic, religious, and political background: 'the first Gothic Revival and the culture of Georgian England'[1] – serves as a potent reminder of the pitfalls we find in applying the term too generally. But even Lévy lacks any faith that the suitably chastised critics will return to a purer use of this determinedly impure and extravagant term. The idea of the 'postmodern' has attracted scathing denunciations from Christopher Norris and Alex Callinicos to name only two of its most articulate and persuasive prosecutors.[2] Whatever the virtues of such cogently argued corrections, it is difficult to see them as other than Canute-like attempts to stem the rising tide of this Sargasso sea of the new, with its flotsam of junk culture and its eddies of modernism or even, in the wilful eclecticism of the supposed postmodern order, currents of romanticism, fragmentary spars of classicism; the coexisting wreckage of all cultures, universally available but equally emptied of meaning; traversed and exploited by the cruise ships of bloated consumers of the image, for the profit of a transnational 'late' capitalism. Let us not, however, be carried away into a Baudrillardian ecstasy of communication in addressing these points; the intention is merely to point out the curious parallel of a paradoxically legitimated illegitimacy, whereby the very hostilities and objections to both the postmodern and the Gothic have become, in the event, further endorsements of their effectiveness, their credibility as subversive and wilfully contradictory taxonomies.

In what follows I intend to suggest some rather more significant parallels, first with a concentration on the Gothic and then in a review of some postmodern fictions, reserving for the moment the question of what connections there may be between the two. In this dual focus some new perspectives can be offered on both.

Indeterminacy

The first of the more serious parallels that I wish to point up is in the quality of indeterminacy which, if it is the stock in trade of the Gothic mode, is surely the very *raison d'être* of the postmodern. In the Gothic, indeterminism is a narrative necessity, providing the essential possibilities of mystery and suspense and, at a deeper level, it is also an epistemological necessity involved in the proto-romantic reaction against classicism and the Enlightenment. For the postmodern, indeterminism is an intellectual inevitability, following from the working through of modernist aesthetics towards a valorising of partial orders in opposition to comprehensive structures and orderings, and the oft-diagnosed breakdown of meta-narratives, in science, religion, and society.[3] In both models we find the proliferation of competing non-privileged narratives and contradictory discourses; a tension of explanation versus complication and mystery; elaboration, complexity, excess, scandal, desire. In both we confront the embattled, deconstructed self, without sureties of religion and social place, or any coherent psychology of the kind observable in both the Enlightenment or modernist traditions.

Epistemology/ontology

One of the more convincing interpretations of Gothic scenarios focuses upon the epistemological crisis of the late eighteenth century in which characters struggle to adjust their perceptions of sensory experience against the rational structures that sustain their world view. The novels of Charles Brockden Brown, for example, are constructed out of this opposition between the irrational but intractable facts of experience and the beliefs in benevolence and order that should make such facts impossible. In *Wieland* (1798) Wieland's sister Clara struggles for most of her narrative to accommodate what she knows with what she thinks she knows: her brother is a deranged murderer of his family and attempting to murder her too, but since this cannot be the case for Clara's intellectual understanding she resists the knowledge and puts herself at further risk;

Wieland himself embraces the supernatural instead of perceiving his own madness. Much the same can be said of *Edgar Huntly* (1799), and, to an extent, of *Arthur Mervyn* (1799, 1800).[4] Similarly, in Mary Shelley's *Frankenstein* the monster is shown as endorsing eighteenth-century principles of reason and benevolence, until his own painful experience of the irrational cruelty of the humans he meets – including the admirable de Lacey family as well as his creator – determines his choice of implacable revenge.

By contrast a major difference in perspectives has been identified by Brian McHale, who argues that the 'dominant' in postmodern texts is ontological rather than epistemological. That is, postmodernist fiction deploys strategies which engage and foreground 'postcognitive' questions such as 'Which world is this? What is to be done in it? Which of my selves is to do it?'[5] But readers of the Gothic will recognise that the situations of mystery, suspense, and not-knowing in such texts are precisely those in which such questions are foregrounded. Furthermore, the Gothic also foregrounds other issues like those identified by McHale as bearing on the ontology of the literary text itself: in its tendency towards narrative digressions, opposition of various stories and registers, disputes of veracity; and an excessiveness in language, gesture, and motive that could be anachronistically labelled as 'camp'. Equally, the insistence of the Gothic on surfaces and sensation inclines me to apply to it McHale's dictum that 'although it would be perfectly possible to interrogate a postmodernist text about its epistemological implications, it is more *urgent* to interrogate it about its ontological implications' (11). Leaving aside the question of 'urgency', it is also possible to observe that the ontological focus of postmodernist fiction is grounded in certain epistemological issues which may, as in Pynchon's *The Crying of Lot 49* (1966), dominate plot thematics and fictional discourse.

Surfaces/affectivity

Postmodernist art has an aesthetics of the surface, dominated by the depthless image, divorced from attendant complications of reference. At the same time, the postmodernist aesthetic involves a manipulation of response, in which free floating 'intensities' substitute for more coherent sets of feelings.[6] Similarly the question of the surface features of the Gothic has been brought to critical attention recently by the work of Eve Kosofsky Sedgwick who points out that criticism of the Gothic has tended to be impatient with its surface material – variously labelled as 'clap-trap', 'decor', 'stage-set' – in its desire to grasp the Gothic novel 'whole' in a thematics of depth and a psychology of depth, but that this has left largely unexplored 'the most characteristic and daring areas of Gothic convention, those that point the reader's attention back to surfaces'.[7] The use of colour, landscape, music, and characteristic turns of plot, as well as 'repetitiveness and fixity' and the two-dimensionality of character in its 'draining but irreducible tension with a fiction of physical, personal presence' (142), are the unexplored areas that Sedgwick returns to prominence, along with the suffusion of the surface features with sexuality in, for example, the use of the veil motif. The veil, in her analysis, is not simply a concealment and inhibition of sexuality, it comes, by a process of metonymy, to represent the thing covered and is then 'a metaphor for the system of prohibitions by which sexual desire is enhanced and specified' (143). This attention to 'metonymic contagion' (149) seems generally applicable to Gothic writing in such matters as 'writing on the flesh', or the recognition (often misrecognition) of identity through facial characteristics, matters which are easily overlooked by criticism's habitual models of depth psychology but constitute important elements of Gothic coding.[8] Sedgwick concludes that:

> A truly dynamic or economic reading of these novels would discern the rules of circulation of conventional 'material'. It would . . . have to discuss sexual desire and, more generally, the will or motivation of individual characters – the illusion of individuality, in fact, and the wracking, dominant struggle between that illusion and the fascination of the hieroglyphic – first as a disorder of rhythm, a disease of expectation, of the sort we have discerned in Ambrosio in his approaches to veils and the veiled, and only then in terms of a typology of characters. (168)

Certainly one might respond that this reappraisal of the surface of the Gothic has more to say about the contemporary redirecting of the critical gaze (which itself may be a product of the postmodern condition) than about the Gothic itself, or that the surface is conditioned by the underlying structures prioritised in earlier criticism. But my own view is that in some way Gothic fiction *is* about its surfaces, its acts of representation and positioning, and its affectivity in relation to the reader. Other recent writers on the Gothic have explored related areas. Susan Wolstenhome in *Gothic (Re)Visions: Writing Women as Readers*, takes up some of Sedgwick's ideas in focusing on staged scenes in the Gothic, examining how visual structuring suggests the gendering of these texts through such issues as who or what becomes a spectacle, and for whom; and where the narrator and reader are situated in relation to the spectacle and the spectator.[9] Coral Ann Howells in *Love, Mystery, and Misery: Feeling in Gothic Fiction* discusses the disconnected affectivity of Gothic texts, how the writers 'tend to concentrate on external details of emotional display while leaving readers to deduce for themselves complex inner psychological movements', so that the splendid displays of strong feeling only add to the mystery of whatever feelings or imagination could have provoked them. That is, the violence of emotional expression is recorded but at the same time the author offers only a shocked withholding of sympathy or perplexed incomprehension.[10] Like postmodern fiction, then, the Gothic foregrounds issues of ontology in reader and text, while subduing or subverting the explanatory structures that might, in a realist or modernist text, control, explain, or direct affectivity.

Nostalgia/archaism/history

John Hawkes once said that 'history and the inner psychic history must dance their creepy minuet together if we are to save ourselves from oblivion'.[11] This motive seems shared across the Gothic and the post-modern writers for that incessant conjuring of the past that defined the Gothic novel is also a mixture of attraction and repulsion, desire and fear. Thus, as David Punter remarks, 'in Gothic the middle class displaces the hidden violence of present social structures, conjures them up again as past, and falls promptly under their spell'.[12]

> what is being talked about is always double: these other barbarities have an intrinsic connexion with the hidden barbarities of the present, the social and economic barbarities of injustice and forced labour. Capitalism has specific taboos, or specific forms of taboo, just as particular primitive societies vary in their taboo structure: what has been most important during the last two centuries emerges quite clearly from Gothic – the family, the concepts of creation and work, the claims of the individual, the power of the repressive apparatus of church and state. These are the areas where to probe too deeply would be to risk tearing the social fabric itself, and these are precisely the areas in which Gothic fiction locates itself, and where it tortures itself and its readers by refusing to let dead dogs lie. (419)

But he goes on to admit, the writers who asked these difficult questions 'asked them in a very diffident way . . . and often, after having asked them, they hastily apologised and produced normative endings to their books' (420). Indeed so, and I would add that the Gothic is also, more than this appalled anxiety; it is a playful admixture of inaccurate histories, versions of feudalism and medievalism restaged for the amusement of an age of industrial capitalism. Though a product of history, in the sense that its charades were doubtless generated by contemporary pressures – as symptom – it is not itself historical in the sense of displaying any informed historical consciousness. Instead the tokens of pastness are exhibited without discrimination, as a fancy dress worn by contemporary sensibility and consciousness. The Inquisition and the practices of the monastery or convent feature not in the context of catholic Europe but as a horrifying affront to protestant sensitivity; the feudal aristocracy is not understood within its own world view but simply as an eighteenth- or nineteenth-century nightmare; the supernatural horror derives more from Fuseli than authentic folk tradition; and the castle or monastery interiors owe more to Piranesi than to extensive architectural knowledge. In this sense we can describe the Gothic as ransacking an imaginary museum of pastness, or rifling a Baedeker of 'foreignness' to deck out its touristic exoticism.

The same, if more extensive, imaginary museum of pastness characterises the postmodern cannibalisation of images from the detritus of global history in which the past, in Jameson's words, has itself become a vast collection of images, a 'multitudinous photographic simulacrum'. Its consequences, however, may be more dire than those of the games of the Gothic, since this image addiction, as he elaborates it, 'by transforming the past into visual mirages, stereotypes, or texts, effectively abolishes any practical sense of the future and of the collective project, thereby abandoning the thinking of future change to fantasies of sheer catastrophe and inexplicable cataclysm, from visions of "terrorism" on the social level to those of cancer on the personal'.[13]

Pastiche/reflexivity

Jane Austen parodied the Gothic in *Northanger Abbey* (1818) in perhaps the only way possible: by opposing reason and moderation to its vehement excesses. For the Gothic was already in some sense a parody of itself, being composed of elements borrowed from other forms and its own earlier examples. Pastiche is I think the preferable term for this, because the essence of the mode was to incorporate such imitations without observable parodic implication. Folk tales, songs and superstitions, scientific enquiries, theology, graveyard poetry, *Sturm und Drang* German romanticism, the literature of sensibility, theories of the sublime, travel guides, dictionaries, legal and religious testimony, melodrama; all were welcomed by this omnivorous form whose capacity to incorporate mixed elements took to an extreme the eclecticism of the novel. Equally, all were ingested without too much reworking and reappraisal; we find them presented largely at face value, commented on only by the development of plot or sometimes, as in Ann Radcliffe's novels, an ultimate disposition and dispersal by postscript.

Pastiche similarly seems to be the dominant mode of postmoderist aesthetics where competing discourses jostle together in explicit avoidance of the modernist conception of a unique style. As Jameson puts it:

The disappearance of the individual subject, along with its formal consequence, the increasing unavailability of the personal style, engender the well-nigh universal practice today of what may be called pastiche . . .

. . . parody finds itself without a vocation; it has lived, and that strange new thing pastiche slowly comes to take its place. Pastiche is, like parody, the imitation of a peculiar or unique, idiosyncratic style, the wearing of a linguistic mask, speech in a dead language. But it is a neutral practice of such mimicry, without any of parody's ulterior motives, amputated of the satiric impulse, devoid of laughter or of any conviction that alongside the abnormal tongue you have momentarily borrowed, some healthy linguistic normality still persists. Pastiche is thus blank parody, a statue with blind eyeballs: it is to parody what that other interesting and historically original modern thing, the practice of a kind of blank irony, is to what Wayne Booth calls the 'stable ironies' of the eighteenth century.[14]

The notion of the 'disappearance of the individual subject' prompts me to comment on an apparent paradox, that despite their importance to plot development, the individuality of characters in Gothic fiction is usually much less than in the novel generally; they are universally remarked to be flat, two-dimensional, without development, except as representative of various neuroses and tabooed desires.[15] And the 'stable ironies' of the eighteenth century were what the Gothic called into question as not stable, and certainly not ironic. The Gothic mode cannot afford irony (except, of course, in the larger sense of its playing with the familiar conventions).

Is there, possibly, a similar motive in this choice of pastiche form? The postmodernist writer deliberately sets out to produce an undecidability: 'This is the textual strategy of postmodernist fiction, to produce systematic uncertainty of signs by locating each of them within more than one interpretative framework, thereby frustrating the reader's will to interpretative synthesis.'[16] The Gothic writer, working to produce incredulity, mystery, and suspense, sets off one account of events against another, usually subsumed within a moralised but generally incompetent master-narrative whose function is to *fail* to explain and thereby allow access to subdued or repressed realms of knowledge and experience. Multiple pastiche without enabling commentary is doubtless self-cancelling, yet, at the same time, each element of pastiche calls into temporary being what and why it imitates. Both engage the reader's desire to create meaning, only to frustrate it and leave us with obscure but significant fragments that engage and yet short-circuit affectivity.

Inevitably along with pastiche we find ourselves engaged with issues of self-reflexiveness, as the fictions selfconsciously speak in other voices and employ techniques that undermine the coherent reader–author relationship of the realist novel. *The Castle of Otranto* (1764) began a tradition of exaggeration beyond all credibility that culminates in Bram Stoker's wilful absurdities, placing the Gothic decisively in the tradition of fantastic literature. It also set a new standard for incoherence in fiction, as Walpole 'set the Gothic novel on a course both self-contradictory and seemingly self defeating', as Haggerty puts it.[17] Where this may be compared with recent writers' Gothicism is in two different respects, first the stylised flat repetition of Gothic narrative structures as in the novels of Susan Hill, especially *The Woman in Black* (1983), or *Mrs De Winter* (1993), John Banville's *Ghosts* (1986) or *The Book of Evidence* (1989); and secondly in the more momentary incursions of the Gothic into novels by broadly non-Gothic writers as in Paul Auster's *City of Glass* (1985), Kurt Vonnegut's *Mother Night* (1966), Don DeLillo's *White Noise* (1984) and *Libra* (1988), William Gaddis's *Carpenter's Gothic* (1985) or Thomas Pynchon's *V* (1963), *Lot 49* (1965) and *Gravity's Rainbow* (1973). In these latter fictions the Gothic appears as one element among many: as a particular setting, an epiphanic moment, a distorted and threatening environment, subdued supernaturalism, a sudden and grotesque violence. Here again I find Jameson's remarks useful, when he proposes (apropos a postmodern house in Santa Monica!) that:

> if the great negative emotions of the modernist movement were anxiety, terror, the being-unto-death, and Kurtz's 'horror,' what categorizes the newer 'intensities' of the postmodern, which have also been characterized in terms of the 'bad trip' and schizophrenic submersion, can just as well be formulated in terms of the messiness of a dispersed existence, existential messiness, the perpetual distraction of post-sixties life. Indeed, one is tempted . . . to evoke the more general informing context of some larger virtual nightmare, which can be identified as the sixties gone toxic, a whole historical and countercultural 'bad trip' in which psychic fragmentation is raised to a qualitatively new power, the structural disintegration of the decentered subject now promoted to the very motor and logic of late capitalism itself. (117)

The parallel between the 'sixties gone toxic' and the late-eighteenth-century reaction to revolutionary excesses will not escape students of the Gothic, although a reservation on behalf of the 1950s claim to its own earlier 'bad trip' might have to be entered – what about John Hawkes, for example – and then again, what of the forties' disposition towards noir? There are always difficulties in periodising too exactly. Still the point may be allowed to stand, with the always convenient proviso that avatars of the postmodern will be rediscovered in its eerie afterlight.

Comedy/burlesque/grotesque

The relentless incertitudes of the postmodern and its refusal to alloc-
ate coherent values generally produces comic effects but terror is an
equally possible option, and not infrequently the two are combined in
black humour at the expense of benighted protagonists as in Nabokov's
Laughter in the Dark (1961), *Bend Sinister* (1948) or *King, Queen Knave*
(1968), Vonnegut's *Slaughterhouse-5* (1969) and *Mother Night* (1966), John
Hawkes' *Cannibal* (1949) and *The Lime Twig* (1968), Heller's *Catch-22* (1961),
Flannery O'Connor's novels and stories, and all of Pynchon's fictions.
Obviously a world without evident values or signposting lends itself to
comic or even burlesque treatments of innocence or ignorance, and to a
morbid humour in the ironies of plot. Much the same is true of the
Gothic, which, as Elizabeth Napier points out, was 'widely imitated and
often (even by its own practitioners) mercilessly burlesqued'.[18] Victor
Sage's exploration of Gothic laughter concludes that the *danse macabre*
of 'readerly doubt, unease, and horror, codified in bathos – in the stag-
geringly banal mechanisms of exaggeration, mistaken identity, misunder-
standing and cross purposes' seen in Ann Radcliffe, Le Fanu, and Bram
Stoker is the very stuff of theatrical farce.[19]

Criminality/the unspeakable/excess

One reason to pursue these similarities between such different fields as
the Gothic literary tradition and the broader postmodern – period, phase
of production, aesthetic style? – is that postmodernists seem to have
borrowed certain particular qualities of the Gothic to pursue their own
agendas. John Hawkes remarks: 'It seems to me that fiction should achieve
revenge . . . it should be an act of rebellion against all the constraints of
the conventional pedestrian mentality around us. Surely it should destroy
conventional morality. I suppose all this is to say that to me the act of
writing is criminal. If the act of the revolutionary is one of extreme
idealism, it's also criminal. Obviously I think that the so-called criminal
act is essential to our survival.'[20] There are shades of the Surrealist manifesto here, and some questions for us about differences between criminality
and the Gothic, but I think his comment will serve to point up the way
that Gothic has proved to be the literary tradition that contemporary
writers have found most resonant in their attempts to break up 'conventional pedestrian mentality and morality'. Postmodernist writing has
frequently – not always, of course – attended to the unspeakable and
the criminal: violent and perverted desires, in Bret Easton Ellis's *American
Psycho* (1991), Pynchon's *Gravity's Rainbow* (1973) or Capote's *In Cold Blood*

(1966); atrocities of war in Herr's *Dispatches* (1977), the shock of assassination or terrorism in DeLillo's *Libra* (1988), *Players* (1989) and *Mao II* (1991). And the tendency is equally explicit in postmodernist films such as Lynch's *Blue Velvet* (1986) or Demme's *Something Wild* (1987), where sadomasochistic elements are virtually part of the *mise en scène*. Postmodernism draws from Gothic its populist tendency, its lurid, low-rent sensationalism and exploitation of affect, its opening up of tabooed realms and giving voice to the other, its embrace of the fragmentary, its use of paranoia. The culture of the spectacle, whipping on a culture of 'waning' affect, produces close parallels to the sensationalism of the Gothic.

But one difference to observe is that whereas the modern Gothic depends as much as its originals on the construction of evil, as Jameson has observed, the evil of the postmodern version is 'the emptiest form of sheer Otherness (into which any type of social content can be poured at will)'.[21] Finally then, even transgression undoes itself and is relieved of its Gothic portentousness (I had almost said seriousness, but that was never quite at stake and in any case we may not be sure how 'serious' the construction of evil in Gothic ever was).

Science/technology/paranoia

The Gothic flourished in the period of early industrialisation, when Enlightenment science began to translate itself into social change at every level. It occurred alongside social upheavals and revolutions in political thought and action. Similarly the postmodern condition seems to be occasioned by transformations determined by technology, and it is here, I think, that the real point of making these comparisons begins to come into view. If it is true that the shift from the technology of production to the technology of information (which includes the changes in global circulation of economics) offers some similarities to the shift that occurred at the end of the eighteenth century, then there is reason to think that the parallels may be more than fortuitous. The challenge of understanding the implications of change on this scale, of responding to its catastrophes, and of imagining the consequences, links Mary Shelley's *Frankenstein* (1818) with William Gibson's cyberpunk, or Bram Stoker's Transylvania with Pynchon's Zone.

The information revolution, by providing too much information and boundless signs without referents, subjects the protagonist to a sensory disarray comparable to the confusions of a Gothic victim and promotes a similar sense that 'they' somewhere, somehow impossibly in control of all this, are competently plotting like the Inquisition or a Gothic villain. As Punter notes, it seems 'impossible to make much sense out of Gothic fiction without continual recourse to the concept of paranoia'.[22] What is the parallel in postmodern fiction to the superstitious dread of catholicism, monkishness, and the Inquisition? Contemporary scientific materialism opens the possibility of what exceeds our understanding; the system running itself, for itself; and hence generates antihumanism, plots beyond comprehension. Either there are plots or, perhaps worse, there are none, an unendurable void of meaning. Enlightenment reason generated the opposing question of unreason and superstition; whereas in the postmodern condition the paranoia is induced by the system of late capitalism, giving rise to the sense of plots within history, and the fear of technology as anti-human, conjoined with the terrified recognition of the human as itself provably anti-human. Benny Profane's conversation with the cyborg SHROUD in *V* explores that avenue: when Benny suggests that the robot ought to be junked, it replies:

> Of course, like a human being. Now remember, right after the war, the Nuremberg war trials? Remember the photographs of Auschwitz? Thousands of Jewish corpses, stacked up like those poor car-bodies. Schlemiel: it's already started.
> 'Hitler did that. He was crazy.'
> Hitler, Eichman, Mengele. Fifteen years ago. Has it occurred to you that there may be no more standards for crazy or sane, now that it's started?
> 'What, for Christ sake?'[23]

Victor Frankenstein's monster searched for answers, Profane's cyborg gives them, with the postmodernist spin. At some point, too, the development of technology merges with mysticism and superstition: at a sufficiently refined level technology itself becomes uncanny and reopens the symbol system of the Gothic.

In William Gibson's *Neuromancer* series the dead – like Jane – return as electronic memory constructions, and the computer matrix recuperates the traditional Gothic interior:

> The tunnel wound in on itself like a gut. The section with the mosaic floor was back there now, around however many curves and up and down short, curving stairwells . . . Up another stairwell they hit a straight stretch that narrowed to nothing in the distance, either way you looked. It was broader than the curved part, and the floor was soft and humpy with little rugs, it looked like hundreds of them, rolled out layers deep over the concrete . . . The ones on top, nearest the centre, were worn down to the weave, in patches. A trail, like somebody'd been walking up and down there for years. Sections of the overhead striplight were dark, and others pulsed weakly.[24]

The punk element in Gibson's cyperpunk is in his registration of the gritty human detail both in the streets of the future underclass or, as here, in the corridors of the virtual construct. But there is equally a technological exoticism:

> 'The Villa Straylight,' said a jewelled thing on the pedestal, in a voice like music, 'is a body grown in upon itself, a Gothic folly. Each space in Straylight is in some way secret, this endless series of chambers linked by passages, by stairwells vaulted like intestines, where the eye is trapped in narrow curves, carried past ornate screens, empty alcoves . . .'

> 'At the Villa's silicon core is a small room, the only rectilinear chamber in the complex. Here, on a plain pedestal of glass, rests an ornate bust, platinum and cloisonné, studded with lapis and pearls. The bright marbles of its eyes were cut from the synthetic ruby viewport of the ship that brought the first Tessier up the well, and returned for the first Ashpool . . .'[25]

The head is actually a ceremonial terminal. Shades of late Bram Stoker return in high tech and virtual reality, because there is no difference between the virtual world and necromancy, where voodoo distorts the psychic space (*Count Zero* (1986)). The effects of Gothic plotting result in pain and damage for venturers into the virtual realm, or emerge as strange new shapes in the cyberspace matrix of world economic information displays (*Mona Lisa Overdrive* (1983)).

In *Count Zero* (1986) the final, transcendental, machine appears as the boxmaker, an obsessive collage constructor, collecting items of the human past which it endlessly assembles into exquisitely moving yet meaningless boxes:

> Eyes wide, Marly watched the uncounted things swing past. A yellowing kid glove, the faceted crystal stopper from some vial of vanished perfume, an armless doll with a face of French porcelain, a fat, gold-fitted black fountain pen, rectangular segments of perf board, the crumpled red and green snake of a silk cravat . . . Endless, the slow swarm, the spinning things.[26]

'When it changed' is the key phrase of this doyen of postmodern Gothicists. In a Pynchonesque exchange 'simstim' star Angie asks her electronic mentor Continuity about the odd beings in the matrix called *the loa*, a secret voodoo spirit group whose voices she hears:

> 'How do the stories about' – she hesitated, having almost said *the loa*, '– about things in the matrix, how do they fit into this supreme being idea?'

'They don't. Both are variants of "When it Changed". Both are of
very recent origin.'
'How recent?'
'Approximately fifteen years.'[27]

My argument is that the sense of 'When it Changed' is what underly-
ingly links the Gothic with the postmodern in an aesthetic of anxiety and
perplexity, as similar responses to the confusing new order – or should
that be the new *disorder*?

Notes

1 M. Levy, '"Gothic" and the Critical Idiom' in *Gothick Origins and Innovations*,
   ed. Allan Lloyd Smith and Victor Sage (Amsterdam: Rodopi, 1994), pp. 8, 2, 4.
2 C. Norris, *What's Wrong with Postmodernism: Critical Theory and the Ends of
   Philosophy* (London: Harvester Wheatsheaf, 1990); Alex Callinicos, *Against
   Postmodernism: A Marxist Critique* (Cambridge: Polity Press, 1989).
3 F. Jameson, in *Postmodernism: Or, The Cultural Logic of Late Capitalism* (London:
   Verso, 1991), points out that there never were any 'master narratives' but
   rather 'eschatological schemata that were never really narratives in the first
   place' (p. xi).
4 For example, Donald Ringe, *Charles Brockden Brown* (New York: Twayne, 1966).
5 B. McHale, *Postmodernist Fiction* (1987, London: Routledge, 1989), pp. 10, 11.
6 Jameson, *Postmodernism*, p. 6. Jameson speaks of 'a waning of affect' (p. 11),
   but it might be better to think of the decoupling of affect from its familiar
   patterns.
7 E. Kosofsky Sedgwick, *The Coherence of Gothic Conventions* (London and New
   York: Methuen, 1986), pp. 140, 141.
8 *Ibid.*, p. 160, where Sedgwick notes how the coded discriminations of features,
   i.e. the Gothic conventions of countenance, overwhelm any non-coded
   distinctions, so that 'there seem to be no non-coded differences between persons
   that could not also occur in any one person over time'.
9 S. Wolstenhome, *Gothic (Re)Visions: Writing Women as Readers* (Albany: State
   University of New York, 1993), p. 7.
10 C. A. Howells, *Love, Mystery, and Misery: Feeling in Gothic Fiction* (London:
   Athlone Press, 1978), p. 15.
11 'Hawkes and Scholes: A Conversation', *Novel*, spring 1972, p. 205.
12 D. Punter, *The Literature of Terror* (London: Longman, 1980), p. 418.
13 Jameson, *Postmodernism*, p. 46.
14 *Ibid.*, pp. 16, 17.
15 See, for example, Elizabeth Napier, *The Failure of Gothic: Problems of Disjunction
   in an Eighteenth-Century Literary Form* (Oxford: Clarendon Press, 1987), pp. 32,
   33.
16 J. Mepham, 'Narratives of Postmodernism' in Edmund J. Smyth, ed. *Postmodernism and Contemporary Fiction* (London: Batsford, 1991), p. 150.
17 G. E. Haggerty, *Gothic Fiction/Gothic Form* (University Park and London:
   Pennsylvania State University Press, 1989), p. 2.

18 Napier, *Failure of Gothic*, p. x.
19 V. Sage, in *Gothick Origins and Innovations*, ed. Allan Lloyd Smith and Victor Sage (Amsterdam: Rodopi, 1994), p. 203.
20 'Hawkes and Scholes', p. 204.
21 Jameson, *Postmodernism*, p. 290.
22 Punter, *Literature of Terror*, p. 401.
23 T. Pynchon, *V* ((1961) Philadelphia: Bantam, 1968), p. 275.
24 W. Gibson, *Mona Lisa Overdrive* ((1988) Glasgow: Harper Collins, 1994), pp. 233, 233.
25 Gibson, *Neuromancer* ((1984) Glasgow: Harper Collins, 1993), pp. 206, 7.
26 Gibson, *Count Zero* ((1986) Glasgow: Harper Collins, 1993), p. 299.
27 Gibson, *Mona Lisa Overdrive*, p. 139.

The politics of petrifaction: culture, religion, history in the fiction of Iain Banks and John Banville

To see a ghost is to be, as we say, 'petrified'; and to petrify a culture –
to arrest it in the stony space of its own superstition – is a characteristic
imaginative manoeuvre of the contemporary Gothic. Once petrified, that
culture's history, even its contemporary history, can be replayed and all
its defensive, exclusive mechanisms laid bare either as Past or Other;
the reader's habitual assumption of the opposite position (as Present, or
Otherless) is then challenged in the act of reading.

Castles and estates, citadels of the Old Gothic, still litter the contemporary landscape of these divided islands, potentially embarassing collections of standing stones, which testify to the failures and exclusions,
the excitements and the victories, of the insularities we live amongst. And
the strain of allusion to the Gothic in significant areas of contemporary
writing, particularly in Scotland and Ireland, is equally and correspond-
ingly alive. Such writing is organised around consciously static, backward-
looking moments, decorative and often fetishised digressions which act
as selfconscious pastiche; but this trait, far from symptomatising a loss
of history, as Fredric Jameson would have it,[1] is a way of giving their
own history back to a readership. These narratives threaten constantly
to collapse into *motif* – an endless labyrinth whose disorientating spirals,
instead of obeying that horizontal syntagmatic selection from the rules
of narrative which allows readers to feel on their pulses an experience
of biography or history, seem to follow the vertical architectonics of allegory; and by doing do, arrest the flow of time and imprison it in a space
of the past.

Towards the end of Iain Banks' most recent ('mainstream') novel,
Complicity, there occurs a remarkable set piece. It is a description of Mary
King's Close, Edinburgh's literal heart of darkness, the shared grave of
plague victims whose bodies were walled up and left to rot in the sixteenth
century. Down in this alien place, for a joke, the narrator's friend Andy
has the caretaker suddenly switch off the lights:

But in those moments of blackness you stood there, as though you yourself were made of stone like the stunted, buried buildings around you, and for all your educated cynicism, for all your late-twentieth-century materialist Western maleness and your fierce despisal of all things superstitious, you felt a touch of true and absolute terror, a consummately feral dread of the dark; a fear rooted back somewhere before your species had truly become human and came to know itself, and in that primaeval mirror of the soul, that shaft of self-conscious understanding which sounded both the depths of your collective history and your own individual being, you glimpsed – during that extended, petrified moment – something that was you and was not you, as a threat and not a threat, an enemy and not an enemy, but possessed of a final, expediently functional indifference more horrifying than evil.[2]

This Gothic digression (which acts as an interesting riposte to Scott's *Heart of Midlothian* (1818)) is mediated and modernised by a hint of Conrad. The cultural allegory sets place against progress: it opposes eighteenth-century, rationalist, progressive, Euro-Edinburgh, to its own past and the 'feral dread of the dark' witnessed by the narrator; the 'superstition' (also suggested as a counterpoint to the narrator's maleness) enshrined ironically in this moment is utterly proscribed by contemporary 'reason': the blind worship of technology, the bright consumer-surfaces of contemporary finance capital, and the continuing atmosphere of greed and corruption in post-Thatcher Britain alluded to in the title of the novel, *Complicity*.

In the narrative, Andy Gould, the joker, is a childhood friend, but also the Other of voyeuristic journalist, Cameron, the narrator (hence the 'you' of the narrative address, which has a peculiar, reflexive ring). Andy is a Man of Action, a warrior, a Falklands veteran, and a multiple murderer, a man who has taken retribution for the state of the world upon himself. At one point he cries out in his own defence:

'Oh I know there's goodness in the world, too, Cameron, and compassion and a few fair laws; but they exist against a background of global barbarism, they float on an ocean of bloody horror that can tear apart any petty social construction of ours in an instant.'(302)

It is evident in the context of this novel as a whole that Cameron's 'extended, petrified moment' in Mary King's Close goes beyond both its picturesque writerly occasion and its immediate topical frame of reference. It is an example of a preoccupation throughout Banks' work with the nature of social, cultural, political, and psychological evolution. For Banks, the dialectic, a paradoxical struggle still dynamically present in the highly technologised Western culture of the late seventies, eighties and nineties, the decades of the Falklands and the Gulf War, is between the

Civilised and the Barbarian. The Gothic strain in his writing, the interest in horror, and the tendency for the books to reflect their own architecture in the cultural 'blind spot' of a static labyrinth, is strongly and self-consciously related to this central dialectic.

I say a paradoxical struggle, because not even the sexually contemplative, drug-taking, lefty, post-sixties computer-game addict, Cameron, is beyond the apparently archaic evil and the horror he perceives. The darkness is, and is not, a part of him. This paradox is something which pervades Banks' writing from the beginning of his career and shapes many of his narratives. For me, the paradigmatic form of the dialectic appears in the earlier science fiction novel, *The Player of Games*.[3] This work narrates a crisis in the life of a highly evolved imperial culture, called 'The Culture', which embodies many of the supposedly humanist, technologically based values of contemporary society. The Culture is an empire based on a commitment to peaceful evolution, a galactically successful version of the 1960s, which has replaced war by sex and sex, at least in the form of gender conflict, by erotic technology. Everything has become a game. By a series of subterfuges which give the impression of his own free choice in the matter, The Culture recalls into service one Gurgeh, a highly advanced player of games (sexually, as well as mentally) in order to deal with a backward alien (1950s? Provincial?) empire which chooses its supreme ruler by a unique game played (in their version of it) according to a barbarian, warrior ethic. The game is not simulated, and real death for the players and defeat for either culture will result. From its own point of view, the imperial mission of The Culture will be put back an appreciable amount of time, if Gurgeh is defeated by the Emperor. The paradox is that, during the finals of the game which are played in a place called Castle Klaff, Gurgeh and the Emperor change places: the Emperor impersonates the characteristically non-aggressive, cerebralist moves of a Culture player, and in order to win, Gurgeh finds he has to play like a barbarian. He has to play the game for real. Thus he is obliged to betray the culture whose ambassador he is and to which he is morally and psychologically committed (or so he believed). To uphold the values of civilisation, he has to become a barbarian. From the other more political end, the paradox still holds good: the culture needs his streak of barbarian, male, warrior values in order to win and further its own ends.

Castle Klaff, the site of this particular novel's 'extended petrified moment', is a recurrent image in Banks' work. The action of his books, regardless of genre labels, tends to revolve around, or to end up in, a decaying feudal/imperial structure in which the future is often being decided, a pastiche of Kafka, Borges/Calvino, and the labyrinth of Mervyn Peake's Gormenghast. To give a few examples: *Walking on Glass*[4] has one of its tripartite, genre-crossing plots devoted to a person called Quiss who is condemned to play a game in a labyrinthine structure called the Castle of Bequest; the hero and narrator of *Espedair Street*,[5] a disillusioned rock-star millionaire, lives in a place called Wykes' Folly in the centre of Glasgow, an imitation of a high Gothic church, a Victorian religious joke created by a Poe-like eccentric ex-catholic; *The Crow Road*[6] is dominated by the image of a Castle, the site of Prentice the narrator's family's child-hood games, which is bought and refurbished by Fergus, the capitalist and which is the conduit for an unexpected and violent return of the past; *The Bridge*[7] (which includes another memorable warrior character called The Barbarian who narrates, joke-appropriately, in a phonetically reproduced lower-class Glaswegian Scots) substitutes another static, infinitely layered Victorian structure, the Forth Bridge, beside which Iain Banks was born in North Queensferry, for the dense and labyrinthine Castle, on whose many allegorical levels the conscious and unconscious fates of the char-acters are decided; and a striking recent novel, *Fearsum Endginn*,[8] which takes place in a technological future, in which humans are replete with the ability to defy death by shifting away from 'base reality', as the children of the 1960s learnt to do in the New Maths, into a series of other bases called the Krypt; this novel envisages the planet itself, in a contradictory, regressive, backward-looking Gothic metaphor that is a characteristic expression of Banks's political and moral scepticism, as reduced (by pollu-tion, political decadence and paranoia) to a huge Fastness in a desert, this time a sort of Hispano-North African Moorish Citadel so big it has its own weather, whose Krypt (hidden script) by the law of pun is its Crypt (Basement) and in which universal Denmark something is deeply rotten.[9] Even from a survey as crude as the above, one can see how narrative quotations from the Gothic tradition are constantly present in a variety of cultural contexts. As in the Old Gothic (as opposed to Scott's modern-ised, rationalised, and conservative historical romance), the environmental symbolism is the living witness that the Past haunts, critically, ironically, and embarassingly, the Present. And the cultural politics of this also includes the question of evil, the nature of the soul, and the survival of religion. Many of Banks' narratives form a kind of stock-taking of the value and the failures of Science-based Humanism in post 1960s popular culture and the ironic presence of religious values in the psyche of his characters, ironic because what often appears in his settings as sites of (Scottish) petrification – bracketed, apparently, in Gothic and picturesque set pieces of citadels – as the half-life of the past, turns out to be a fictional meditation on the continuing, dialectical relationship between humanism and religion. Hence Cameron's 'superstition' in the passage from *Complicity*.

Cameron feels his moment of superstition despite his 'materialist

Western maleness'. This in its turn connects with Banks' sexual politics: women (even if they are people's parents) tend to be sexually liberated, post 1960s humanists; men are either converted to the female in themselves (through sex, drugs, and rock-and-roll, like Cameron) or they belong to an (apparently) historically outmoded barbarian, male, warrior-culture, essentially religious and ritualistic in nature, based on violence and retributive justice (like Cameron's friend Andy). Hence the relevance in the corpus cited above of *Canal Dreams*,[10] which appears at first sight mysteriously unrelated to any of the above. Culturally dislocated, it has none of the Gothic I have been talking about. And yet, the choice of a delicately beautiful Japanese female cellist who discovers warrior violence in herself when made the victim of male terrorists in Panama, has a very obvious and logical, if an unexpected, symbolic relevance to the dialectical analysis of postwar culture in the other books. Japan's set of logical exposures of Western culture proves as fascinating to Iain Banks, as it was to Angela Carter in *Fireworks* (1976).

From *Complicity* to Banks' first published novel, his *succès de scandale*, *The Wasp Factory* (1984) may seem a large and unncessary step backwards, but this is the other novel which at first sight doesn't appear to fit and I'd like to use briefly the above sketch of what I see as a central dialectic in his work as a framework in which to read *The Wasp Factory*, because there are signs in the reviews that the novel is often misread. Thom Nairn has complained about the way English reviewers have missed the jokes in the novel, because they aren't Scots, but I think the reason might also be that they read it over-naturalistically.

The narrator of the novel, Frank, is the Barbarian in Banks' cultural dialectic and the whole narrative is told from his point of view. Or at least, that's how we are compelled to read it first time round. In fact, Frank's voice is not at all pure and this novel is a highly skilled piece of literary ventriloquism which, technically, is a parody of Defoe's method of the unconscious first person in *Robinson Crusoe* (1719). Like Defoe, Banks is an excellent voice-thrower and in this case, it is a double-bluff across the gender divide: it transpires that Frank is Frances, a woman, all along. The novel's Gothic comes from its other major literary forebear, Mary Shelley's *Frankenstein* (1818), and in particular Shelley's brilliant device of a first-person Godwinian parody of Rousseau's idea of the 'natural man'. Both of these experiments in the first person are to do with myths of origination; first, the myth itself in Defoe, and then the parody of its later Enlightenment power in Shelley: and this is what we get updated in the story of Frank: contemporary parody of the myth of origins. Frank's is the story of Frankenstein's monster written ironically from the monster's deceived point of view, and set in the world of the 1980s.

Isolated in the family home on an island (just) off the north-east coast of Scotland, Frank is compelled by his 'hippy anarchist' scientist Father, an apparently insane and cruel survivor of the 1960s who retired early from the world to his family home on the island, to invent his own world from scratch with the aid of a few primitive 'facts', almost all of which are lies. Frank's 'education' consists of a whimsical and arbitrary set of jokes. When Frank is little, his Father tells him the world is not spherical but a Moebius strip; that Pathos is one of the Three Musketeers, Fellatio is a character in *Hamlet*, Vitreous a town in China, and 'that the Irish peasants had to tread the peat to make Guinness'. More importantly, he tells him that he has been castrated by a bulldog, and this is why he can't stand up to pee like other boys. Actually, as both he and the reader learn later, Frank is Frances, a girl, and Father has been feeding him male hormones all along in the horrible stews he insists on making for him in order to suppress his secondary sexual characteristics.

Neither Frank nor the reader has any choice at first but to believe the lie. Ironically, Frank proceeds not only to invent himself as a male, but also a whole religion and cosmology which will explain and justify the microcosmic barbarian world he imagines himself to be the centre of. Combining the animism of a savage out of *The Golden Bough* (1922) and the sensibility of a sergeant in the Royal Engineers, Frank becomes a super-male, an insular warrior, whose enemies are Women and the Sea:

> My greatest enemies are Women and the Sea. These are the things I hate. Women because they are weak and stupid and live in the shadow of men and are nothing compared to them, and the Sea because it has always frustrated me, destroying what I have built, washing away what I have left, wiping clean the marks that I have made. And I'm not all that sure the Wind is blameless either.
>
> The Sea is a sort of mythological enemy, and I make what you might call sacrifices to it in my soul, fearing it a little, respecting it as you're supposed to, but in many ways treating it as an equal. It does things to the world, and so do I; we should both be feared. Women . . . well, women are a bit too close for comfort as far as I'm concerned. (43)

It takes two readings to understand the double irony of this last remark. Frank's voice is not the voice of the text.

The gender ambiguity is not simply a mechanical switch for the purposes of a surprise ending. The topography of Frank's little world of death and retribution is the topography of his own unconscious self-denial: as Thom Nairn said, there's nothing he likes more than building dams. Even Frank's Gothic Sublime is conditioned by the continuous petrified fiction of his own maleness:

> I got to the island eventually. The house was dark. I stood looking at
> it in the darkness, just aware of its bulk in the feeble light of the broken
> moon, and I thought it looked even bigger than it really was, like a
> stone-giant's head, a huge moonlit skull full of shapes and memories,
> staring out to sea and attached to a vast powerful body buried in the
> rock and sand beneath, ready to shrug itself free and disinter itself on
> some unknowable command or cue. (86)

This flash of the Old Gothic looks back to Mervyn Peake, and, behind
his topography, Blake's Druid or Celtic Sleeping Albion, imprisoned in
the stone until the moment to arise. But even as he dreams of liberation, Frank is also busy mythologising the defensiveness and secrecy of
his relationship with his father. Frank and Father have made the house
into what he calls 'mutual citadels' – Frank's is the attic to which his
father can no longer climb, and Father's is his study, always locked,
where he keeps the secret about Frank he is continually hinting at.

The rest of Frank's defensive citadel, the island off the east coast of
Scotland, in which he is God and Adam at once, is ruled by weird animistic
recyclings, cargo-cult rituals. Frank is the creature of his own imagination,
a barbarian warrior. He is the Adam (and, unknowingly, the Eve) of his
boy's own *Treasure Island* world (Banks is particularly witty in this novel
on the analogy betwen the fetishism of adolescent boys and primitive
religion), naming his trowel 'Stoutstroke', his catapult 'Black destroyer'
(it's safe, he explains, if no one knows its name), his bike 'Gravel', etc.

Frank even contrives to rescue the head of the dog he is told castrated
him, and turns it into a precious relic, praying to the skull, its sockets full
of candles, on a special altar down in a Second World War bunker by the
shore, in order to gain telepathic knowledge of the future. His father has
named the dog Old Saul, and Frank, who recycles most of the knowledge
he acquires, one way or the other, retains the name for the skull, insisting
on explaining to the reader his father's religious joke:

> Now, I did eventually get my father to tell me this; and according to
> him, it was just as he choked the last struggling life out of the dog that
> he heard another scream, this time from above, and inside the house,
> and that was the boy they called Paul, being born. What sort of twisted
> thoughts went through my father's brain at the time to make him
> choose such a name for the child I cannot start to imagine. (107)

It's clear from this that Frank knows all about his Father's parody of bib-
lical revelation and conversion, even though he doesn't understand that
the bit which applies to himself is a lie. A votive of Old Saul, Frank murders Paul in a particularly sadistic fashion, living out his own microcosmic
1980s barbarian parody of the civilisation of Science and Technology of

the sixties, in what he thinks of as an inner rebellion against his Father. In fact, he is enacting Father's experiment, beautifully, all along, inventing religion on the way.

Actually, it's not clear what Frank's Godlike Frankenstein of a Father (if, that is, anything exists beyond his own sadism – he actually gives Frank *Myra Breckinridge* as a present) is trying to test out. Banks doesn't give us his reaction to the end of the experiment, but what he succeeds in establishing in the case of Frank is the paradox that (1) gender is socially, not biologically, determined; but that (2) if religion and the Law of the Father were proved to be historically unnecessary, they would have to be re-invented.

Frank's superstitious world of death, in which he kills without compunction, and which he has sold to himself and to the reader as his own self-defining Gothic reality, is a simplified compensatory fiction, a counter-dream born of the historical fiction of being socially, geographically, and anatomically, 'cut off'. The novel's Gothic is a brilliant parody of the weird insularity and the warrior-culture atmosphere of the Falklands campaign, with Frank's self-constructed Oedipal biography as 'a small image of the ruthless soldier hero almost all I've ever seen or read seems to pay homage to'.

There is, however, a metaphysical allegory left in the story which moves, dialectically, in the opposite direction. The novel takes its title from Frank's creation in the attic: a particularly elaborate kind of wasp trap, in which the wasps 'choose' their own deaths. According to this destiny machine, the wasps crawl round the face of a clock, and enter one of the many gates he has constructed, each with a different death behind it. From being the God of the Machine, Frank sees at the end of the book that he's now just another wasp:

> Believing in my great hurt, my literal cutting off from society's mainland, it seems to me that I took life in a sense too seriously, and the lives of others, for the same reason, too lightly. The murders were my own conception; my sex. The factory was my attempt to construct life, to replace the involvement which I otherwise did not want.
>
> Well, it is always easier to succeed at death.
>
> Inside this greater machine, things are not quite so cut and dried (or cut and pickled) as they appeared in my experience. Each of us, in our personal Factory, may believe we have stumbled down one corridor, and that our fate is sealed and certain (dream or nightmare, humdrum or bizarre, good or bad), but a word, a glance, a slip – anything can change that, alter it entirely, and our marble hall becomes a gutter, or our rat-maze a golden path. Our destination is the same in the end, but our journey – part chosen, part determined – is different for us all and

changes even as we live and grow. I thought one door had snicked shut behind me years ago; in fact I was still crawling about the face. *Now the door closes, and my journey begins.* (183–4)

This destiny machine is another citadel-like labyrinth. No one escapes choosing their own particular kind of un-freedom, but the historicism which Frank invents (called 'my experience') in order to justify his choices is revealed as a fiction. In knowing this, Frances is about to enter life and her own real (i.e. present) history at last.

At the heart of John Banville's narrative quotations from the Gothic lies a certain aesthetic celebration of decay. The site, the focus of many of his narratives, is a large delapidated house set either in a provincial estate or on an island, often unnamed or renamed. This building, frequently inhabited by alien grotesques, rats which have gravitated by a perverse law of culture to the sinking ship, becomes a domestic inversion of the 'natural', an anti-world feeding with all the massive energy of the parasite, on the ruins and the absences of the past. Consider the part played by decay in the readerly pleasures of the following sequence:

> We came to the house, and climbed the steps to the front door. Sophie produced a huge iron key from a pocket of her skirt. In the hall a rhomb of sunlight basked on the floor, like a reclining acrobat. The wallpaper hung down in strips, stirring now in the doorway like bleached palm-fronds. There was a dry, brownish smell, as of something that had finished rotting and turned to dust. On the theshold a barrier seemed to part before me, an invisible membrane. The air was cool and dry. There was no sigh of life. Dust lay everywhere, a mouse-grey, flocculent stuff, like a layer of felt, cushioning our footfalls. We went into a large, darkened room. The shutters were drawn, bristling with slanted blades of sunlight. There was a skitter of tiny claws in a corner, and then silence. An armchair leaned back, its armrests braced, in an attitude of startlement and awe. We stood looking about us for a moment, and then abruptly Sophie took my hand and drew me after her out of the room and up the wide staircase. She ran ahead of me through the shuttered bedrooms, flinging them open to the radiant day. She laughed excitedly, making gagging noises, her chin up and jaw thrust out as if to prevent something in her mouth from spilling over. I could still feel, like a fragment of secret knowledge, the cool moist print of her hand in mine. I followed her from window to window. The hinged flap of a shutter came away in my grasp like a huge, grey, petrified wing, another collapsed in a soft explosion of rotted wood and paint flakes and the brittle husks of wormwood larvae. Higher and

> higher we went, the house becoming stylised outdoors around us, with all that light flooding in, and the high shadowy ceilings the colour of clouds, and the windows thronging with greenery and sky. (44)[11]

This ambivalent, liminal moment is a primal scene in Banville's writing; rich in psychological, but also cultural meaning. The hinge between the erotic excitement of a transgression, and the reader's final ascent into an anti-nature of the imagination; between an intrusion into a forbidden history and the perception of an ideal outside (or perhaps inside the husk of) Time becomes overt in the strangely exhilarating 'soft explosion of rotted wood and paint flakes'.

In Irish history and culture, of course, this particular icon – the decay of the 'rich man's flowering lawns' – carries a built-in political and religious complexity. Banville's novels are replete with this ambiguous moment of 'intrusion': the narrators stare at the ascendancy manor, the demesne, 'from the other side', that is, either from the catholic, lower middle-class, excluded side, or from the later twentieth century, marginalised, post-catholic side, a perspective which tends to drop register, its language full of a bawdy, vulgar, and bizarre energy that constantly threatens to carnivalise the bland surface of these texts' mandarin allusions to poetic tradition; and yet the half-life of this gaunt house full of alien (often European) grotesques is fetishised at the same time in a series of arresting romantic conceits, as if the Mallarméan self had nested, finally, in the House's progressive attentuation and loss of substance, metonymically semi-incarnate, and could be known there, through the negative hints and sensory signatures of its decaying labyrinthine structure.

The lyric subjectivity of this (male) point of view in the passage above is obsessive throughout much of Banville's work and there are certain aspects of Neoplatonism's traditional obsession with light and harmony (an idealist reading of *The Tempest* and some of Donne's and Marvell's lyrics, the strange miniaturised life of the House and the Garden in the latter, for example), the perceptions of a later tradition of romantic idealism from Berkeley, Wordworth, Coleridge, and Shelley, through to Yeats and Samuel Beckett (Moran's return to his decaying house in *Molloy* (1951)), and perhaps Banville's favourite of all, Wallace Stevens, which form an obsessive 'pull' in much of the writing – the ascent, the secret knowledge, the nature of what Arthur Koestler in *The Sleepwalkers* (1959) calls the 'walled-in universe' in the history of thought – Banville establishes a self-conscious relation between this and the narrative imagination. A dialogue with lyric poetry is visible everywhere in the cadences of the prose. This literary undertow, which one feels in the stately gravity of the style, pulls towards light, silence, and stillness; and it is here, in the notion that the phenomena of nature are 'haunted' by absences, that Banville's 'ghosts' make their appearances, as twins of the historical present, substantial, perceptible – entering the world through the two-way shutter of decay. These 'presences' – known only by their their traces – occur within the walls of a House apparently abandoned by its own history.

At the level of form, this ambivalence presents itself characteristically as a struggle between lyric entropy, ironically enshrined in the selfconscious but egoistic fictionalising of a male narrator, and the processes of a historical, or even a historicised, perception – the syntagm of the novel's very form, its onward movement into time, sequence, causality. This central tension governs the distinctive pacing, the dreamlike expansion of the static moment, in Banville's writing. Narrative, for Banville, is a kind of puppet-stage on which, to give credibility to others, the narrator has first to imagine his own absence, to come to terms with his own evident unreality, to accept and even to celebrate his role as 'the pretext of things'. Sometimes this can only be done by the reverse process: imagining the others first, as if he were forced to live and remember a past, and then deducing his own absence from the afterglow of their images. Stylistically, this results in the struggle of the novel itself to expand beyond its own initial premises, the narrator himself often having to leave the House and wander abroad, in an aimless and carnivalesque journey.

I want to give two concrete examples of this process at work, one relatively simple, the other more complex. The first is from *The Newton Letter*, a novella of 1981. The narrator is a scholar, a kind of historian/biographer, writing a book about Sir Isaac Newton, who retreats (in a reprise of the traditional ghost-story opening – compare Maturin's *Melmoth* (1820) or Bram Stoker's 'The Judge's House' (1914)) from a city one assumes to be Dublin to the provinces to finish his book. Curiously weightless, he becomes the tenant in the gatehouse, the lodge to Ferns, the big house. His displacement is both social and metaphysical:

> What possessed me? Ferns was hardly that Woolsthorpe of my vague dreams, where, shut away from the pestilence of college life, I would put the final touches to my own *Principia*. Time is different in the country. There were moments when I thought I would panic, stranded in the midst of endless afternoons. Then there was the noise, a constant row, heifers bellowing, tractors growling, the dogs baying all night. Things walked on the roof, scrabbled under the floor. There was a nest of blackbirds in the lilacs outside the parlour window where I tried to work. The whole bush shook with their quarrelling. And one night a herd of something, cows, horses, I don't know, came and milled around on the lawn, breathing and nudging, like a mob gathering for the attack.

But the weather that late May was splendid, sunny and still, and tinged with sadness. I killed whole days rambling the fields. I had brought guidebooks to trees and birds, but I couldn't get the hang of them. The illustrations would not match up with the real specimens before me. Every bird looked like a starling. I soon got discouraged. Perhaps that explains the sense I had of being an interloper. Amid those sunlit scenes I felt detached, as if I myself were a mere idea, a stylised and subtly inaccurate illustration of something that was only real elsewhere.[12]

The narrative takes the form of a letter to 'Clio' (a real person who doubles for the muse of history), and the tone is comic, but the self-displacement, the sense of a haunting in our self-styled historian, is strongly present. He becomes obsessed by the family at the House, the Lawlesses (an allegorical name which, as we shall see, Banville uses elsewhere) and abandons work on his book, content only to fill the vaccuum of his own non-existence with the pleasures and the torments of what he calls his 'remote prurience'.

The socio-political level of the text is full of teasing reversals. The narrator appears the confident novelist, confirming the reader's prejudices about the Lawlesses; through the frank medium of his first-person testimony we are invited to be amused by the allegorical fitness between their name and their economic condition, history's revenge against a decayed and impoverished Protestant Ascendancy:

> I had them spotted for patricians from the start. The big house, Edward's tweeds, Charlotte's fine-boned slender grace that the dowdiest of clothes could not mask, even Ottilie's awkwardness, all this seemed the unmistakable stamp of their class. Protestants, of course, landed, the land gone now to gombeen men and compulsory purchase, the family fortune wasted by tax, death duties, inflation. But how bravely, how beautifully they bore their losses! Observing them, I understood that breeding such as theirs is a preparation not for squiredom itself, but for that distant day, which for the Lawlesses had arrived, when the trappings of glory are gone and only style remains. All nonsense, of course, but to me, product of a post-peasant Catholic upbringing, they appeared perfected creatures. (12–13)

Through his eyes, we are forced to watch the drama of their decline: Edward, it seems, is a drunk who brutalises the delicate Charlotte his wife, with whom the narrator falls hopelessly in love, and to whom he attempts to declare himself. But we learn gradually, through a series of reversals, that he has woven their biography from his own fantasies. He has mis-read everything: not only only are the Lawlesses Catholics, but Edward is dying stoically of stomach cancer while Charlotte, devoted to him but unable to cope, is full of drugs, which explains that strange remoteness in her which the narrator insists on idealising and employing as the sign of his own unrequited love. Edward, we learn, is the lawless and landless one, and Charlotte's maiden name, Grainger, is the name of the estate.

Ironically, Ferns, the house itself, surrounded by the constant whiff of decay, its greenhouse a 'dead and standing pool of air' (this unforgettable phrase is Marvell's from 'The Mower Against Gardens'), the arthritic branches of its rhododendrons giving off 'a smell of mossy rot reminiscent of the tang of damp flesh' is described, unexpectedly at first, as 'hynotically vivid in its unreality'. Only the indefatigably bodily, but sad Ottilie, Charlotte's daughter, with whom he has a real sexual affair, and whom he treats callously, is not a 'ghost':

> I took her for granted, of course, except when, exhausted or bored, she forgot about me. Then, playing the radio, brooding by the stove, sitting on the floor picking her nose with dreamy concentration, she would break away from me and be suddenly strange and incomprehensible, as sometimes a word, one's own name even, will briefly detach itself from its meaning and become a hole in the mesh of the world. (29)

Only the stubbornly incarnate Ottilie exists with any certainty outside the tissue of fictions with which the narrator's own imagination, like Prospero's magic, has endowed his own history, and this is because she thinks of *him* as non-existent: 'She laid her forehead against my cheek. "You know," she said, "sometimes I think you don't exist at all, that you're just a voice, a name."' (67)

This faint but audible echo of Donne's 'Aire and Angels' is a crucial indicator of the pattern of metaphysical irony in Banville's masterplot. The incarnation works in reverse: the narrator turns out to have been not an angel who took fleshly form, but an anthropologist excluded, by his misreading of it, from a ritual. For Ottilie refuses to be anything other than a historical being, and in doing so, she proves to the narrator his own (divine, but embarrassing) insubstantiality, she witnesses his 'ghostliness', which corresponds on the moral plane to a callow narcissism. On all levels this is a paradox: at the point, he implies, of knowledge of his own exclusion from it, his own history can be written. Prospero had drown'd his book, it seemed, but now he can take it up again and finish the narrative of Isaac Newton's strange crisis which has become his own.

Birchwood, one of Banville's earlier (1973) and more complex versions of this plot, also plays out this tension between the entropy of lyric idealism and the processes of incarnate history. This central struggle is reflected in the novel's three-act structure: Part I, subtitled 'The Book of the Dead' is a magnificent Gothic set piece contained entirely within the walls of the

decaying corpse-like mansion, Birchwood, which narrates the conception and childhood of Gabriel Godkin, and his existence amongst his
savage and unholy family of Beatrice, Martha, and Joseph, and the hilari-
ously hideous Smallweed-like Granda and Granny Godkin, who dies of
spontaneous combustion she is so dickensianly horrible, assassinated by
the House itself. Part II, 'Air and Angels', narrates Gabriel's incarnation
in history, his leaving of the dead womb of the house and his carnivalesque wanderings through Ireland with Prospero's Magic Circus. Part
III, 'Mercury', narrates the completion of the orbital journey of this starry
messenger; his return 'home' as a stranger and his confrontation with
his twin brother Michael, from which 'historical' point (the narrative is
set back to the post-Treaty period), Gabriel, immured once again in the
decayed House, has begun to tell the story.

The ultimately circular stasis which describes a magic ring of 'ram-
shackle dream' around the novel's plot, which the characters can neither
fully enter (the archangels are not part of human history) nor fully exit
from, has some relation to the central predicament of Yeats' last, metaphysical tragedy, *Purgatory* (1938). But the plot of Banville's novel is poised
between allegory and farce: a blasphemous parody of theological and
religious determinants in Irish history. Gabriel and Michael are identical
twins, the product of the secret incest of Joseph and Martha; one of them,
Michael, has been brought up as a 'Catholic', deliberately excluded from
his inheritance, Birchwood, while the other, Gabriel, the 'Protestant', has
spent his childhood and adolescence at Birchwood as the son and heir of
the estate of the Godkins. The deal between brother and sister was that,
as the price of Martha's silence, Michael would come into the estate and
Gabriel, finally, be excluded, but before his death Joseph altered the will,
betraying Martha and her son, and making Gabriel the rightful (i.e. legal)
heir of Birchwood. The novel is narrated by the archangel Gabriel, all
taking place at the beginning of the end of history. The roles of the identical twins have been randomly reversed: Gabriel, the angel who initiates
the end of history with a blast on his horn, inherits the dead protestant
past, while Michael, the catholic nationalist, who comes with fire and
sword to divide at the last day, inherits the nameless future.

The novel's Gothic, its obsession with the decaying House, is the
point at which this apparently concrete historical world turns inside out
before the reader's eyes. The cultural satire is foreshortened by the inertial
pull towards light and silence which Gabriel's point of view implicitly
reveals:

> Papa no longer tried to hide his helplessness. He gazed on the dissolu-
> tion of his kingdom in a kind of daze, humming distractedly under his

breath. He was rarely sober, and sometimes at night I would hear him stumbling up the stairs, cursing and belching, and kicking over the jamjars which Mama had so carefuly placed under the leaks in the ceilings. Nockter disappeared one night, and in the morning the police came looking for him. It seems he was in the movement. Papa was profoundly shocked. The rot of rebellion was no longer distant and therefore manageable, but had spread under his own roof, had flourished among the innocent flowers of Birchwood. I remember him in his armchair, in the library, gingerly opening the morning newspaper, holding his face away from it as though he feared that a fist might lash out from between the pages and punch him on the nose, and then there was his look of awe and bafflement as he read of the latest disasters and assassinations. Surely it was all a dream? The world was solid, god damn it![13]

Joseph, the protestant head of the Birchwood estate, has been living in a dream, and so, naturally enough, it appears solid to him. He learns even here that he has been selling off the estate all along to his old enemies the Lawlesses, Beatrice's family, a decadent wing of the protestant tribe fallen into trade. The equation is between the rotting of the building and the dissolution of the historicity of the protestant inheritance. Even here, when the historical perspective of the book appears so concrete (compare the 'empire Gothic' of J. G. Farrell's *Troubles* (1970), which is similar in its wildly comic, yet Gothic and grotesque, celebration of the decay of the ascendancy class, but finally very different in the more political role it assigns to 'history') Banville's idealising cadence is from Shakespeare's *Tempest*, and Prospero's cloud-capped towers ('The world was solid, god damn it!'). We tend to forget until such moments that the whole novel is narrated by an angel, a being whose presence in the world is preincarnate, only a formal fiction, after whose 'arrival' (he keeps his birth from us, just as it was kept from him) at Birchwood, a 'hollow horn of silence sounded through the house'.

This entropic pull in Gabriel's language towards light and silence, in which it comes to him, with the clarity and beauty of a mathematical statement that 'all movement is composed of an infinity of minute stillnesses', is totally unreconcilable with a fully achieved presence in the world. Most dynamic processes, including Gabriel's sexual initiations into the organic cycle, what he calls 'the damp dark side of life', are seen, intermittently but persistently, 'from the other side' as ghostly absences, stylised in form, strange petrifications of life's most vital moments. So Gabriel remembers the consternation at Granny Godkin's death:

The front door stood open. Three dead leaves were busy chasing each other round and round on the carpet. I saw all this in a flash, and no doubt that precise situation took no more than an instant to swell and flow into another, but for me it is petrified forever, the tapping finger, Mama's dripping hair, those leaves. (76)

Gabriel's haunted vision of his family, which appears simply to be a memory of the past, is also Prospero's revelation that his fictions are wearing thin, refusing to witness him any longer: 'They were all fleeing into themselves, as fast as they could flee, all my loved ones.'

While Gabriel is absent on his *Wanderjahre*, the Lawlesses eventually take possession of, and refurbish Birchwood, only to have the Catholic Nationalists, a strange murderous branch of whom, the Molly Maguires, who dress in women's clothing and with whom Michael seems to be loosely associated, slaughter them all. The final confrontation between the twins takes place in the empty house. Gabriel is crouched in the attic, holding a Sabatier knife. It is another moment of 'petrification', whose elaborately built dramatic suspense and Gothic allusions to horror and temporal decay seem curiously lightened of substance, robbed of their expected effects in the act of narration itself:

> The day waned. Rain fell, and then sun again briefly, then twilight. The tenants of the little room, a brassbound trunk, the dusty skeleton of a tricycle, that stringless tennis racket standing in the corner like a petrified exclamation of horror, began their slow dance into darkness. My face with its staring eyes retreated stealthily out of a grimy sliver of mirror, and then I knew he was in the house, for I could feel his presence like a minute tremor in the air. I waited calmly. The stairs creaked, and the spokes in the wheel of the tricycle tingled, and the door swung open. Michael, with his legs swaying and the wide skirts falling round him, stood on his hands out on the landing like a huge white mushroom upside down. I could have killed him then, with ease, I even imagined myself flying at him with the knife and plunging it down into his heart, but he was, after all, my brother. (75)

Michael is a murderous parody of the luminous, ideal sister Gabriel went in search of, not understanding that he had a twin brother all along, but the scene is one of armed reconciliation between Abel and Cain, not armageddon after all. Michael takes him to the summerhouse and shows to Gabriel the throttled corpse of their father, Joseph, whom their catholic tenant, Cotter, has risen up and personally killed, mocking the body with the blasphemous parody of the Lord's prayer: 'Our father, which art dead.'

Hovering between allegory and farce, this scene is a parody of the 'family romance' of Irish history, because the incestuous twins, Gabriel thinks, have probably been chosen for the wrong roles: this answers the puzzle for the reader of a false symmetry in the two archangels: Michael appears to be 'in' history, immersed in it, whereas Gabriel, the son and heir, seems only to inhabit the threshold of a biography, endlessly negotiating through the act of memory to join his own own past, and endlessly failing, his narrative a 'hollow horn of silence'. The answer is that these roles are arbitrary; comically, by whatever fiction Joseph and Martha chose them, they chose the wrong twin for each role, and, as Gabriel puts it, 'thereby came their ruin'.

But Gabriel's 'failure' is finally his success: we remember Prospero had a brother too, and the wizard's narrative, his reincarnation of history as a fiction on an empty stage allows him to understand the provisional nature of all of the past, its schizophrenia and absurd tragedies. It is in the nature of Prospero that he must leave and we must stay, but Gabriel, speaking both to his father as he buries him, and slyly to the reader too, concludes: 'so I became my own Prospero, and yours' (172).

I have been arguing that the texts of these two very different, contemporary, much-read, and widely praised authors carry a persistent strain of allusion to the characteristic environmental symbolism of the Gothic tradition. Both Iain Banks and John Banville are concerned with moments of the sublime, raised and cancelled in the structural metaphor of 'petrification'; the metaphor is structural because, far from being a mere question of linguistic or stylistic detail, or even of setting alone, its recurrence is part of a cultural code in these texts. The ironic petrifying of historical and psychological processes into dank, Gothic spaces is a way of laying bare what Roland Barthes calls 'the ideology of time'. The castle or fortress in Banks's *Complicity*, *The Crow Road*, *Fearsum Endginn*, and *The Player of Games*, self-confessedly a pastiche, represents a vertical arrestation of time, a barbarian labyrinth of darkness that takes the reader outside the comfortably depthless, cliché-ridden, so-called 'postmodern' landscape of 'heritage', and holds up to ransom easy notions of secular humanism and social progress since the 1960s; in Banville's Ferns and Birchwood, in the house in his *Mephisto*, *The Book of Evidence* (1980), and in *Ghosts* (1995), we trespass in the houses of a Protestant inheritance arrested in a lyrically evoked state of petrified decay like a fleet of becalmed ships – houses, always dying but never dead, whose shabby, vilely energetic array of tenants, lodgers, squatters, violators, hangers-on, circus people, and latecomers in general, reveals in a repeated scene of transgression the fictive arbitrariness of all exclusive genealogies and sets up, for characters and readers alike, a critical estrangement between the present and the past.

Notes

1 See Jameson's essay, 'Postmodernism and Consumer Society', in H. Foster (ed.), *Postmodern Culture* (London: Pluto Press, 1985), pp. 114–18.
2 Iain Banks, *Complicity* (London, 1994), p. 310. All quotations from this edition.
3 Iain M. Banks, *The Player of Games* (London: Macmillan, 1988).
4 Iain Banks, *Walking on Glass* (London: Macmillan, 1985).
5 Iain Banks, *Espedair Street* (London: Macmillan, 1987).
6 Iain Banks, *The Crow Road* (London: Scribners, 1992).
7 Iain Banks, *The Bridge* (London: Macmillan, 1986).
8 Iain M. Banks, *Fearsum Endginn* (London, Macmillan, 1994).
9 This general survey of Banks' dialectic reflects conversations in the summer of 1994 with Philip Gaskell. Iain Banks, *The Wasp Factory* (London: Abacus, 1984). All quotations from this edition.
10 Iain Banks, *Canal Dreams* (London: Macmillan, 1989).
11 J. Banville, *Mephisto* (London (1986), 1993), pp. 43–4.
12 J. Banville, *The Newton Letter* (London (1982), 1992), pp. 4–5. All quotations from this edition. This section is a modified version of a paper given to the Postgraduate Studies Group in the School of English and American Studies at the University of East Anglia in February 1995.
13 J. Banville, *Birchwood* (London: Minerva, 1973), p. 85. All quotations from this edition.

The pre-Oedipal father: the Gothicism
of *Blue Velvet*

My starting point is an observation by Stuart Hall:

> There are many different metaphors in which our thinking about cultural change takes place. These metaphors themselves change. Those which grip our imagination, and, for a time, govern our thinking about scenarios and possibilities of cultural transformation, give way to new metaphors, which make us think about these difficult questions in new terms.[1]

Western culture has extracted different metaphors of cultural change from the Oedipus myth's single story. Oedipus himself undergoes personal transitions of status, from those of the folk tale rite of passage (Propp) and the monomyth of accession to kingship (Goux) to the tragic developments of *Oedipus Rex* and the ultimate spiritual apotheosis of *Oedipus at Colonus*. Deviations from the norm in the early narrative phase indicate that the Oedipus story itself, as myth in its own right beyond the personal tale, stands on the threshold of wider social and symbolic transformations. And, in turn, these transformations acquire a renewed significance in the post-Enlightenment period, when Oedipus became a privileged emblem of tension between rational consciousness and the return of the repressed, the persistence of the irrational unconscious. It was, of course, in the last decade of the nineteenth century when Freud was writing *The Interpretation of Dreams* (published 1900), that Oedipus acquired his modern persona in the emblematic narrative of psychoanalysis. Writing now, in the year of the centenary of cinema, the image of Freud in 1995 seems uncannily juxtaposed to the Lumières' first projections. My analysis of *Blue Velvet*, as a site of the strange persistence of the Oedipus myth into twentieth-century popular culture, uses the film as a site, not only of Oedipal drama, but of the uncanny and the Gothic. My argument focuses first on the villain as father figure, a trope of Gothic fiction to which *Blue Velvet* gives an Oedipal origin; then goes on to consider the Sphinx as a figuration of the marvellous, who can return to popular imagination through the technologies of projection which first became a popular form in the Gothic period.

The cinema, with its ability to render visible the invisible, and conjure up meanings outside the precision of language, creates a cat's cradle of semiotic, symbolic, metaphoric, and all the other terms by means of which human culture has struggled to work through, and find representations for, the imprecise and invisible workings of the human mind. The post-Enlightment culture of the Gothic was important for Oedipus, as it was then that he came to represent the site of tension between the unconscious and conscious mind. But it was also the period in which phantasmagorias, prototypical of the cinema, became massively popular, appealing to the contemporary tension between the rational and the irrational. *Blue Velvet*, directed by David Lynch, released in 1986, allows a number of these issues to be discussed together.

In addition to the references and citations surrounding its Oedipal hero, *Blue Velvet* provides a spatial, or topographical, realisation for the Oedipal narrative and protagonists. It exploits the cinema's ability to provide a visualisation of narrative. The hero undergoes a horizontal transformation of status across a social spectrum by means of a vertical, metaphorical journey into the lower depths of the psyche. The horizontal journey is a movement towards the future, while the vertical suggests a return towards the past. A criminal 'underworld' provides the setting for the story's Oedipal drama, in which the 'repressed' of the law and the 'repressed' of consciousness converge. For Freud, the insistent pressure of a repressed past on the conscious mind may be displaced onto imagery of ruins or the archaic. He comments, for instance, on the imagery of Pompeii in the Gradiva story. The Gothic genre is, of course, literally haunted by the past, by its gloomy ruins, its subterranean passages, by its archaic superstitions and the 'returns' that mark its narratives. It is, perhaps, for this reason that it has never been easy to depict the archaic landscape and beliefs of the Gothic within the so-called New World. This is one of *Blue Velvet*'s most significant achivements. Its narrative topographies manage to install a 'nether' world within small town America, above all through the villain, a materialisation of the archaic father from the Oedipus legend. The openness of this link, and the use of 'returns' from the past of Hollywood cinema, both in casting and in generic reference, suggests a new figuration for Gothic themes in American popular culture.

Blue Velvet is a film which knowingly uses the interface between persistent popular iconographies and psychoanalytic theory. The critic does not have to 'read in', or 'read against the grain', as the both generic and psychoanalytic references are clearly marked. The film's interest lies in the way that it uses the 'symptomology' of popular culture to illuminate the place of unconscious fantasy in persistent, emblematic figures and stories. It is probably only out of the selfconsciousness of contemporary, postmodern, Hollywood in conjuncture with Lynch's own influences, such as Surrealism, and interests, such as psychoanalysis, that such a film could appear.

Transitions

The transitional, hybrid nature of the Oedipus story, from folk tale pattern to psychological drama, demands that the figure of the 'villain' should also change from the mythological, or marvellous (the Sphinx), to an anthropomorphic monstrous, a projection of infantile fears of the father.

My interest in *Blue Velvet* was first aroused by its overt exploitation of the hybrid temporality of the Oedipus story. First, there is the narrative that is patterned around a young man's rite of passage from adolescence into maturity. Secondly, there is the story of infantile Oedipal desires and conflicts. The two are linked by the hero's curiosity and his fascination with the enigmas of the nether world, which relates to the detective genre. The first of these stories is obviously based on the resolution of an essential conflict between hero and villain. *Blue Velvet* throws light on the psychoanalytic implications of the villain through its embedding of the Oedipal drama. And this, in turn, may throw light on the Gothic tradition of story-telling, with its particular conflation of father figure with villain. At the same time, the film's citation of film noir allows it to use the detective theme in order to create a conflation between infantile curiosity (Sandy's first initiatives and then Jeffrey's illicit voyeurism) and the investigative drive of the law.

The story of a hero's adventures on a journey, which takes him through a rite of passage from youth into maturity, has carried an important motifs from the folk tale into popular cinema. Film theorists, originating with Peter Wollen's analysis of *North by Northwest* (1959, d. Hitchcock),[2] have used Vladimir Propp's *Morphology of the Folktale* (1928) to identify the characters and motifs that are associated with this narrative pattern. The story is one of social transformation, a narrative rite of passage. A young male hero, unmarried, poor, and of low social status, leaves his childhood home to undergo a series of adventures and trials in which he has to prove himself. The crucial phase of transformation takes place around conflict with and the ultimate defeat of a villain. At the end, in the Proppian model, the hero rescues the princess who has fallen into the villain's clutches (a dragon, a giant, a wicked witch). As a reward, he marries the princess and the king, his father-in-law, bestows upon him half of his kingdom. He thus ends up mature, married, rich, and of a higher social status. He is now the owner of a new home, a palace indeed, in which he is the representative of the Law (represented as the power of the king).

Propp himself noticed that the first part of the Oedipus myth conforms closely to the structure that he had identified in Russian folk tale and he discussed the similarities and divergences of pattern in his article 'The Oedipus Myth as Folktale'.[3] He argued that the deviations in the Oedipus story bear witness to a social transformation. Thus, a story which is itself an account of a hero's transition to a new social status, reflects a wider, historical transition. While the old folk tale pattern is determined by a system of inheritance based on marriage, from father-in-law to son-in-law, the Oedipus story records the traumatic transition to a system of inheritance based on birth, from father directly to son. Oedipus seems, on the face of it, to follow the folk tale pattern, leaving home, embarking on a journey, conquering a monster, the Sphinx, and being rewarded by the hand of the Queen in marriage and the kingdom of Thebes. He has, in fact, returned to the place of his birth, from which he was banished as an infant, and actually inherited his own father's kingdom, in direct patrilineal descent. And he has, of course, killed his father to make way for this perverse aberration of the folk tale pattern, placing parricide and maternal incest at the very moment at which patrilineal inheritance is instigated.

Jean-Joseph Goux, in his book *Oedipus, Philosopher*[4] draws attention to the Oedipus story as a version of an initiation rite, analysing its structural similarity to, in his terms, the 'monomyth' of the hero's rite of passage to royal investiture. He considers the Oedipus story to be aberrant in the hero/villain relation. The Sphinx, structurally situated as the creature that must be defeated for the tale to reach its appropriate conclusion, is a female monster and is thus related to the other monsters of Greek legend, the Gorgon and the Chimera, who are also defeated by heroes on their way to kingship, Perseus and Bellerophon. Goux argues that the female monsters stand in for a 'monstrous maternal', whose murder is essential for the rite of passage to take place. Thus the heroes' victory represents an act of matricide that necessarily precedes their ascension to kingship and marriage. The male initiate celebrates his separation from the archaic and overpowering mother. The monstrous mother is archaic in that she belongs to an earlier epoch, both in terms of the psychological development of child/subject and the social development of patriarchy. She is also literally monstrous, part animal, part bird, part human, belonging to an ancient realm of myth that would pre-date the humanoid appearance of the Olympian gods and goddesses.

41

Feminist film theorists have pointed out that this 'monstrous maternal' persists into contemporary popular culture. Teresa de Lauretis has analysed the topographical significance of the mythic monster figure, who stands, static, in the path of the hero's trajectory as a space that must be crossed.[5] And Barbara Creed has identified the mother alien in the *Alien* trilogy (1979, 1986, 1992) as a return of this figure.[6] However, the Oedipus myth is once again sited on a threshold. The story bears witness to a transformation in the villain function that will be of central importance in later popular cultures. Oedipus fails to kill the Sphinx. He answers her riddle and thus, as Goux points out, omits the initiate's act of matricide leaving the Sphinx to self-destruct. The maternal monster is thus only present as a weak function; her challenge is reduced to the verbal and her defeat is reduced to suicide.

The Sphinx is placed in the narrative to mark the defeat of the villain by the hero and his reward with the hand of the princess (Jocasta) and the kingdom (Thebes). But, placed immediately before this motif of victory/defeat, is another which the Proppian narrative cannot acknowledge in its true transformative sense. Oedipus has been confronted, just previously, at the fork in the road, by a terrifying old man who threatened to run him down and kill him. Oedipus, acting as he later claimed, in self-defence, kills him instead. Laius and the Sphinx are doubled in the narrative structure. The Sphinx is present as a remnant of an archaic world and belief system. Laius introduces a new psychic element, inaugurating, perhaps, a new personification of villainy that would survive beyond the villain functions of dragons, witches, giants, and so on. Thus, the function 'villain', once the maternal as static, archaic monster, is transposed onto a monstrous paternal, human in shape and, rather than static, in competition with the young man for space on the road. It is, in fact, only by eliminating the old king that Oedipus is able to marry Queen Jocasta and inherit Thebes.

The Oedipus Complex, in Freud's theory, is also a narrative of a rite of passage. It marks the transition from infancy to childhood, from a boundaryless attachment to the mother in which her body and the infant's are inextricably intertwined in a complementary duality, to the child's assertion of autonomy from the mother, achievement of a sense of self, and an understanding of his/her place in the cultural order of the family. For Freud, this transition was achieved only through a painful and never to be erased threat of castration, which emanates from the father. Lacan theorised the castration complex in the Oedipal trajectory more specifically as a traumatic, but necessary, passage on the way to an initiation into the symbolic order of culture, through acquisition of language and understanding of the Name of the Father as the signifier of Law.

In the process, the infant abandons his desiring and deeply erotic feeling for his mother, murderous jealousy of the father, identifying with the 'promise' (as Althusser puts it) that he will grow up to take his father's place within the symbolic order.

Blue Velvet negotiates a merger of the two versions by embedding the Oedipal narrative of transition within the story of passage from youth to maturity. The hero's 'adventures' are not simply those of the folk tale's triumphant encounter with danger and victory over evil. Following the Proppian pattern Jeffrey Beaumont is, at the beginning of the story, still a callow youth. By the end of the movie, after his 'adventures', he has acquired a new maturity and is able to claim Sandy as his future wife. He has also, through his struggle with the villain and victory over him, inherited the place of the father and the father-in-law. He has moved into the position of authority, associated with the patriarchal function, and the Law.

However, the doubling, or distribution, of narrative functions between characters indicates the presence of the second, Oedipal, narrative pattern. While Sandy represents the Proppian princess 'to-be-married' as a reward for the villain's defeat, in the Oedipal story Dorothy represents the princess who must be rescued from the villain. The opening sequence gives an Oedipal twist to Jeffrey's father's collapse. And Mr Beaumont's subsequent illness allows two other figures to occupy the place of the paternal. One is literally the representative of the Law, Sandy's father (Detective Williams), while Frank Booth, the villain who focuses the conflict between hero and villain, emerges as a disturbing perversion of the paternal. His iconography conflates the underworld of the criminal, the netherworld of the city at night, with the unconscious of the Oedipal drama.

David Lynch makes use of specific psychoanalytic scenarios and citations in order to give Frank paternal as well as brutal attributes. The film's most famous and most shocking sequence is a vivid rendition of Freud's concept of the 'primal scene'. Jeffrey, hidden in the wardrobe, witnesses Frank's violent, sexual attack on Dorothy. According to Freud, when a child's first witnesses his/her parents' sexual intercourse, the sight is terrifying and probably traumatic. The child interprets the scene as one of violence, in which the father, the stronger partner, carries out a brutal attack on the mother, the weaker. The mother, who is also, of course, the child's main love object, needs to be rescued. Within the perspective of the primal scene, Frank personifies all that is perceived as brutal in the father, and Dorothy personifies the mother's vulnerability. In the child's fantasy, the mother would infinitely rather 'be married' to him/her than persecuted by such a monster, and she only undergoes such horrific humiliation to protect him from the father's attack. Jeffrey is the horrified witness of the primal scene, but its emotional impact and implications are extended and reiterated into the story as a whole. Jeffrey understands Frank's hold over Dorothy to be the direct result of her need to protect little Don, her son. And Dorothy sometimes calls Jeffrey 'Don'.

Jeffrey's hiding place, the wardrobe, accentuates his status in the scene as both infant and 'infantile voyeur'. The scene therefore condenses a fantasy enactment of the primal scene with a fantasy of desire for the mother. Before Frank arrives, Dorothy has entered her appartment, and started to undress. The film intercuts between the room and the wardrobe to emphasise Jeffrey's voyeuristic look. Dorothy's body is not, however, presented to the spectator in any way enhanced by the usual conventions of cinematic eroticism. When she answers the telephone and speaks to her son she is stamped as mother, and as vulnerable. But when she discovers Jeffrey's illicit presence in his hiding place, she threatens him with a knife, suddenly shifting from the vulnerable to the castrating mother. She infantilises him by forcing him to undress and then seduces him. Dorothy's is not a single, coherent, fictional, characterisation. She moves through contradictory, unconscious, iconographies of motherhood, from vulnerability to the father's aggression, to castrating and threatening the helpless boy, to the image of absolute incestuous desirability. Furthermore, the eroticism into which she initiates Jeffrey is perverse; she teaches him the sadistic sexuality that is associated with Frank. This scene, in all its permutations, is acted out with such extraordinary and shocking violence and eroticism, that it is truly suffused with the horror and attraction of a fantasy scenario.

These psychoanalytic references place Dorothy and Frank within the realm of the unconscious, as the 'father' and 'mother' of the Oedipal child. *Blue Velvet* sends Jeffrey, not on the folk tale's adventure into the liminal space away from home, or outside the city, but on a journey into the Oedipal unconscious, to confront incestuous desire and the villainous father figure. In this sense, Frank represents the 'pre-Oedipal father'. The lifelessness of life in the small town home, contrasts with Dorothy's shockingly direct sexuality, her immediate seduction of Jeffrey, and Frank's horrific restless energy, always torn by violent emotion. But Frank is also, in a way, impotent. He is as dependent on his amyl nitrate fix for potency as Mr Beaumont is dependent on his oxygen apparatus for breathing. His rape of Dorothy is closer to Freud's vision of infantile sexuality as polymorphously perverse, than to adult genital sexuality, even at its most violent. He is far from a figure of mature masculinity. This is emphasised by his 'regression' to babyhood (his desire to 'go back home'), his orality, voyeurism, sadism, acting out of the child's understanding of the female body as castrated, and finally, and most significantly, his fetishistic fixation on the blue velvet. He is incapable of coherent speech and almost completely inarticulate in his repetition of obscenities. He is simultaneously an infant and the monstrous paternal.

In my 1987 article on the myth of Oedipus,[7] I was reminded of Frank Booth while writing about Laius. In the pre-story of Oedipus, which Freud has been accused of repressing, Laius had been exiled, temporarily from Thebes and taken refuge in the court of King Pelops in Sparta. There he had fallen in love with the king's young son Chrysippos, raped him, and attempted to kidnap him. In revenge for this act of brutal violence, the king pronounced a curse, that Laius would be killed by his own son who would then have an incestuous relationship with his mother. It was in order to escape this fate that Laius, in another act of brutality, had his baby son Oedipus exposed and left to die. The joy-ride scene in *Blue Velvet* uncannily reproduces these themes. Frank seems to recognise some affinity with Jeffrey when he says: 'You're like me' and before beating him up he puts on lipstick and kisses Jeffrey passionately on the lips. The brutal father seems to threaten the son, not only with violence, but with a sexualised violence that approximates to rape. There is a sense in which Frank, like Laius, is pre-Oedipal. Laius in literal, generational chronology pre-dates the Oedipal trajectory lived out by his son. Frank stands in polarised opposition to the Law, culture, the symbolic order, and, to all intents and purposes, verbal language.

Raymond Bellour, the French film theorist who was one of the first to articulate the Oedipal pattern of Hollywood narrative, puts the argument like this:

> the bad father must die, in the final confrontation, so that the couple can be formed; he even has his double, his reverse image, the good father, who makes possible the entry into the genealogy, the continuity between generations . . . It's the movement from the adventurer, sans foi ni loi as we say in French (lawless and faithless) to the husband, the future father and the good citizen . . . The American cinema thus finds itself enacting the most classic paradigms elaborated for the subject of Western culture by Freudian psychoanalysis . . . My constant surprise was to discover to what degree everything was organised according to a classic Oedipal scenario which inscribed the subject, the hero of the film, in a precise relation to parricide and incest and to observe that his itinerary, his trajectory corresponded to a strict psychic progression which engaged the hero in the symbolic paths of Oedipus and of castration.[8]

Although Bellour draws attention to the persistence of the Oedipal narrative, he also describes how the generic versions (the Western, in this case) erase the threat of the unconscious as the villain is erased from the story. The conclusion seems to indicate that the traces of Oedipal desire are easily abandoned in the story's lawless, liminal phase. The hero's erasure of the monstrous paternal allows the story to come to rest under the aegis of a new moral order. *Blue Velvet*, on the contrary, implies that the Symbolic Order is imbricated with the monstrous paternal. The story records Jeffrey's transition into maturity but, at the same time, the Oedipal figures of fear and desire have inscribed themselves into the psyche. When the camera emerges from Jeffrey's ear at the end of the film, the implication that everything else has been 'only a dream' is undercut by Jeffrey's new darkness. It is clear that Frank Booth and Dorothy Vallens will live on in his unconscious, erupting into the symptomatic behaviour that characterises, and is repressed by, the patriarchal psyche.

The terrible violence and irrationality of the father/villain lies at the heart of the Gothic genre. The founding novel of the genre, Horace Walpole's *The Castle of Otranto* (1794) is a story of three failed fathers, but its narrative development is centred on Manfred's autocratic power. At the untimely death of his son, Manfred decides to marry his future daughter-in-law himself and the novel then unfolds in the aftermath of his monstrous fixation. Isabella's escape takes her into a 'nether world', the characteristic Gothic *mise-en-scène* of underground passages, through which Manfred pursues her. Theodore, the young peasant whom Manfred also persecutes, rescues Isabella and it turns out that Manfred had usurped the estate to which Theodore is the rightful heir. Here again, a young man reaches maturity through a confrontation with a figure of the monstrous paternal, whose autocratic, irrational, and instinctual tyranny belongs to a pre-Enlightenment age.[9] In Mrs Radcliffe's *A Sicilian Romance*, the Count imprisons his daughters' mother in an underground cave, directly under the deserted wing of his castle. The civilised surface life of the castle carries dark secrets beneath it and the father's behaviour oscillates between the darkness of the pre-Oedipal villain and the Oedipalised patriarch.[10]

Jane Austen's famous comment on the fashion for the Gothic, *Northanger Abbey*, written during the late nineties at the height of Mrs Radcliffe fever, focuses both on the *mise-en-scène* of the Abbey and the heroine's semi-erotic terror of General Tilney, who, for her, becomes a figure of the villainous paternal. Breaking into a sudden parody of the Gothic's syntax, punctuation, and use of the 'free indirect', Jane Austen suggests that the genre played on a state of mind, a propensity to fantasy in its young women readers:

> Catherine's blood ran cold with the horrid suggestions which naturally sprang from these words. Could it be possible? – Could Henry's father?

– And yet how many were the examples to justify even the blackest suspicions! – And, when she saw him in the evening, while she worked with her friend, slowly placing the drawing-room for an hour together in downcast thoughtfulness, with downcast eyes and contracted brow, she felt secure from all possibility of wronging him. It was the air and attitude of a Montoni! – . . . Unhappy man![11]

Jane Austen makes fun of the Gothic, but she takes seriously her heroine's desire to believe in the irrational evil conjured up by the genre. This rational, psychological portrait internalises Catherine's fears and renders them as figments of her imagination. This tension between the exterior and the interior, the rational and the irrational, brings back the figure of Oedipus as an emblem of transition in the post-Enlightenment period.

The Enlightenment's unconscious

It was with the publication of Horace Walpole's dream novel, The Castle of Otranto (1764) that the demonic found a literary form in the midst of Augustinian ideals of classical harmony, public decorum and restraint. Unreason, silenced through the Enlightenment period, erupts into the fantastic art of Sade, Goya and horror fiction.[12]

Jean-Joseph Goux emphasises that Oedipus defeats the Sphinx purely 'on his own', that is, without help from the gods essential to the other heroes' victories. Oedipus makes use of his own intelligence rather than magical objects donated by supernatural beings. He is thus poised on another threshold. He stands between a world inhabited by fabulous impossible creatures and gods and goddesses who intervene in the lives of men, and a world in which Man is at the centre and the 'marvellous' is equated with superstition. Oedipus does not deign to do battle with the Sphinx. She self-destructs when the riddle is answered, signifying that the epoch of credulity that had conjured up such creatures, had come to an end.

When Oedipus was confronted with the riddle of the Sphinx: 'What speaks with one voice, walks on four legs in the morning, on two legs at noon and on three legs in the evening and is weakest when it has the most?' He answered, as everyone knows, with one word 'Man'. This moment was adopted by post-Enlightenment thinkers as the founding moment of a subjectivity that is centred on human consciousness, that is, on man's awareness of his own rationality. The relation between the question and its answer is not simply that of riddle and solution. The two terms are separated by the vast conceptual gap that represents the difference between meanings that are coded and obscure and those produced by man's ability to think philosophically.

In Hegel's discussion of Oedipus, he uses this moment in the myth as a point of transition between two cultures, in which one is characterised by the philosophical abstraction of Greece and the other by 'Egyptian' symbolism. Again, the Sphinx epitomises the pre-rational. She is archaic and monstrous, a creature composed out of three different parts, human, animal, and bird. She is a riddle and she poses a riddle. With a slight manipulation of geography and myth, Hegel conflates the Greek with the Egyptian Sphinx thus enabling her to represent a culture of symbols, in which meaning is concealed in allusion. He says: 'In Egypt, on the whole, almost every shape is a symbol and a hieroglyph not signifying itself but hinting at another thing with which it has an affinity and thus a relationship.' Meaning has to be deciphered out of enigma. For Hegel, Oedipus, on the hand, inaugurates the triumph of rationality. He is the proto-typical philosopher, for whom thought can be expressed without mediation and obscurity. It is the anthropocentric answer 'Man' that causes the Sphinx to throw herself from the rock and kill herself.

Goux points out that the Cartesian revolution is itself Oedipal in its insistence on the autonomy of the individual subject, its insistence on the inherent ability of man to achieve rational thought without tradition or teaching. He says:

> Descartes's patricidal gesture is incommensurable, in its import and its radicality, with any individual killing of any individual father. Descartes is a principal and abstract Oedipus. He denies the ontological dimension of paternity. He attempts to establish truth in the absence of that dimension, taking on himself, as an 'I' the function it purported to fulfil.[13]

The spirit of the Enlightenment thus attempts to assert the subject's pure power of reason and complete the transition inaugurated so long before by Oedipus. The traditional power of the priesthood, which held people in fear, ignorance, and ritualised belief, could be swept away by the spirit of self-sufficient knowledge. The gods and goddesses, spirits and fairies, the saints and superstitions of Catholicism, even the purified, post-Reformation God himself, could all be dismissed as emanations of the human mind, simply figments of the imagination.

From this perspective, Freud's theory of the unconscious appears on the intellectual scene as a final act of the Enlightenment. And psychoanalysis, from this perspective, constitutes a rational theory of the irrational, which could bring human fears, anxieties, and credulities into a framework of articulate explanation. Even dreams could be translated out of their enigmatic language, interpreted, and revealed to 'make sense'. But there is, of course, a further dimension to Freudian theory which is encapsulated in the next phase of the Oedipal trajectory. Although Freud posited a theory and a vocabulary which describes and analyses the unconscious, its place in the human psyche is not dissolved or even necessarily mitigated as a result. The unconscious continues to haunt 'Man' even at his most rational. Oedipus stands on the threshold, as an emblem of transition between the world of the supernatural belief and rational understanding, but he also stands on the threshold where the conscious mind learns the intractable presence of the unconscious. The Sphinx commits suicide, but Oedipus marries his mother. He then becomes the emblem of the human psyche subject to 'the return of the repressed'.

Freud uses the Sophocles play *Oedipus the King* as his source material and his interest focuses on the events that take place within the spatial and temporal rules of the Greek tragedy, rather than on the wandering structure of the folk tale type story. This section of the story told in the play, comes long after Oedipus' encounter with the Sphinx, his marriage, and ascension to the throne, and concentrates on the traumatic repressed of his rationality. Freud transforms Oedipus from a figuration of human reason into a figuration of the human subordination to unreason. The Oedipal intelligence is, as the play progresses, at first clouded by resistance and then, through determined investigation and analysis, confronted with the real monster in the story: his unconscious acts of patricide and incest.

Freud made several contributions to the accumulating significance of Oedipus as he recurs metaphorically through Western culture. First of all, he detached the story from its hero/rite of passage narrative, cutting loose its archaic accoutrements. Secondly, he transformed the modern, rational Oedipus of Enlightenment iconography into a powerful example of the force of the unconscious, with its intractable formation in the subject's relations with its father and mother, refracted through infantile sexuality and anxiety. Finally, he replaced the story's transitional or liminal motif back in time from that of a passage between youth and manhood, to that of a passage from infancy to childhood.

To summarise in Jean-Joseph Goux's words:

> It is not surprising that Freud discovers the unconscious and the two Oedipal drives at the same time. The modern subject's self-consciousness is constituted as 'Oedipus's response', which leaves in obscurity, as a counterpart, the two never-extinguished drives that shape Oedipus's destiny. It is not just self-consciousness, reflective ego-centering that is Oedipean, as Hegel masterfully noted; it is also the unconscious and desiring counterpart that this response engenders, as Freud discovered. If consciousness is constituted 'in response to the Sphinx', the

unconscious is the obscure, pulsional side of that response: patricide, incest.[14]

Oedipus thus becomes a double, Janus-faced, figure. He represents simultaneously humanity's utopian aspiration to the rational and to transcendent knowledge; and, its impossibility, the necessary failure, even the tragedy-laden fate accompanying such arrogance. It is important to emphasise that, although Freud's discovery is, indeed, one of the essential intractability of the unconscious, it is still formulated and articulated within an Enlightenment aspiration. He not only notes that figures of fear and desire are strictly emanations of the human mind, but provides a language and a conceptual framework within which their meanings can be analysed.

In *Blue Velvet*, Jeffrey's rite of passage into maturity is also simultaneously a journey into the Oedipal unconscious. David Lynch does not allow the story to exorcise its demonic forces and return to the surface as the natural and normal site of being. The shots of the trees with the camera tracking into darkness, a candle flame, or a curtain blowing in the wind, suggest that the exorcised psychic forces live on in Jeffrey's unconscious mind. The hero's rite of passage into patriarchal maturity is built on his internalisation of the forces he overcame in the course of the story. And the last shot of the film shows mother and son, happily reunited in their ideal dyad, waiting for the whole process to begin all over again.

The return of the Sphinx

Lacan's emphasis on the abstract, signifying nature of the father's symbolic authority links to both Propp's and Hegel's conception of the Oedipus story. Propp saw the Oedipus story as a transitional moment to patrilineal inheritance, and Hegel 'Europeanised' the story by setting up a polarised distinction between an abstract and a symbolic system of representation. But it is essential to remember that, for Lacan, language cannot escape from the effects of the unconscious mind. His use of semiotics, his concept of the instability of meaning and its slippage from sign to sign, is a reminder that the Law is always fraught with unconscious effects. If the disposal of the Sphinx is, at one and the same time, the disposal of the 'monstrous maternal' and of 'Africa', her suicide acts as a metaphor for the repression of both the mother and the cultural Other under the patriarchal Symbolic Order. But the repressed returns, in disguised forms which are necessarily outside immediate, transcendent understanding and demand interpretation which Freud compared to the deciphering of a rebus.

Hegel's beautiful characterisation of the Egyptian signifying system alters in the light of later psychoanalytic theory. He points out that the symbol and the hieroglyph are 'not signifying but hinting at another thing' and thus evoke the 'disguised' language of the Freudian unconscious, which makes use of condensation and displacement to find means of articulating meanings unacceptable to the conscious mind. And when Hegel goes on to say: 'Egypt is the country of symbols, the country which sets itself the spiritual task of the self-deciphering of the spirit, without actually attaining to the decipherment',[15] he could be evoking the psychoanalytic project, in which the process of analysis deciphers signs, for instance, the language of dreams, attempting to restore them to their original point of unconscious reference. But Hegel foresees the Lacanian warning of the ultimate impossibility of the task of decipherment; while signifiers form links and slippages of meaning, pure reference constantly gets lost under excess of signification.

The Sphinx belongs to the world of the marvellous, beyond nature, a world in which disbelief is suspended in the face of supernatural phenomena. While Oedipus represents the unconscious, those elements in the human psyche that the Enlightenment could not exorcise, the Sphinx represents its propensity to credulity and the persistent fascination with the marvellous and the supernatural that the Enlightenment, equally, failed to exorcise. Her image and the story of her fate can provide an appropriate metaphor for the culture of phantasmagoria that has always, technology permitting, fascinated credulous spectators. The story of projected phantasmagorias emerges as an accompaniment to the story of tension between rationality, superstition, and the unconscious. It leads towards to its twentieth-century apotheosis in the projected images of cinema which could also tell stories as well as simply amaze.

An important accompaniment to the culture of the Gothic was a fashion for ghosts, summoned up by phantasmagoric projections. The Enlightenment, illuminating the dark relics of religious belief with science and reason, banished ghosts and other terrifying manifestations only to have them crowd back through the culture of the Gothic. So, just as the old beliefs of the spirit world were swept away, their forms materialised onto Magic Lantern screens. The Gothic is closely tied to the protocinematic. Just after Matthew Lewis had become a best-selling author with the publication of *The Monk*, in 1795, the Belgian showman Etienne Robertson was entertaining Paris with his phantasmagorias. Set in the labyrinthine underground vaults of the former Capuchin convent, Robertson put on a ghost show in mechanical projection. While the show overtly demystified superstitious belief, it used every trick of *mise-en-scène* to fill the audience with a sense of the 'horrid'. Terry Castle has argued that these phantasmagoric effects acted as a bridge between the spirits that people, once upon a time, believed existed in the world around them, and their relocation into the interiority of the human mind as symptoms of mental disorder. The phantasmagorias showed, she says: 'that although one knew ghosts did not exist, one saw them all the same, without precisely knowing how'. She continues: 'The rationalists did not so much negate the traditional spirit world but displace it into a realm of psychology. Ghosts were not exorcised but only internalised and re-interpreted as hallucinatory thoughts.'[16] And thoughts could take on the haunting reality of ghosts. The supernatural marvellous is relocated in the mechanical uncanny which can then become a metaphor for the persistence of human belief in the irrational. This link between the proto-cinematic projection machine and the proto-psychoanalytic return of the irrational are identified by Christian Metz as specific to cinema. Suspension of disbelief, he says, is a similar mental mechanism to that of fetishism: 'I know these images are not real, but all the same . . .'

It was just as Freud was working on *The Interpretation of Dreams*, that the first film projections took place in 1895. This moment reiterates the earlier conjunction between the Enlightenment and the phantasmagorias. Just as Freud extended rational investigation to the world of dreams, they returned on the movie screen, with the phantasmatic stories and scenarios that can recreate the marvellous and make any hybrid monster come to life. However, the cultural impact of Freud's unveiling of the human unconscious and its language can be seen in its appeal to the Surrealists, who were totally opposed to Enlightenment rationality and saw the cinema as a materialisation of the dream life. André Breton was himself an admirer of both the English Gothic and cinema. In his introduction to the catalogue of the 1930 Surrealist exhibition, he commented on Walpole's account the origins of *The Castle of Otranto* in a dream, in which a hand of an enormous scale appeared inside a house.[17] Breton describes the the cinema in dream terms: 'From the instant he takes his seat to the moment he slips into a fiction evolving before his eyes the spectator passes through a critical point as captivating and imperceptible as that uniting waking and sleeping.'[18] And Brunius describes cinema as: 'an involutary simulation of a dream. The darkness of the auditorium, tantamount to closing the eyelids on the retina, and, for thought, to the darkness of the unconscious.'[19] Fragmented words and images appear on a screen.

> Neither chronological order nor relative values of duration are real. Contrary to the theatre, film, like thought, like the dream, chooses some gestures, defers or enlarges them, eliminates others, travels many, hours,

centuries, kilometers in a few seconds, speeds up, slows down, goes backwards.[20]

The Surrealists' passionate invocation of the irrational creates a link between the Gothic aesthetic, Freudian theory, and the dream-like qualities of the cinema. They are also an acknowledged influence on David Lynch.

Blue Velvet manifests these links through its narrative structure, and in its organisation of narrative into a topographical system. The Oedipal narrative unfolds in a *mise-en-scène* of the uncanny. In his 1919 essay,[21] Freud analysed the uncanny as the 'unheimlich', the unhomely, and located the strangeness of its effect within the home itself, ultimately locating it in the womb, the first home, and the tomb, the last.

The power of cinematic language juxtaposes spaces and images which disturb the familiar with strangeness and the uneasy intimations of fear and desire. The uncanny is closely associated with place, or with the projection of unconscious unease into a fantastic topography. The Gothic is, quite obviously, a genre of uncanny *mise-en-scènes*: ruins, tombs, labyrinthine underground passages give material visibility to the presence of the past, doubling up the way that the stories are actually set in past historical time. The uncanny also occupies the underworld of the nineteenth-century city, celebrated in the detective genre that investigates its enigmas. The uncanny topography extends to the 'underworld' of crime, the nether side of law and order. All these spatial representations, the ruins of the past, the criminal milieu, make use of the division between surface and nether world.

Blue Velvet's opening sequence is designed around these intricate topographical metaphors, but in such a way as to make its implications as apparent as possible. The binary opposition between the everyday and nether worlds is there for all to see and to grasp. The sequency begins with a sunlit, leafy, small town street, inhabited by school children and the benign authority of the fire brigade; it ends in the darkness of the undergrowth, where, invisible to the normal eye, hideous insects are locked in mortal combat. This opposition is easy to understand and forebodes the topographical organisation of the story that is to come, between light/day and dark/night, the institutions of law and the criminal underworld, conscious perception and unconscious experience, and between hero and villain. However, the surface world is depicted as 'surface'. It has the immaterial, itself uncanny, quality of the cliché which speaks of appearance and nothing else and the impermanent, almost comic, quality of the postcard which has no substance other than connotation. On the other hand, unlike the flatness and colour saturation of the opening images, the darkness draws in the camera with the force of fascinated curiosity.

The sequence sets up a spatial configuration around the home itself, that is suspended between the opposition of surface and under-world. First, there is a shot of a house, the small town home, white, with a picket fence. This image of the homely is quickly rendered uncanny. Mother and father are located one on the inside and one on the outside, the father waters the garden and the mother watches television. Suddenly a knot forms in the garden hose, and the father collapses with a heart attack. As he lies on the ground, the hose spurts water in a phallic stream and a toddler appears walking towards him, like a manifestation of the Oedipal death threat. Small drops of water are reduced to slow motion as a little dog snaps at them over the man's prone body. Inside, a gun appears in close-up on the television screen, as the mother sips her tea. The collapse of the homeliness of the scene is accentuated by the cine-matic effects, the slow motion in particular, and the sound effects which, as the camera follows the line of the hose pipe towards the undergrowth, drown out the strange, melancholic 'Blue Velvet' song, which prefigures the erotic element in the story, with noise of an indecipherable nature.

In *Blue Velvet*, the story buries a narrative of the unconscious within a frame that belongs to a world of normality. This latter world is, in fact, deeply implicated with its other, and exists as a fragile bulwark set up to keep out the forces of darkness. Given that *Blue Velvet*'s setting is small town America, the film has to construct its 'Gothic' iconographies and *mise-en-scènes* out of generic and psychoanalytic references. The film excav-ates a topography of the fantastic, of an underworld, out of a social set-ting which appears to repress its very possibility. A vocabulary of visual and rhetorical devices and a syntax of story-telling appear on the screen like phantasmagoric shapes whose immanent, misty, smokey material congeals gradually into visibility. (David Lynch uses this vocabulary and syntax in such a way that it should be readable to anyone in the audience who is prepared to think about it.)

These images make a demand on the audience to figure out their relationship, to register the patterns set up between the opposing motifs that appear on the screen, while noting the imbrications between them as enigmatic and mysterious, as material that will have to be deciphered by the plot. In this way, as, during the main line of the story, Jeffrey will have to pursue and investigate the clues to the mystery of Dorothy Vallens and Frank Booth, so the audience will have to follow a parallel process of decipherment which cannot find full resolution within the conscious-ness of the characters themselves. For Freud, the topographical metaphor that he used, in his early formulation of his theories, to evoke the relation between the conscious and unconscious aspects of the psyche was only the beginning of the story. There was no simple movement between the two. The unconscious manifested repressed desires in the conscious mind through a translation, or disguising of ideas, by means of the processes of condensation and displacement. The displacements activated by the images of the uncanny set up the more complicated displacements activated by the Oedipal narrative.

The specific formal properties of cinema play a crucial part in creating this, further, textual level, in the film. They reverberate resonances across images, setting up links, which tie together into a chain of significance, rather as Frank's obsession with the blue velvet leaves fragments of the material scattered across the development of the drama. This is a point where the mechanisms of the dream work (condensation and displacement) find an equivalence in the cinema. In cinema, shifts in scale, or repeated camera movements, can tie together images to create linked meanings, either opposing the two in a binary opposition or carrying the significance of one image over and onto another. In this sense the language of cinema can set up meanings that inform each other not only through the nature of their content but through the rhetoric of their visualisation.

David Lynch uses psychoanalytic theory quite blatantly, almost a 'dollar book Freud' as Orson Welles said of *Citizen Kane* (1941), to bring a Gothic uncanny home to roost in the mythology of small town America and its amorphous temporality, a 1950s 'once upon a time'. Traditionally and innovatively, with a camp wit, he suggests that the cinema screen has been the site of phantasmagoric projection, which reached its perfection in Hollywood. With its stars, its genres, and its technological perfection, Hollywood recreated the marvellous, in glamour, in its supernatural effects, and in the sutured surface of the world of its story-telling. It is only with the decline of the Hollywood system, perhaps, that the cinema, once upon a time the guarantee of modernity and the progressive orientation of the New World, can become the archaic for American popular culture. The cinema always had something of the android in its fascination; its beauty and naturalism were only a mechanical effect, the animation of still frames, that could grind only too easily into stasis. And as the great stars grew old and died, their images continued to shine from television screens in a perpetual state of animation from beyond the grave.

Blue Velvet was released in 1986, the high point in the reign of the United States' first movie star President, whose own formation and self-image were grounded in the last moments of the Hollywood studio system, as well as the political paranoia and white suburban spread of the fifties. The year 1986 also saw a small plane shot down over Nicaragua, leading to the disclosure of the labyrinthine underworld known as 'covert operations'. The topographies implied in the metaphors suggest an uncanny underside to the surface presented by the President, himself an image of the uncanny: made-up, artificial, and amnesiac. *Blue Velvet* restores an uncanny to American culture that the uncanny President disavows. In Freud's definition the uncanny is simultaneously located in homeliness and is the eruption of something that should remain hidden. *Blue Velvet* uses the cinema's own rhetoric to acknowledge its uncanny as, for instance, when Sandy first appears on the screen in a long fade up from black and accompanied by a swelling score. The film also depicts the forces of the unconscious through a repeated topography which is decipherable to any spectator while, at the same time, evoking shades of the Gothic. The hidden is brought to the surface to trace its persistence rather than its erasure.

Notes

1 S. Hall, Introduction to Allon White, *Carnival Writing Hysteria: The Essays and Autobiography of Allon White* (Oxford: Clarendon Press, 1993).

2 P. Wollen: 'North by Northwest: A Morphological Analysis' in *Readings and Writings* (London: Verso, 1982).

3 In Lowell Edmunds and Allan Dundas (eds.), *Oedipus. A Folklore Casebook* (Garland Publishing Inc.: New York and London, 1984).

4 J.-J. Goux, *Oedipus, Philosopher* (Stanford University Press, 1993).

5 T. de Lauretis: 'The Desire for Narrative' in *Alice Doesn't: Feminism, Semiotics, Cinema* (Bloomington: Indiana University Press, 1982).

6 B. Creed, *The Monstrous Feminine: Film Feminism and Psychoanalysis* (London: Routledge, 1993).

7 L. Mulvey, 'The Oedipus Myth: Beyond the Riddles of the Sphinx', *Visual and Other Pleasures* (London: Macmillan, 1989).

8 'Alternation Segmentation Hypnosis', Interview with Raymond Bellour by Janet Bergstrom, *Camera Obscura* 3/4 (1979).

9 H. Walpole, *The Castle of Otranto: A Gothic Story* ((1764) New York: Macmillan, 1963).

10 A. Radcliffe, *A Sicilian Romance* ((1790) Oxford University Press, 1993).

11 J. Austen, *Northanger Abbey* (Harmondsworth: Penguin Books, 1972), p. 190.

12 R. Jackson, *Fantasy: The Literature of Subversion* (London: Methuen, 1981), p. 95.

13 Goux, *Oedipus*, p. 161.

14 *Ibid.*, p. 179.

15 Quoted in *ibid.*, p. 164.

16 T. Gastle, 'Phantasmagoria: Special Technology and the Metaphorics of Modern Reveries', *Critical Inquiry* (autumn 1988), p. 52.

17 André Breton, Introduction to the Catalogue of the Surrealist Exhibition, 1930, trans. Sir H. Read, repr. in V. Sage (ed.), *The Gothick Novel: A Casebook* (London: Macmillan, 1991), pp. 112–15.

18 A. Breton, 'As In A Wood' in Paul Hammond (ed.), *The Shadow and Its Shadow* (London: British Film Institute, 1978), p. 43.

19 J. Brunius, 'Crossing the Bridge' in Paul Hammond (ed.), *The Shadow and Its Shadow* (London: British Film Institute, 1978), p. 61.

20 *Ibid.*, p. 61.

21 S. Freud, 'The Uncanny' in *The Standard Edition of the Complete Works of Sigmund Freud* (London: Hogarth Press, 1955), vol. 17.

Wild nights and buried letters: the Gothic 'unconscious' of feminist criticism

'As dream or nightmare, or both at once, [sexuality] reigns in our lives as an anarchic force, refusing to be chastened and tamed by sense or conscience to a sentence in a revolutionary manifesto.'[1] Cora Kaplan here announces the 'agenda' of feminism in its 'second-wave' from 1970 onwards, the attempt to analyse the role of sexuality as the key to both the oppression and liberation of women. That her pursuit of the disturbing signs of sexuality in feminist writing lights upon Mary Wollstonecraft's *Vindication of the Rights of Woman* (1792) is by no means coincidental, for feminist criticism has consistently found its own 'unconscious' in what might be dubbed 'female Romanticism'.

Two important articles of Anglo-American feminist criticism, Mary Jacobus' 'The Buried Letter: *Villette*', first published in 1979, and Cora Kaplan's 'Wild Nights: Pleasure/Sexuality/Feminism', first published in 1983, locate the origin of the modern construction of 'woman' as overdetermined signifier of sexuality in late-eighteenth- and early-nineteenth-century culture, understanding Wollstonecraft's polemical writing as both symptom and analysis of that construction. For Kaplan and Jacobus, Wollstonecraft's *Vindication* dramatises the tension between desire and reason in terms of the return of a primal complex in the adult ego, figured through the discursive tactics of 'sensibility', that the text struggles imperfectly to repress. Jacobus concludes her analysis of Charlotte Brontë's *Villette* (1853) by locating it in the feminist tradition of Wollstonecraft's *Vindication* which though 'directed against the infantilising Rousseauistic ideal of feminine "sensibility"':

> not only advocates the advantages for women of a rational (rather than sentimental) education, but attempts to insert the author herself into the predominantly male discourse of Enlightenment Reason, or 'sense.' Yet, paradoxically, it is within this shaping Rousseauistic sensibility that Mary Wollstonecraft operates as both woman and writer – creating in her two highly autobiographical novels, *Mary* (1788) and ten

years later, *The Wrongs of Woman*, fictions which, even as they anatom-
ise the constitution of femininity within the confines of 'sensibility,'
cannot escape its informing preoccupations and literary influence.[2]

Kaplan, too, understands Wollstonecraft's writing as bedevilled by the inescapable language of sensibility (apparently coterminous with sexuality):

> Woman's reason may be the psychic heroine of *A Vindication*, but its
> Gothic villain, a polymorphous perverse sexuality, creeping out of every
> paragraph and worming its way into every warm corner of the text,
> seems in the end to win out. (45–6)

In these accounts, then, 'sensibility' has an uncanny facility of reappear-
ing at the point when its repression is most powerfully asserted; it functions as a form of childhood memory for the rational woman author,
but, significantly, both Jacobus and Kaplan stress that this is not a pre-
linguistic feminine semiotic pressure on symbolic paternal language,
but acknowledged as itself a construction *of* the symbolic which must
be overcome by the woman writer as the origin of her oppression rather
than source of her liberation.

Both Kaplan and Jacobus understand the problematic of this division between the passionate and the rational self in the female writing
subject as symptomatic of modern feminist theory in general. Jacobus
suggests that in attempting to trace the process of repression at work in
fiction the feminist critic can find a mirror for her own sense of the tension between the 'prevailing conventions of academic literary criticism'
and the political urgency of her own 'anger, rebellion and rage', a process
that Lucy Snowe's struggle to narrate her 'self' in *Villette* vividly figures
(60). Kaplan insists that the feminist project must forsake its pursuit of a
'feminist humanism' that argues for the possibility of women being released
into a 'natural' sexuality outside the ideological distortions Wollstonecraft
so effectively exposes. Locating Adrienne Rich in a continuum with
Wollstonecraft in that her account of 'compulsory heterosexuality', like
Wollstonecraft's of 'sensibility', is one of a complex and multivalent system of male power that alienates women from their true desire (for Rich
the desire for other women, for Wollstonecraft the desire for rationality
which she identifies as synonymous with power), Kaplan points out that
Wollstonecraft's Enlightenment project for feminism 'never had much
going for it – not because an immanent and irrepressible sexuality broke
through levels of female self-denial, but rather because the anti-erotic
ethic itself foregrounded and constructed a sexualised subject' (50).

Female Romanticism, then, finds itself relocating women as subjects
only in terms of their relation to the sexuality/sensibility it seeks to deny.

Sexuality here might be seen as structurally equivalent to Freud's understanding of the role of the unconscious in the construction of subjectivity. Though it exists only in relation to the ego it is ultimately *determining*. The critic's or analyst's task is to pursue the traces of its presence in the symptomatic text, a presence which is manifested in *repression* rather than *expression*. This essay seeks to evaluate and question the role of sexuality as the determining 'unconscious' of feminist criticism which is most powerfully felt in the centrality of the Gothic to Anglo-American critical appropriations of a psychoanalytic and post-structuralist feminist tradition from France. If, in feminist psychoanalytic literary theory, the Freudian 'hysteric' emerges as a proto-feminist (writer), struggling to bring into expression through displaced bodily (or textual) signs her experience of the denial of female agency in a patriarchal culture, then it is the Gothic heroine who most powerfully and explicitly 'represents' this hysterical condition to the feminist reader. This version of the Gothic 'heroine' profoundly restricts the possibilities of a feminist account of the representational architectonics of women's oppression.

Ann Radcliffe's Gothic novels importantly distinguish between material oppression and psychic confusion; her heroines are explicitly criticised for seizing on 'supernatural' explanations which prove easier for them to accept than the realities of male power and material exploitation in the adult world they are being forced to enter. Emily St Aubert, the heroine of Radcliffe's *The Mysteries of Udolpho* (1794), not only learns that seemingly supernatural phenomena have rational material explanations but also that it is not sexual desire that motivates her male oppressor, Montoni, but material gain and political power in which he views women simply as a means rather than an end. Emily's dangerous lack of knowledge is not solely sexual innocence but *political* ignorance. Imprisoned in Montoni's castle in Italy she comes to realise that he is the head of a group of *banditti* and assumes he 'meant to retrieve his broken fortunes by the plunder of travellers'.[3] Radcliffe adds that this supposition 'however natural, was in part erroneous, for she was a stranger to the state of this country and to the circumstances, under which its frequent wars were partly conducted' (358). Montoni's ambition goes beyond the acquisition of wealth to the acquisition of political power, in which his marriage to Emily's aunt and his pursuit of control of Emily's person is only a small part itself. The spectre, then, that haunts *Mysteries of Udolpho* is the possibility that the Gothic sense of female terror may be a recognition that in the pursuit of politico-material power women are no more than exchange tokens between men; the 'hidden' supernatural and sexual causes which the text puts into play may be nothing more than displacements or smokescreens which provide the Gothic heroine with an illusory sense of the possibility of a political agency or significance from which she is, in reality, excluded. Feminist literary critics have tended to repeat this movement of wilful 'misprision' on the part of the Gothic heroine, finding it easier to explore questions of psychic division and sexual repression in women's writing than material social and political oppression. The article concludes by offering a consideration of one of Isak Dinesen's most complex and disturbing *Seven Gothic Tales* (1934), 'The Monkey', to highlight the ways in which Gothic fiction inscribes its own understanding of the dangers of reading a repressed desire as determining origin rather than symptom of women's alienation from social agency.

Eve Kosofsky Sedgwick suggests in her 1986 preface to the reprint of her 1980 *The Coherence of Gothic Conventions* that psychoanalysis appears to 'make sense' of the Gothic because, like the Gothic, it too is engaged in a distinctively Romantic 'propagation of a . . . problematics of individual "character" '.[4] Sedgwick posits that Gothic fiction of the late eighteenth century falls into a gender division that can be equated with Freud's gendered distinction between the paranoid and the hysteric:

> Call for convenience's sake, the heroine of the Gothic a classic hysteric, its hero a classic paranoid. The immobilising and costly struggle, in the hysteric, to express graphically through her bodily hieroglyphic what cannot come into existence as narrative, resembles in this the labor of the paranoid subject to forestall being overtaken by the feared/desired other, by himself mimetically reproducing the perceived or projected desire/threat of the other in a temporarily paralysed form. (vi)

Two distinct traditions, male and female, might then be understood to co-exist in the Gothic most strongly marked perhaps in the distinction between Matthew Lewis' tormented Faustian hero, Ambrosius in *The Monk* (1796) and Ann Radcliffe's dutiful sensibility-sated Emily in *The Mysteries of Udolpho* (1794). Mary Jacobus' essay, 'The Buried Letter', points to the 'hysterical' structure of Charlotte Brontë's mid-nineteenth-century novel which 'mirrors' the hysteria of its heroine, Lucy Snowe. The representational 'order' of the Victorian realist text is repeatedly punctured by a spectral Romanticism which cannot be put into narrative except in the shape of a disturbance of linear historicised courtship to marriage plot. It is the 'ghost' of the nun of the Rue Rossette which 'triggers' in the narrative the pressure of hysterical desire in Lucy's narrative. The nun, Jacobus argues, can be only understood as 'the alien, ex-centric self which no image can mirror – only the structure of language' (52). Similarly, Kaplan's account of Wollstonecraft's *Vindication* understands the hidden presence of sexuality (bearing in mind Freud's gloss to the term 'unheimlich' drawn from Schelling that it is 'what ought to have remained secret and hidden but has come to light'[5]) as visible only in terms of disturbance of the rational structure of argument in the text.

Disturbances of language are, then, a register of the struggle of repressed desire to signify just as the hysteric's physical disturbances (failures of physical function in particular) indicate a repressed childhood trauma which cannot be directly 'spoken'. In the case of both hysteric and paranoiac, internal psychic contradiction is mirrored in narrative through the use of techniques that point to duality. In the paranoid text the figure of the double serves as a projection outward of self-division (most often in the case of the Gothic 'monster' or 'villain' who 'acts out' the hero's repressed desires); in the hysterical text the narrative itself takes on the features of the internal split within the heroine (the puncturing of narrative realism with dream sequences or the explosion of an excessive Romantic rhetoric in the linear progress of the tale). However, the double is, I would argue, not exclusive to the male Gothic nor is the hysterical disturbance of language exclusive to the female Gothic.

In what follows I argue that Isak Dinesen's short story 'The Monkey' selfconsciously deploys the use of the device of the double in a narrative that might be understood otherwise to follow the hysterical conventions of the female Gothic.[6] In so doing, she begins to construct a version of a female 'uncanny' that is expressed through paranoid projection rather than hysterical introjection and leads her reader back to a recognition of the material social and economic grounds of women's oppression rather than the psychosexual contradictions that in the Romantic period of the Gothic had served to displace or conceal those grounds.

Isak Dinesen's 'The Monkey' powerfully dramatises the complexity of the position of women in Gothic fiction. In this story, set in the first half of the nineteenth century, a young guardsman named Boris comes to visit his aunt, the Prioress of Closter Seven (a secular convent in Northern Europe for widowed and unmarried mature women), to request her aid in arranging a marriage for him that will serve to dispel the rumours circulating at court of his involvement, along with others in his regiment, in crimes connected 'with those romantic and sacred shores of ancient Greece' (77). His aunt suggests Athena Hopbehallus, the daughter of a Polish Count, whose estates border the convent, and Boris duly visits to make his offer. He finds the Count celebrating his success in a lengthy law-suit over his lands in Poland and delighted to propose the match to Athena 'a strong young woman of eighteen, six feet high and broad in proportion, with a pair of shoulders which could lift and carry a sack of wheat' (92). The following day, however, the Count writes to both Boris and the Prioress to express his regret that Athena will not comply. The Prioress plans to compromise Athena, inviting her to dinner at the convent, plying her with drink and then sending Boris to the state rooms where she is sleeping. Boris is to seduce her inspired by a mysterious draught the Prioress administers to him. However, the seduction becomes a violent physical struggle which ends when Boris forces Athena into a kiss that causes her to faint. The next morning the Prioress summons both to her office and persuades the innocent Athena that she has been so compromised that she must marry Boris, but Athena swears to kill him as soon as the knot has been tied. At this point, the Prioress's pet monkey returns from one of its regular and mysterious absences, appearing at the window and finally breaking the glass. The Prioress struggles to escape but after a brief scuffle:

> The old woman with whom they had been talking was, writhing and dishevelled, forced to the floor; she was scrunched and changed. Where she had been, a monkey was now crouching and whining, altogether beaten, trying to take refuge in a corner of the room. And where the monkey had been jumping about, rose, a little out of breath from the effort, her face still a deep rose, the true Prioress of Closter Seven. (119–20)

Athena's glance at Boris affirms that what they have seen means that 'an insurmountable line would be for ever drawn' (120) between them and the rest of the world.

'The Monkey', in terms of both plot and narrative structure, makes visible much that conventionally remains hidden in Gothic fiction. Plot, narrative voice, and symbolic language alike all point to the 'disappearance' of women just when they seem to be most visible. The reasons for Athena's resistance to marriage to Boris are obscure. The possibility that hers is a hysterical refusal of sexual feeling is aired by the Prioress/ Monkey who describes her rejection of Boris' proposal as that of 'a fanatical virgin' (99). Her response to Boris' kiss is excessive: '[a]s if he had run a rapier straight through her, the blood sank from her face, her body stiffened in his arms like that of a slow-worm when you hit it' (113). Dinesen's use of a third person 'personal' narration from Boris' perspective makes it impossible to determine whether Athena's response here is that of orgasm or rape victim. Athena is only ever seen and interpreted, most often by analogy with animals: the slow-worm here, earlier as having the eyes of 'a young lioness or eagle' (92), 'a young she-bear' in her conflict with Boris (113). Boris' interpretation of Athena is also, however, the key to her rejection of him and symbolically of the function of exchange object of which his proposal makes her aware. This is Athena's loss of innocence, her coming-to-knowledge, that, despite being brought up in 'an atmosphere of incense burnt to woman's loveliness' (93), ultimately she is for her prospective husband nothing other than the 'exquisitely beautiful skeleton' he fantasises she may become after death:

> Less frivolous than the traditional old libertine who in his thoughts undresses the women with whom he sups, Boris liberated the maiden of her strong and fresh flesh together with her clothes, and imagined that he might be very happy with her, that he might even fall in love with her, could he have her in her beautiful bones alone . . . Many human relations, he thought, would be infinitely easier if they could be carried out in the bones alone. (107)

The 'bones' of the relationship between Athena and Boris is, of course, an exchange in which sexuality is precisely a 'cover' or 'flesh', which conceals the reality that Boris' desire is not for a woman at all.

This is made clear in an inset narrative rendered as Boris rides to Hopballehus to make his proposal. He recalls travelling with a friend and a doll theatre six months previously. On Walpurgis night, when the two young men are lodging in a farmhouse, three girls enter their room and strip naked in front of a mirror in accordance with the tradition that they will catch a glimpse of future husbands. Boris, we are told, in response to this memory:

> thought with deep sadness of all the young men who had been, through the ages, perfect in beauty and vigour – young Pharoahs with clean-cut faces hunting in chariots along the Nile, young Chinese sages, silk-clad, reading within the live shade of willows – who had been changed, against their wishes, into supporters of society, fathers-in-law, authorities on food and morals. (86)

Boris understands relations between men and women as purely functional, indeed destructive of the romance, poetry, and beauty that exist between men. The reduction of women to nothing more than a function is not, the story makes clear, a product of a homosocial/heterosexual exchange system that Boris seeks to enter in order to conceal his homosexuality. Homosexuality, in Luce Irigaray's terms, acts out visibly the law of a homosocial order (desire for relations between men), not attempting to veil the mediating function of women between men behind 'romantic' or 'sensual' displays of feeling:

> The 'other' homosexual relations, masculine ones, are . . . forbidden. *Because they openly interpret the law according to which society operates*, they threaten in fact to shift the horizon of that law. Besides, they challenge the nature, status, and 'exogamic' necessity of the product of exchange. By short-circuiting the mechanisms of commerce, might they also expose what is really at stake? Furthermore, they might lower the sublime value of the standard, the yard-stick. Once the penis itself becomes

merely a means to pleasure, pleasure among men, *the phallus loses its power*. Sexual pleasure, we are told, is best left to those creatures who are ill-suited for the seriousness of symbolic rules, namely, women.[7]

Athena's father, a worshipper of women, who, it is hinted, conducted a romance with Boris' mother in his past, also understands marriage as a contract which allows the continuation of male property and power through the bodies of women. His letter to Boris complains:

> She has been to me both son and daughter, and I have in my mind seen her wearing the old coats of armour of Hopballehus. Too late I realise that she is wearing it, not as the young St George fighting dragons, but as Azrael, the angel of death, of our house. (98)

The association of Athena with death is here explicitly connected with her refusal to enter into reproductive relations with a man. Boris' desire for Athena as skeleton is made into a reality on the morning after her 'seduction' when we are told '[s]he had in reality a death's-head upon her strong shoulders' (115).

Both homosexual and heterosexual men associate women who refuse to enter the exchange relations of marriage with death. And yet, Athena's response makes it clear that it is these very relations that are death-bringing for her as social agent. It is her conviction that she has been compromised into marriage which makes her appear to be a death's-head. The fear of 'disappearance' in marriage which Athena's fierce determination to follow the lesson of the Great Bear that she and Boris admire on the evening of his visit to Hopballehus to 'keep your individuality in the crowd' (94) indicates, is mirrored by the ambiguous transfer of identity between the Prioress and the monkey. The monkey is a profoundly over-determined signifier in Dinesen's tale, associated with primitive culture (through its origins in Zanzibar), with sexual lust, and social cunning (in its machinations to bring about an alliance between Athena and Boris). Its associations and the difficulty of interpreting its function in the tale are further expanded in the rendering of the evening conversation at Hopballehus. The Count's solicitor in Poland (who has just secured his inheritance for him) also owns a pet monkey we are informed and in the Count's country of origin there are 'Wendish idols . . . of which the goddess of love had the face and façade of a beautiful woman, while, if you turned her around, she presented at the back the image of a monkey' (93). Significantly, it is Athena who asks 'how . . . did they know, in the case of that goddess of love, which was the front and which the back?' (94). Like most Gothic 'monsters', of which Frankenstein's monster is the archetype, the monkey is a double which troubles the notion of secure autonomous identity.

The double, as Sedgwick notes, is a significant feature of the 'masculine' paranoid Gothic narrative, functioning as a dangerous projection of the masculine psyche and enabling the displacement of homosocial desire into a homophobic construction of 'otherness'. However, the monkey's doubleness is not easily explicable within this model and does not seem to be particularly 'uncanny' for the male hero of the tale; Athena is its target. 'The presence of some unknown danger', Boris meditates over dinner, 'was impressed upon the girl by the Prioress's manner toward her' (103). That the monkey doubles for the Prioress also suggests that 'uncanniness' is specific to women. Dinesen's tale, I would suggest, offers the prospect of reading its heroine as a hysteric, only to put in its place a feminised version of the traditionally 'masculine' plot of paranoia. The monkey literalises Athena's fear, not of her own sexual desire, but of her own status as 'doll' in a narrative scripted by mysterious forces beyond her control.

Speculation about the possibility of a specifically female 'uncanny' has only recently begun to surface in discussion of the Gothic.[8] Helene Cixous in her essay 'Fiction and its Phantoms: a Reading of Freud's *Das Unheimliche*' is a significant, if oblique, contribution to that speculation.[9] Cixous draws out attention to Freud's refusal to countenance the importance of the figure of the doll Olympia in the uncanny effects of Hoffmann's story, 'The Sandman', which he takes as his example.[10] Freud asserts: 'I cannot think – and I hope most readers of the story will agree with me – that the theme of the doll Olympia, who is to all appearances a living being, is by any means the only, or indeed the most important element of uncanniness evoked by the story' (348). Uncertainty over whether a figure is living or inanimate is, according to Freud, far less 'uncanny' than the hero, Nathaniel's, fear of losing his eyes at the hands of the Sandman, itself a displaced fear of castration, which is the punishment he fantasises will be the result of his jealousy of his father. If she stands for anything, Freud concludes, '[t]his automatic doll can be nothing less than a materialisation of Nathaniel's feminine attitude towards his father in his infancy' (354). Cixous teases out her own understanding of Freud's text as necessarily repressing the image of the doll through a process of 'inverted repetition' (533), because the process of his own writing is that of 'a kind of puppet theatre in which real dolls or fake dolls, real and simulated life, are manipulated by a sovereign but capricious stage-setter' (525). Cixous supports her argument by noting Freud's tactical exclusions of the involved narrative structure and heterogeneous points of view of Hoffmann's tale in order to manipulate it into the linear Oedipal account of the construction of masculine paranoia he seeks. It is, then, Cixous concludes, precisely the fictionality of Hoffmann's tale that

Freud seeks to repress, a fictionality associated with the figure of the doll, which is in turn associated with death: 'Neither real nor fictitious, "fiction" is a secretion of death, an anticipation of nonrepresentation, a doll, a hybrid body composed of language and silence that, in the movement which turns it and which it turns, invents doubles, and death' (548).

This long detour through Freud and Cixous returns us to Dinesen's 'The Monkey' and its preoccupations with theatricality, death, and the double, at first associated with femininity but gradually revealed to be a construction of male homosociality which, far from threatening *masculine* identity, uncannily poses the problem to women that they may be dispensable, that what appears to be the front (the female form, sexuality, love) may be the back (the monkey, trickery, statecraft). The monkey, then, rather than doubling for the repressed desire of the unmarried woman (the Prioress/Athena), may be doubling for the pursuit of male power in the form of statecraft (with which the monkey is most often symbolically associated in the tale). Dinesen's refusal to give us access to the perspectives of the Prioress/Monkey or Athena only serves to reinforce the text's dramatisation of the reduction of women to exchange function in patriarchal culture which Boris' attempt to conceal his homosexuality through heterosexual marriage only makes more visible because he does not seek to conceal the property relations behind a rhetoric of desire or idealisation. The nuns of Closter Seven, we are told, are disturbed by the rumour of Boris' Greek sins because:

> To all of them it had been a fundamental article of faith that woman's loveliness and charm, which they themselves represented in their own sphere and according to their gifts, must constitute the highest inspiration and prize of life. In their own individual cases the world might have spread snares in order to capture this prize of their being at less cost than they meant it to, or there might have been a strange misunderstanding, a lack of appreciation, on the part of the world, but still the dogma held good. (77–8)

Dinesen's deployment of a paranoid Gothic narrative of the double to extrapolate the conventionally 'hysterical' Gothic text of the unmarried heroine's fear of enclosure/live burial allows her to make explicit what Jacobus and Kaplan suggest has to remain hidden in the tradition of post-Romantic feminist versions of the Gothic originating in Wollstonecraft – that it may not be female sexuality that requires correction, control, or release in the new bourgeois order but the masculine desire for power. '*Villette*', Jacobus comments, 'can only be silent about the true nature and origin of Lucy's oppression' (46) because it continues to enshrine marriage as a form of spiritual resolution of division and doubleness of the human psyche. Similarly, Kaplan complains that Wollstonecraft finds herself unable to pursue her argument in the *Vindication* to its logical conclusion because the polemical trajectory of the *Vindication* is to an assertion of women's right to claim a different construction of subjectivity, that of bourgeois 'masculine' reason, for themselves:

> What the argument moves towards, but never quite arrives at, is the conclusion that it is male desire that must be controlled and contained if women are to be free and rational. This conclusion cannot be reached because an idealised bourgeois male is the standard towards which women are groping, as well as the reason they are on their knees. (46)

In the female Gothic, then, it seems to be the case that what cannot be said is what is remarkably obvious, that women in patriarchal culture are accorded only one function, that of mediating male power, to which their own sexual desires are immaterial. In this formulation, hysteria becomes not a mode of resistance but a means of concealing these relations of power and property by displacement into internalised struggle over the repression of sexual desire. Ellen Moers, whose influential work *Literary Women* placed the Gothic at the centre of feminist literary history, astutely recognises the ways in which the female Gothic facilitates the internalisation of struggle and contradiction within its hystericised heroines:

> The savagery of girlhood accounts in part for the persistence of the Gothic mode into our own time; also the self-disgust, the self-hatred, and the impetus to self-destruction that have been increasingly prominent themes in the writing of women in the twentieth century. Despair is hardly the exclusive province of any one sex or class in our age, but to give *visual* form to the fear of self, to hold anxiety up to the Gothic mirror of the imagination, may well be more common in the writings of women than of men.[11]

Dinesen's use of the figure of the double in 'The Monkey' allows her to explore the possibility of women's externalisation of their fears, just as the 'masculine' Gothic's paranoid structure privileges projection over introjection as a resolution of contradiction. Athena's 'unlikeliness' as a Gothic heroine is her strength; she externalises rather than internalises her fear of being reduced to an exchange function, engaging in ferocious hand-to-hand combat with her suitor, literally 'fighting off' his advances. Athena attempts to make herself visible as *subject* in a 'plot' which is premised upon the absence or exclusion of women from the mechanisms of power (the monkey has substituted for its mistress).

Returning to Kaplan's and Jacobus' analogy between female Romanticism and feminist criticism, then, it might be argued that for both the urgent 'unconscious' fear that haunts the writing process is that the construction of the possibility of female agency through an investigation into the specificity of a repressed female desire may be to reproduce rather than challenge the ideology of patriarchal power. As Michel Foucault points out in his *History of Sexuality*, the modern 'hysterisation' of women's bodies 'whereby the feminine body was analysed – qualified and disqualified – as being thoroughly saturated with sexuality' is one of a number of discursive techniques that serve to maintain control over and secure the consent of subjects to existing power relations.[12] Athena's 'trial of strength' (115) in 'The Monkey' is to resist the negation of her agency, to exceed the imposition of the status of pure function in an exchange; that her resistance is 'read' (by the Monkey/Prioress and Boris) as a refusal of sexuality is a means of relocating women solely as sexual rather than political subjects. There can be no easy negotiation out of the complexity of the relation between sexual and political identity for women, as both the Gothic/Romantic texts and their critics that have been under discussion here make abundantly clear. To resort to the image of the hysteric as revolutionary sexual subject is, however, no solution precisely because by definition the hysteric signifies nothing beyond the suffusion of the female body with the displaced signs of sexual desire. What the hysteric signifies is the desire for political agency itself for which, as Dinesen's short story demonstrates, sexuality is itself a displacement or substitution. To be 'free' for women is then not to be 'sexual', but to be free not to signify sexuality alone.

Notes

1 C. Kaplan, 'Wild Nights: Pleasure/Sexuality/Feminism', *Sea Changes: Culture and Feminism* (London: Verso, 1986), p. 32.

2 M. Jacobus, 'The Buried Letter: *Villette*' in her *Reading Woman: Essays in Feminist Criticism* (London: Methuen, 1986), p. 59; Charlotte Brontë, *Villette* (Harmondsworth: Penguin Books, 1979); Mary Wolletonecraft, *A Vindication of the Rights of Woman* in *Mary Wollstonecraft: Political Writings* (Oxford University Press, 1994).

3 A. Radcliffe, *The Mysteries of Udolpho* (Oxford University Press, 1980), p. 358.

4 E. Kosofsky Sedgwick, Preface, *The Coherence of Gothic Conventions*, 2nd edn (London: Methuen, 1986), p. vii.

5 S. Freud, 'Das Unheimliche', *Art and Literature*, ed. Albert Dickson, vol. 14, Penguin Freud Library (Harmondsworth: Penguin Books, 1985), p. 345.

6 Isak Dinesen, *Seven Gothic Tales* (Harmondsworth: Penguin Books, 1963).

7 L. Irigaray, 'Commodities Among Themselves', *This Sex Which is Not One*, trans. Catherine Porterwith Carolyn Burke (Ithaca, New York: Cornell University Press, 1985), p. 193.

8 See, in particular, Claire Kahane, 'The Gothic Mirror', *The (M)other Tongue:*

Essays in Feminist Psychoanalytic Interpretation, eds. Shirley Nelson Garner, Claire Kahane, Madelon Sprengnether (Ithaca and London: Cornell University Press, 1985), pp. 334–51.

9 H. Cixous, 'Fiction and Its Phantoms: A Reading of Freud's *Das Unheimliche* (The 'Uncanny'), *New Literary History*, vol. 7:3 (1976), pp. 525–48.

10 Ernst Theodor Amadeus Hoffmann's short story 'Der Sandmann' first appeared in his *Nachstücke* (1816–17). For a modern translation see *Tales of Hoffmann*, ed. and trans. R. J. Hollingdale *et al.* (London: Penguin Books, 1982).

11 E. Moers, *Literary Women* (London: Women's Press, 1978), p. 107.

12 M. Foucault, *The History of Sexuality: Volume One*, trans. Robert Hurley (Harmondsworth: Penguin Books, 1981), p. 104.

Postmodern feminine horror fictions

When pop-goddess Madonna ceremoniously flashed her bra on the top celluloid stage in Cannes,[1] the 1200 camera images of that moment conserved the self-made *femme fatale* of postmodernism: the image of a daring beauty, publicly transgressing conventions but – unlike her mythical model – no longer provoking fear or outrage. The fantasy-art-construct of 'the sexual woman', once tempting and threatening in her own – the erotic – domain, has come into fashion: minus the threat of death, minus the inevitable self-destruction, minus the related subversive powers. The perfectly stylised incorporations of this feminine type banalise, even domesticate these qualities – qualities that had marked the *femme fatale* and her emancipatory potential. Heartless Sadeian beauty visions construct the erotics of our advertisements and other everyday aesthetics. Cruel vamp styles construct the erotics of the female top star's pop video art: synthetic, surface-suggestive. What they evoke are gazes from a secure distance: look, don't touch. Postmodern culture's images of the sexual woman have come to mean no more than superficial entertainment for bored eyes.[2]

By contrast, a typical Gothic image of the sexual woman reads like this:

> In the deep shade, at the farther end of the room, a figure ran backwards and forwards: what it was, whether beast or human being, one could not, at first sight tell: it grovelled, seemingly, on all fours: it snatched and growled like some strange wild animal: but it was covered with clothing, and a quantity of dark, grizzled hair, wild as a mane, hid its head and face.[3]

Such is the appearance of Bertha Mason-Rochester in that feminine Gothic classic – and cult text of feminism – *Jane Eyre* (1847). The 'madwoman in the attic' is seen as 'clothed hyena', crazy, imprisoned – and *voiceless*. Her presentation in *Jane Eyre*'s attic scene as antipode – and Other – to the 'proper' Jane betrays a remarkable – and, as it turns out, typically feminine

Gothic[4] – narrative construction: it occurs within the powers of the hero's gaze. Rochester's view of his wife that controls this passage – including its focaliser Jane – casts Bertha as 'monster'. As various critics have shown, this view – and the resulting imprisonment – is related to social fears of the sexual woman and her 'passions', adult sexuality, affirmation of physical pleasure, expression of desire.[5] The figure of Bertha Mason has thus become a prototype of the sexual woman in the feminine Gothic: affirmative femininity turned into the monstrous – or, in narratological terms, into a voiceless textual *object*, controlled by the male gaze. This imprisoned position of the sexual woman figure has become one of the most powerful horrors that shape feminine Gothic texts.

While earlier feminine Gothic texts like *Jane Eyre* have used Gothicism to expose the imprisonment through the male gaze – not only of the 'monstrous' woman (Bertha) but also of the 'proper' one (Jane) – this imprisonment is radically put on trial when the silenced 'madwoman' starts to speak. Only recently has she been given a voice: in Jean Rhys' *Wide Sargasso Sea* (1966). This fragmented metonymic, dark Gothic fiction is one example of the ongoing intense intertextualisation of feminine Gothic writing; moreover, it is one of the first modernist versions of that writing that tells the sexual woman's story. Meanwhile, the 'madwoman in the attic', the sad figure of the Gothic *femme fatale*, has reappeared in contemporary feminine fictions as a changed textual figure: a female speaking subject. Reflecting upon contemporary women's writing, Margaret Atwood has asked: 'What about that madwoman left over from *Jane Eyre*? Are these our secret plots?' Such dark, horrific plots around 'madwomen' like Bertha Rochester indeed seem to shape much of contemporary feminine writing. This might surprise in a (feminist) critical context that has distinguished two different modes as representative of that contemporary literary culture: that of autobiographical confession and that of an experimental feminine language. However, the works of authors such as Margaret Atwood and Jean Rhys, but also of Lynne Tilman and Diane Johnson in the USA or Angela Carter and Fay Weldon in Great Britain or Alice Munro and Jane Urquhardt in Canada lead us back to questions of the relations of Gothic and gender. They might also lead to a two-fold view of Gothic effects in a contemporary feminine literary culture: (1) continuity: an ongoing elaboration of the large web of women's Gothic intertextualisations; (2) deconstruction: a challenge to the limits of Gothic form – and especially to the myths of the feminine shaping that form. This last aspect relates to the sexual woman figure who represents a specific challenging potential in these texts: a double or split or unfixed subjectivity. In this essay, I would like to explore the typical formal and stylistic constructions of this figure's challenging effect.

The figure of the sexual woman in postmodern feminine Gothic presents a contrast to the contemporary fashionable *femme fatale* outlined above: her voice addresses (rather than adapting to) the secure surface suggestions of such idealised feminine figures. Formally speaking, this happens overtly in popular punk texts or the so-called 'lower East Side Scene Lit' (Kathy Acker, Catherine Texier). Or it happens 'covertly' – in the shape of what Atwood calls a 'secret Gothic plot' as in the young Canadian writer Aritha van Herk's *No Fixed Address*.[6] This novel is a good example of what I mean by postmodern feminine horror fictions. It is a feminine Gothic in form: the story of a female subject, shaped by the secret plot of the sexual woman and other narratives of horror that develop into a deadly nightmare. It is also a typically postmodern text, with its characteristic double voices that allow for the simultaneous formal complicity and ideological critique that Linda Hutcheon has postulated in terms of the potential politics of postmodern representation.[7]

No Fixed Address's multi-levelled structure announces itself from the start. The female subject's name, Arachne Manteia, signals a first formal quotation of the Greek myth of the mortal woman whose wonderful weaving provoked the goddess to turn her into a spider. It is, as various other narrative strategies in the text, a quotation with a difference: Arachne does not produce a web, she rather travels the web of roads in the Canadian West – selling women's underwear, thereby avoiding at first any sense of the enclosed space that typically characterises the Gothic. But there is more to Arachne's occupation as sales representative for the – very aptly named – 'Ladies' Comfort Limited' company. The novel opens (in analogy to the Madonna image opening this essay) with a reflection on the functions of underwear, depicting its age-old function: 'to aid physical attractiveness, a standard inevitably decided by men' (9) – and the subsequent effect: imprisonment of the female body and the general discomfort of women – until the more androgynous fashions of the 1980s. This introduction sets the tone, in terms of a feminist as well as a comic touch within the text: a combination of gendered critique and ironic humour that marks the postmodern feminine horror fictions. Moreover, it has a structural impact. The hidden shapes the surface: this opening suggestion of double-layers will structure the following in various ways: in terms of the female *subject*, who will develop into more than typical Gothic doubleness, in terms of the text's *form*, incorporating a dark secret plot shaping the surface, and in terms of another, stylistic phenomenon: *irony*.

The double voice of irony marks Aritha van Herk's feminist/comic style: irony's double layers are essential to what is labelled postmodern just as much as to what is called feminine art. Linda Hutcheon's discussion of the trope in *Splitting Images* suggests its value for both 'movements' and their different but related scepticism/s of liberal humanism's values:

> What is it about the situation of women that makes irony such a powerful rhetorical tool? Many feminist critics argue that the condition of marginality (with its attendant qualities of muteness and invisibility) has created in women a 'divided self, rooted in the authorised dualities' of culture. If so, then the 'splitting images' they create through their double-talking ironies are a means of problematising the humanist ideal (or illusion) of wholeness, as well as hierarchy and power. Contradiction, division, doubleness – these are the contesting elements that irony lets in by the front door.[8]

Postmodern irony, characterised by that 'double-talking' structure of complicity and critique 'incorporating that which it implicitly contests' works to emphasise the characteristic dynamics of postmodern feminine narratives like the Gothic: the connectedness to a whole web of feminine writing (through repetition of its traditions) and the simultaneous critique of its traps. The most obvious effect of this ironic double voice is, as has been suggested, a change in tone: from the sublime, dark *Schauerroman* to the comic – albeit no less dark – postmodern Gothic. The more hidden function of the ironic double voice will turn out, I think, as a challenge to traditional forms of genre and subjectivity. Which brings us back to the sexual woman figure: as a challenge to those liberal humanist values that have shaped not only concepts of art and beauty but also of feminine ideals – or illusions. These challenges critically expose what results from such ideals: the horror of imprisonment within 'the feminine' (in Moi's[9] sense of the term).

No Fixed Address is a case in point, with its un-Gothic atmosphere of open space and its comic tone. Its *form* parodies – in postmodern as well as feminist terms – the conventions of Canadian women's travel fiction or the Western, but first and foremost the picaresque novel. Indeed, it is not the generic Gothic romance form that shapes Arachne's story, but that of the adventurous travelling picara[10] who has long transcended the female space of the home, and who abhors – in typical hyperbole – the stasis which that place signifies. But Arachne's story involves further hyperbolic transgressions: as announced above – and as suggested by her name with its allusion to the figure of the 'spider woman' – her figure is that of the sexual woman. Her travels in her fifties Mercedes-Benz are, as the subtitle aptly indicates, an 'amorous journey', as Arachne, with her need to 'stay amused', enjoys sexual encounters with numerous 'road jockeys'. The rendering of her erotic 'amusement' is quickly overshadowed by Gothic traces that typically thicken throughout the text and become grotesque, criminal, violent, unreal. The Gothic in this context recalls Julia Kristeva's 'X-ray' through the concept of love with its layers of eros overshadowed by those of thanatos[11] as the form runs through the interrelatedness of romance/sex/horror. One example is Arachne's completely imagined sexual encounter with the virtual ghost of an airforce man who had drowned in 1944 – an uncanny scene in the last, most obviously dark and death-ridden part of the text (294). That part turns into an associative prose-piece of Gothic border-blurs between a sublime and fearful imagination and a more reliable perception of 'reality'.

Dark and death-ridden is also the relationship with Joseph, Arachne's ninety-year-old lover who is romantically – and ironically – described as a man 'who has been alive for a long time'. His character appears not only as hyperbolic distortion of the traditionally somehow physically maimed Byronic Hero but also provides the possibility of a reversed Gothic elopement when Arachne kidnaps him from an old people's home – one of the truly nightmarish spaces in the text with its 'endless white corridor that seems like an entrance to a dream where walls are terrifying and forever' (225). This affair is also a good example of the functions of irony in this text: when Joseph and Arachne see their reflection in a window, what that mirror shows is the surface gaze: a very old man and a young women – an 'impossible' couple. What the text has constructed, however, is a deep parallel between the two: their shared fascination with motion and fear of stasis and death, their marginality in terms of the 'improper' use of language and as outsiders: Joseph as Hungarian immigrant and Arachne as working class girl. This parallel ironically works to present them as the only matching couple in the text – and thus seriously contests the limitations of convention's gaze.

Arachne's aggressive sexuality has parodic effects:[12] most importantly, it both recalls and critically mocks the traditional *femme fatale*: with her erotic but deadly powers (Arachne does bring love and death, only to different men); with her ideal body (Arachne is 'chunky') and artistic seduction (Arachne 'jumps' men rather than playing games). But this postmodern sexual woman figure also mocks the figure of the modern male macho type – as well as the female versions of that figure: the type of the cruel woman in the above-mentioned punk texts. Thus, she poses a challenge to the attractions of the *femme fatale* without replacing them by a new sexual woman ideal – a typical move (the refusal of new female role models) of feminist texts of the eighties, and especially of postmodern feminine horror fictions.

Moreover, her treatment of men also mocks the myth of romantic love that has always shaped feminine Gothic form – at least on the surface – into the 'heroine's plot':[13] the plot ending in marriage or death.

The feminine Gothic's generic 'happy ending', however, has early been implicitly questioned for example in Ann Radcliffe's *The Mysteries of Udolpho* (1793); Emily's wedding day is described like a fairy tale by the servant Annette. *Jane Eyre*'s 'Reader I married him' introduces a Utopian vision of family life outside of society's possibilities. In *Villette* (1853), the reunion of the two lovers is endlessly deferred. Foregrounded in modernist versions, such challenges mostly work to sceptically highlight love as deadly appropriation of the other, especially in *Wide Sargasso Sea*. As to the postmodern *No Fixed Address*, romance is ridiculed and marriage as immobility abhorred; the text ends in ironic – and Gothic – accordance with the incessant desire for motion.

There is another decisive formal strategy that marks the feminine Gothic's implicit deconstruction of the myths of feminine ideals and 'happy endings': the introduction of a second narrative level that rivals the romance. As early as in *The Mysteries*, the female subject is constructed as 'competent subject' in the sense of a Greimasian actant *not* by romantic love for the hero, but by her quest for the mother. This quest develops in a parallel plot to the surface romance, and comes to question that surface's primacy as well as its (patriarchal) ideology. The mother–daughter plot in the feminine Gothic then functions like a 'mirror plot' in what Catherine Belsey has called the 'interrogative text',[14] a text that offers not one primary discourse or meaning but challenges the reader. Cast in 'Gothic' terms, the myth of romantic love shapes the surface narrative but is relativised by the mirror text which explores the desire for the mother. The subject of the feminine Gothic is neither a (humanist) feminine ideal nor a (seventies') feminist role model, but a divided subject: split between the conscious and socially acceptable movement towards the 'happy ending' with the hero and the unconscious and socially muted desire for a female community. It is the tension thus created that foregrounds – in a typically feminine Gothic move – complex processes of constructing subjectivity, thereby giving room for Gothic horror.

This horror is intensely linked with aspects of female sexuality as represented in the split subject of the feminine Gothic. Lately, Julia Kristeva's[15] concept of horror, 'abjection', has become particularly apt for the discussion of feminine horror fictions in these terms, as its focus is on the physical aspects of horror as related to fears of female powers as well as to an ambiguous attitude towards the maternal. Defined as 'twisted braid of affects and thoughts' without 'a definable object' (1) and as 'above all ambiguity' (9), abjection is formed at precisely the point in biological development – or, as Kristeva emphasises, 'soul formation' – when female desire originates: at the moment of language acquisition. This moment means the loss of the harmonious dyadic unity with the mother through the intrusion of the father and the symbolic order; it means the recognition of the mother as Other, which evokes an underlying extreme fear of female powers – the archaic, overpowering maternal, but also the power of the female body to give life – life that is, however, finite and will end in death (see 'Those Females Who Can Wreck the Infinite', 157ff.).

Feminine Gothic texts, it seems, have early been informed by such a concept of abjection as 'the unbearable side of soul-life' (Kristeva) with the result of physical horror structuring the female subject's romance as well as her quest-for-mother. A closer look at the construction of the female Gothic subject evokes the idea that the Gothic is the form that has not only very early foregrounded 'engendering' processes as such (through an emphasis on dreams, power relations, etc.) but also the horrors related to the development towards such an ambiguous (illusion of) femininity. There is always already a gap between the feminine ideal, the ideal woman – and women's ability to fulfil this ideal.[16] This gap, usually 'naturalised' or 'collapsed',[17] has early been recognised in feminine Gothic texts and consequently constituted much of their horror and monstrosities: Bertha, the sexual woman seen and treated as monster in *Jane Eyre*; birthing, female powers of creativity parodied or perversely transformed in *Frankenstein* (1818); the mother–daughter bond's security questioned as early as in *The Mysteries of Udolpho*.

Postmodern feminine horror fictions emphasise these processes in various ways, and the transformation of the sexual woman figure into the speaking subject is a central example. Moreover, there is the characterisation of the mother–daughter relationship devoid of the myths of mother-love. Abjection is foregrounded just as much as the mirror plot of female desire: for example, thematically by the heroine's fear of becoming the mother, or, structurally, by the ironic double voice. A good example of how this can function is the disruption of a romantic scene involving hero and heroine by her thought: 'All this time I carried my mother around my neck like a rotting albatross' – ! The quote is from Margaret Atwood's *Lady Oracle*,[18] a reverential postmodern parody incorporating various forms of Gothic. Like this example, *No Fixed Address* selfconsciously works out the split-subject idea as well as the importance of the mother–daughter relationship (Arachne's love–hate relationship with her mother Lanie) for the abjection in between 'woman' and the (self-)perception of the enunciating female subject: with its ironic transformations of the romance pattern and with the stress of female desire and feminine relations that will not only challenge form but also unfix the subject.

A look at Arachne's subjectivity in the various layers of narrative is illuminating in these terms. Refusing the romance saves her from being objectivised into a 'proper' heroine, but could easily objectivise her into a Gothic *femme fatale*, victimised and muted. Resisting complete bonding with mother and Thena saves her from the static position they would wish for her but which she abhors – but will make her travels endless, geographical as well as psychological border blurs 'on the edge'. It is this mobility with 'no fixed address' that introduces the 'unfixing' of the subject here: just as Arachne moves through the Canadian West, she moves through the narrative, changing subject positions. Keeping with Emile Benveniste and his view of subjectivity as relational, Arachne's subjectivity must be seen in relation to the enunciating voice that has introduced her in the beginning as a discursive subject, then turns her into an object of desire/knowledge, and lastly loses her – to take her place. This mysterious, disembodied voice introduces an all-inclusive You, interrupts Arachne's story to bring us back repeatedly to research about underwear – and to the search for Arachne. This You, which could be reader, confidante, Arachne herself, or yet another discursive/enunciating subject, functions to shift possible subject positions around – thereby exploding subjectivity and with that the fixing of identification and meaning.

This might sound like a contradiction to the definition of the feminine Gothic as centred around a female subject – however, this unfixed, multiple, mobile discursive female subject is a good example of the work of postmodern feminine 'shape shifters'. Alice Jardine has called this version of subjectivity 'women-as-verbs': the 'putting into discourse of woman as that process . . . intrinsic to the condition of modernity' . . . and as an answer to the profound crisis in legitimation of what Lyotard calls 'master narratives', Truth, Meaning, History, subjectivity – sites of crisis, Jardine adds 'that are not gender neutral: they are crises in the narratives invented by men'.[19] In *No Fixed Address*, this kind of mobile, dynamic female subjectivity also works to explode one version of such a narrative of 'the feminine': the *femme fatale* – and with that the form that had typically placed it in the position of an object.

Subjectivity, thus, is shaped like 'women as verbs', moving through Gothic structure, expanding it, exploding stability. Gothic form, too, is shaped into layers, foregrounded self-consciously by the double voice of irony: and by another extension, the idea of explosion. Horror, itself is multi-faced, inscribing engendering processes.

In our postmodern context, 'Gothic' has come to mean a lot of things, from traces of cruelty in affective art to the musical styles of rock groups like Mission or Sisters of Mercy to a posh London fashion form. Whether all these different aesthetic constructs share a 'secret plot', a darker vision that shapes and challenges their polished popular surface remains the question. Madonna, for example, after some earlier promising hits and videos, seems to have lost it. The postmodern feminist Gothic's disruptions of feminine myths – whether 'proper' or 'fatale' – by a double-layered aesthetics (of subjectivity and form) happens in a cultural context in which such myths have still not lost their power of seduction – even to the self-made woman. As one-dimensional and thus domesticated *femme fatale*, Madonna pays lip- and body-service to the male gaze: lacking the chances of an ironic self-consciousness of feminine double-voiced aesthetics – and its figure of the sexual woman, losing the potential for ongoing challenges and even provocation. However, such lacks and losses are highlighted by the powers of the postmodern multi-layered Gothic. And the popularity of its many well-known, even best-selling, authors indicate its function as powerful sign of – and contribution to – the processes of feminine culture and feminist politics in the eighties and early nineties. So: Who cares . . . about Madonna's underwear anyway? (Arachne, by the way, doesn't wear any . . .)

Notes

1 The reference is to the première of the movie *Truth or Dare/In Bed with Madonna* at the Cannes Film Festival, 1991.

2 My introduction paraphrases the system of the *femme fatale* as shown in Carola Hilmes' study: *Die Femme Fatale. Ein Weiblichkeitstypus in der nachromantischen Literatur* (1990), for brief definitions see esp. pp. xiiif. 10f. The related type of the 'sexual woman' has been discussed by Kay Mussell in 'Beautiful and Damned: The Sexual Woman in Gothic Fiction' (1974).

3 Charlotte Brontë, *Jane Eyre* (Harmondsworth: Penguin Books, 1966), p. 321.

4 I use the term 'feminine Gothic' for the Gothic formed by female subjectivity in the text – in contrast to Ellen Moers' concept of the 'female Gothic', the Gothic written by women.

5 Gilbert and Gubar, *The Mad Woman in the Attic* (New Haven and London: Yale University Press, 1979).

6 Aritte van Herk, *No Fixed Address* (1985).

7 Linda Hutcheon, *The Politics of Postmodernism* (London: Routledge, 1989 repr.).

8 Linda Hutcheon, *Splitting Images* (Ontario: Oxford University Press, 1991), p. 97.

9 T. Moi, *Sexual/Textual Politics* (London: Methuen, 1989), p. 123.

10 L. Hutcheon: *The Canadian Postmodern* (1988), pp. 123ff. However, the picaresque is as intensely connected to the Gothic as is the sentimental romance, as Ellen Moers, who first termed the Gothic written by women the 'female Gothic', worked out: 'In Mrs Radcliffe's hands, the Gothic novel became a feminine substitute for the picaresque, where heroines could enjoy all the adventures and alarms that masculine heroes had long experienced, far from home, in fiction' (*Literary Women* (Garden City, NY, 1985 repr.) p. 126). What this recognition reveals is one of the early twists in the feminisation of the Gothic, namely the reduction of the villain, otherwise the subject of the action,

to a mere function in the female subject's transcendence of 'her proper sphere': the home.

11 Talking about the relationship of her concept of love in *Stories of Love* (1983) and her concept of abjection in *Powers of Horror* (1980), Kristeva used the metaphor of 'an X-ray through love' that avoids the idyllic aspect, highlighting instead the darker aspects of destruction and violence as related to love's passions. (Paris, 15 March 1991)

12 For a definition of parody as 'repetition with critical difference' see Hutcheon, *A Theory of Parody* (London: Methuen, 1985), e.g. p. 32.

13 Moers, *Literary Women* (London, 1976).

14 C. Belsey, *Critical Practice* (London: Methuen, 1980), p. 91.

15 J. Kristeva, *Powers of Horror* (Columbia, New York, 1982).

16 T. de Lauretis' discussion of 'woman' captures the problematics of the ideal feminine: 'a fictional construct, a distillate from diverse but congruent discourses dominant in Western cultures (critical and scientific, literary or juridical discourses), which works as both their vanishing point and their specific condition of existence' in contrast to 'women': 'the real historical beings who cannot as yet be defined outside of those discursive formations, but whose material existence is nonetheless certain' (*Alice Doesn't: Feminism, Semiotics, Cinema* (University of Indiana Press, 1982), p. 5).

17 Moi, *Sexual Textual Politics*, p. 123.

18 Margaret Atwood, *Lady Oracle* (New York: Simon and Schuster, 1976), p. 238. The complexities of these feminine relations can quickly be sketched in two examples of *No Fixed Address*: (1) There is the discursive interaction of the female characters which introduces a liberation from the male-character-oriented plot-motivation. Arachne's sexual affairs, when told to her confidante Thena, reduce their importance, objectivise the males involved. (2) However, there is also the often-uttered wish of mother Lanie's as well as Thena's, that Arachne should marry Thomas, her 'apocryphal lover', the man she lives with between travels. These positions however are ironically underminded as both have suffered from their marriages. This example points to one typical paradox in the engendering processes: the paradox of perpetuating feminine horrors from one woman to the other. The foregrounding of such paradoxes is a typical postmodern feminine Gothic critique.

19 A. Jardine, *Gynesis* (Ithaca and London: Cornell University Press, 1985), p. 24.

Isak Dinesen and the fiction
of Gothic gravity

There is really no getting away from the business of story-telling in *Seven Gothic Tales*.[1] The emphasis on the importance of the telling of tales is precisely and continuously foregrounded and this is the first aspect of the text I'd like to look at in this essay. It is frequently the subject for self-reflexive contemplation as the tales debate and discuss the pleasure, pain, poverty, or wealth which may be at stake behind the labour of just getting the tale told. But this thematic also has a knock-on effect on the way we read the narrative structures themselves. Each tale is comprised of so many different tales, following the tradition of the convoluted historical Gothics of *Melmoth* and *Frankenstein*, that this self-reflexivity and structural complexity merely serves to draw attention to the diegetic apparatus which comprises their narration and hence underlines their fictionality, the 'make-up', the structures of their being made. This all makes the term 'tale-telling' a doubly appropriate one here.

The second pervasive theme I want to look at is that of weightlessness and gravity. When I refer to gravity here I mean it in the sense of gravitational law, though the double meaning implicit in the word holds a pertinence which I hope to come to.

So, to turn to the texts themselves. It is 'The Dreamers' most of all which explores the grandest of heights and the lowest of depths involved in the telling and the acting out of tales. In terms of narrative structure it is also probably the most complex. It is constituted through three levels of narration, of stories within stories (the third person extra-diegetic voice with which the story begins, the intro-diegetic character of Lincoln Forsner who then relays three further hypo-diegetic narratives – Pilot's, the Baron's, and Marcus Cocoxa's). The 'live' and lived nature of the tale and the importance of its oral reworking are implied throughout and this is not without consequence. Lincoln Forsner, a travelling English gentleman and, therefore, an amateur in contrast to the professional and 'much renowned story-teller' Mira Jama, complains that Mira Jama's telling of the story of the sultan and the virgin was much better the first time he heard it. A turn of event or an edge of character may have lost definition in the performance, as a result of the declining fortunes of its teller. The first rule of the tale, then, is that it must be 'live' but as a result it has no life of its own; its production is too contingent with the life of its teller which means it can never possess an essential existence within itself.

Later on, at the point in Lincoln's own memoir where he describes his search for Olalla (Pellegrina Leone, the ex-prima donna of the operatic stage has several pseudonyms) in a mountain blizzard, he pauses for comment:

> 'Do you know, Mira,' Lincoln said, interrupting himself in his tale, 'that this is the first time that I have thought at all of our hour up there? I only remember it now, step by step so to say, as I tell it. I do not know why I have not thought of it before.' (281)

So it's only in the act of a performance that the events of this episode come to be recorded at all. Their existence fully depends on the memory of the apparent narrator who, as we witness, is as inclined to repress and forget as he is perhaps to embroider. The stories, therefore are characterised here by their mutability and this is the second rule of the tale.

It also becomes quite apparent that the next criterion of any good story is that it must not be true, indeed, it must have obtained some tangible distance from lived reality. The real test of the tale's ability to persusade of its own reality is its efficacy in producing passions and emotions in its listeners. To do this, a certain distance must come into play, a distance which, as Mira Jama laments here, he has now lost:

> as I have lived I have lost the capacity of fear. When you know what things are really like, you can make no poems about them. When you have had talks with ghosts and connexions with the devils you are, in the end, more afraid of your creditors than of them; and when you have been made a cuckold you are no longer nervous about cuckoldry. I have become too familiar with life; it can no longer delude me into believing that one thing is much worse than the other. The day and the dark, an enemy and a friend – I know them to be about the same. How can you make others afraid when you have forgotten fear yourself? (239)

If you have lived the passions of the story yourself it ceases to be a real story at all so, almost paradoxically, no on can believe in it or any longer be stirred by it. This the same with anything which involves a performance and is much like Marcus Cocoxa's description of Pellegrina Leone's singing later on in the story: 'Ah Rupia, kama na Majassee it is a very lovely song about true and pure love. Only a whore has ever sung it well, that

I know of' (293–4). Great and effective performance, then, always implies separation and distance from experience.

An offshoot of this necessity is an ongoing and implicit rejection of the narcissism of the Cartesian formula of existence. This is most acutely sent up (or has its gravity removed) through the character of Pilot. For Pilot, everything, to the point of absurdity, becomes meaningful only insofar as it justifies his own identity and existence: 'I prefer Moselle to Rhenish wine; consequently I exist.' 'A person has given me a nickname. Consequently I exist' (255). But the rejection of a stable and determinate relationship between consciousness and being in this Cartesian sense is also a rejection of a particular kind of masculinism which validates the controlling symbolic universe of men at the expense of women. The women who throw open the gap in these tales between identity and existence rely on dream, imagination, acting, and performance. They are at once rejecting this heavy-handed masculinism and are also following an existing model of Gothic character figuration. As Eve Sedgwick has already noted in *The Coherence of Gothic Conventions*: 'It was from the Gothic novel that this drama of substance and abstraction made its way into more easily intelligible, modern-sounding forms.'[2] The decription is of Vashti's stage performance in *Villette*. Vashti is left grappling with the abstractions of her theatrical role but is forced to end her performance when a fire starts in the theatre. It's no coincidence that the point at which Pellegrina Leone abandons the bother of grappling with and instead actually becomes various abstractions of character, that is, begins her life as a real performer, is when a fire during a performance causes the injury which terminates her singing career. This is like a prefiguring of Pellegrina's later comment in 'Echoes', the sequel to 'The Dreamers' in *Last Tales* (1957),[3] when she discovers her voice in the body of a young boy, that 'God likes a *da capo*' (170). This may be a more modern-sounding repetition of the drama described by Sedgwick, but in Dinesen's re-evocation and furthering of the incident, it is the will for abstraction which takes the centre-stage.

The aim of all story-tellers is to pin down, identify and discover the true identity of the woman they all seek, Pellegrina Leone. But with every new layer of narrative, it becomes more obvious that this will be impossible, that finally she will elude them all, because the more that stories are told about her, the more identities she acquires and the more distant and obscure she becomes. Again, this is very much in line with versions of the historical Gothic in which the more attempts are made to describe or discover some unspeakable secret, the more impossible we realise its revelation will be.

Now to move on to the second aspect of the tales I want to look at. All the associations made between females and story-telling in the tales are expressed positively throughout *Seven Gothic Tales* in the form of certain recurrent themes – weightlessness, mutability, fakery, transience, super-ficiality, role-playing, and the deliberate and imaginative denial of the categories of the real and realism in favour of the dreamed and fantastic.

If the female 'Gothic terrorists' of the eighteenth century described by Ellen Moers[4] sought to 'get to the body itself, its glands, muscles, epidermis and circulatory system, quickly arousing and quickly allaying the physiological reactions to fear' then, quite clearly, these texts do not belong to this category of sensationalist Gothic which weigh heavily on the body, both in and outside the text. As D. A. Miller has noted[5] criti-cism has frequently regarded this kind of sensationalist fiction, as liter-ature in which the reading body's hysterical acting out of nervousness both nullifies and naturalises the meaning implied within the narrative. The assertion has been that because such texts generate palpable effects on the body, they merely register the self-evidence of various nervous fears and emotions and thus preclude the activities of interpretation and analysis as though, he says, 'in the breathless body signification expired'. He provides a critical resistance to this approach but also makes the important point that the association of nervous excitability with reading has systematically been linked with femininity. The frequent appearance of plots which thematically involve contagious female neurosis has been identified as a symptom of this. The neuroses both threaten an irrepar-able violation to the equilibrium of some intra-diegetic male and signal the probability that the symptoms, reverberating extra-diegetically, may be passed on to the reader. Miller highlights critical and fictional texts, then, in which body and biology are the designated vehicles for the expression of feminine meanings and are opposed to the distance, intellect, and cerebral dimensions of masculine knowledge. The point I want to make here is that, in Dinesen, the theme of weightlessness and withdrawal from the confinements of the palpable body can be read as being of particular significance, in the context of a feminist debate, because this theme dis-tinguishes her texts from inscriptions of female spectacle and hysteria as they appear in the sensationalist Gothic of the eighteenth century and in doing so they celebrate a particular cerebral rather than biological dimension of the female.

Physically there is frequently something about these characters which defies gravity and there is a definite significance in the double mean-ing which is implicit in this word gravity; that is, they defy the law of nature which keeps our feet on the ground and stops us floating away but, hand in hand with this, seems to go a distinct defiance of the serious-ness associated with the gravity present in the colloquialism of the phrase 'keeping your feet on the ground'. Fransine, in 'The Poet', is attributed with what is described 'in the technical language of the ballet as *Ballon*, a light-ness that is not only the negation of weight but which actually seems to carry upwards and make for flight' (319). Her apparent lack of gravity is described as being at once 'a play on the law of gravitation', a 'piece of celestial drollery', and a 'piece of acting'. She is acting, and she has, unlike the hysteric who is in a relationship of immediacy to her body for expression, a distance, indeed a playful distance, from the body which performs. In both she and Kasparson, the Cardinal's valet in 'Deluge at Norderney', this talent for dance is regarded as being symptomatic of some overall abstraction of existence and a lack of corporeality; both are treated delicately as though they were some untouchable sublime art object. Yet both he and Fransine eventually refuse to go on confirming the gravity (in the sense of (self-)importance) of those who continually define and denigrate them as lightweight and both wreak bloody and murderous revenges.

In 'Deluge at Norderney', amongst the sect at Hernhuten, women's bodies are described as being the registers of a kind of social centre of gravity in a world of masculine entitlement:

> In those days a woman's body had one centre of gravity, and life was much simpler to her on this account than it has been later on. She might poison her relations and cheat at cards with a high hand, and yet be an honnête femme as long as she tolerated no heresies in the sphere of her speciality. Ladies of her day might themselves fix the price of their hearts and minds and of their souls, should they choose to deal with the devil; but as to their bodies, those were the women's stock and trade, and the lowering of the sacred standard price for them was thought of as disloyal competition to the guild of honnêtes femmes, and was a deadly sin. (135)

The attempt here is to fix the value of the female in terms of the ex-change value of her body, yet through the trade union of the 'honnêtes femmes' it is the women who are the brains behind the market, turning its rules on its head so that it functions, not for consumer satisfaction but, through a consensual female code of fair trading, only to glorify the women's own 'stock in trade'. Miss Malin Nat-og-Dag on the other hand is relieved by the distance she attains from the market once she turns fifty and gleefully enjoys sending the whole vulgar affair up. She delights in the little bit of madness she is allowed, a madness which, we are told, took the: 'curious form of a firm faith in a past of colossal licentiousness. She believed herself to have been the grand courtesan of her time, if not the great whore of the Revelation' (138). She is making herself and her value up just like the honnêtes femmes. This is real story-telling. By accepting their terms and then taking things to exaggerated extremes she makes a real comedy out of what was, to her, formerly merely a bad joke. She becomes an etiquette terrorist: 'Fantastical by nature, she saw no reason for temperance, and drove up her price fantastically high. In fact, in regard to the price of her own body she became the victim of a kind of megalomania' (135). Self-deception in this story is always a means of self-defence. Try as they might to target women's centres of gravity in their bodies, to weigh them down through their bodies, taking no account of wit, men always seem to be missing the joke, which is as often as not themselves, as the women bob and smirk above their heads.

So the point I want to make here is that throughout these tales weightlessness is never a diminishing of female presence or a 'making light' of women's intellectual powers as a means to dramatising the fears and fantasies of male narcissism, which have so often been the stuff of Gothic fiction. Rather it is a thematic which invests in a kind of female cerebral superiority, not exactly to men, but to the roles which are offered them by masculinist social orders, most particularly in relation to their bodies. It is a lightness which is powered above all by the energies of wit and humour of the kind so felicitously demonstrated by Miss Nat-og-Dag.

All this frivolity and humour may seem like a far cry from the conventions of a literary tradition which has always seemed more deeply connected to the darker impulses of terror and screams; a series of fictions in which women don't fly in the air but are entrapped in depths. Yet Sybil James[6] points out that the irony and wit of the tales, the emphasis on fictionality and making things up, is an impulse which has always already been implicitly a part of the Gothic (the predictability and staginess of its trappings, its camp associations, its constant repetitions of plot conventions, its stereotypings in characterisation, its contradictory and multiple narrations). It is a feature of the modernism of the text, then, of its twentieth-century status, that this awareness can be brought more explicitly into the foreground. David Punter also describes Dinesen's 'amused awareness that the Gothic to which she refers is itself a glorious fake, doomed to fail in the recapture which it intended.'[7] Much like the superior female characters of her fictions, she can thus be seen as a writer knowingly superior to her genre, the gravity of which in the first place thus becomes thrown seriously into doubt.

As well as a modernist self-consciousness around narrative/narrator/fictionality, it is also worth noting here that her texts seem to fit most appropriately into the critical exigencies of German aesthetic theorists of the Romantic period. The emphasis in Schlegel and Goethe is in the need for art to include both 'gravity' and 'fun'. In Tieck comes the notion that, in irony, not only are the apparent oppositions of play and seriousness in a productive combination but that irony, one of Dinesen's favourite modes, essentially embodies the destruction of illusion, that is, it possesses 'destructive creativity'.[8]

I'd like to finish off now by briefly looking at 'The Poet'. As the last story in the volume, its final moments seem appropriately to crystallise several of the points I've made so far about story-telling and weightlessness. It also provides a good example of 'destructive creativity'.

Until the end of the story Fransine exists between the two male characters, Anders Kube and Councillor Mathieson, only because they have been able to invest in her as a spectacle, as an object for sexual desire and, as a dancer, for entertainment. The release from this state, which by now we know to have been all an act anyway, is coolly stated here: 'She had on a plain nightgown only, put on in a hurry, for she had done with her body' (362). Then again when Mathieson tries to communicate his need for help by touching her foot: 'the girl who had been so sensitive to touch did not move; she had done with her body' (363). At first her body seems to deflate like a balloon, loses its 'ballon':

> Her rounded bosom and hips had shrunk; there seemed to be nothing inside her white garment but a stick . . . her fresh and gentle doll's face was dissolved and ruined by tears; the doll had been broken; its starry eyes and rosebud mouth were no more than black holes in a white plain. (362)

Physically she appears to have been reduced to the image of a barely skeletal frame and yet the figure which has actually disappeared is that of the woman as doll, the ideal abstraction of a woman – the Fransine created and painted by Mathieson. In fact, it seems that the more she is physically abstracted in the text, the nearer she approaches her 'true nature'. After all she is only a fictional character. The last line of this description moves Fransine from the Romantic poet's clichés of womanhood, 'starry eyes' and 'rosebud mouth', to 'black holes on a white plain', and in doing so dramatises the contingency of the embodiment of the fictional figure with the graphic figures on the page through which they are made up within writing – black letters on a white page. Her move into fictionality, then is simultaneous with her liberation from Mathieson. It is Mathieson who wants to eliminate the gap between his word and the reality which it describes, and through this description attempts to shape. But then he is a poet and a Romantic poet at that, whose great hero, his God in fact, is Goethe. The disappearance of rosebud mouths marks the end of his tyrannical domination and allows Fransine to make this decisive realisation: 'He meant to tell her that the world was good and beautiful, but indeed, she knew better. Just because it suited him that the world should be lovely, he meant to conjure it into being so' (363). It is at precisely this point that she cracks him over the head with a large stone boulder, a violence which is accompanied by the most malicious insult she can conjure up: 'You! she cried at him. You Poet!' (364). With these words the gravity and portentousness of the poetic universe is subverted and obliterated in a stroke:

> The blood spurted to all sides. The body, which a second before possessed balance, a purpose, a conception of the world around it, fell together, and lay on the ground like a bundle of old clothes, at the pleasure of the law of gravitation, as it had fallen.
>
> To the Councillor himself it was as if he had been flung, in a tremendous movement, headlong into an immeasurable abyss. It took a little time; he was thrown from one cataract to the other. And meanwhile, from all sides, like an echo in the engulfing darkness, winding and rolling in long caverns, her last word was repeated again and again. (364)

The final text here, then, is the mortality and fallibility of the poet as well as his attempt to convert literary language into real control as order, balance and conception. Inevitably it is the law of gravitation which has the final pleasure of the text, enjoying a joke at the expense of the pretensions of the Godlike author/poet who is usurped by the spirit of story-telling which unburdens the fictional figure from the weight of poetic investment, celebrating its abstraction and mutability in its profane reduction to 'a bundle of old clothes.'

Notes

1 I. Dinesen, *Seven Gothic Tales* (Harmondsworth: Penguin Books (1934), 1988). All page references are to this edition.
2 E. Sedgwick, *The Coherence of Gothic Conventions* (London: Methuen, 1986), p. 170.
3 I. Dinesen, *Last Tales* (Harmondsworth: Penguin Books (1957), 1986).
4 E. Moers, *Literary Women* (London: Women's Press, 1978), p. 90.
5 D. A. Miller, '*Cages aux folles:* Sensation and Gender in Wilkie Collins's *The Woman in White*', in *Speaking of Gender*, Elaine Showalter (ed.) (London: Routledge, 1989), pp. 187–215.
6 S. James, 'Gothic Transformations: Isak Dinesen and the Gothic', in *The Female Gothic*, Juliann Fleenor (ed.) (London: Eden, 1983), p. 140.
7 D. Punter, *The Literature of Terror* (London: Longman, 1989), p. 380.
8 See Kathleen Wheeler's Introduction to *German Aesthetic and Literary Criticism: The Romantic Ironists and Goethe* (Cambridge University Press, 1984), pp. 17–20.

Tearing your soul apart: horror's new monsters

Introduction

The aim of this chapter is to consider the possibilities for the expression of Gothic themes and ideas within the contemporary horror film, with particular reference to the range of monsters and villains available in the genre at this time. Such an enterprise immediately raises some questions to do with the definition and meaning of the term 'Gothic' itself. For example, it is not uncommon in certain contexts for 'Gothic' and 'horror' to be used as if they were more or less interchangeable. Another fairly widespread approach identifies horror as a vulgarised, exploitative version of Gothic. To make matters even more complicated, the term 'Gothic horror' when applied to cinema usually refers to a specific type of horror film, one which has a period setting and which relies for many of its effects upon what might be called here the visual trappings of late-eighteenth- and early-nineteenth-century Gothic, namely ruined castles, dank dungeons, and the like.

As far as an understanding of horror cinema is concerned, I would argue that it is more useful, in broad terms at least, to consider Gothic as a distinctive mode which influences a wide range of cultural forms while horror, and especially the horror film, is best seen as a genre, a much more narrowly circumscribed area of cultural activity. The horror film genre as we understand it today was largely formed in America in the 1930s with a series of films boasting European settings and featuring the likes of Baron Frankenstein (and his creations), Count Dracula, the Wolfman, and the Mummy, all of whom were to become 'classic' movie monsters. These films drew upon Gothic sources for much of their inspiration but the generic framework within which they were housed clearly had the Hollywood studio system's stamp upon it. In particular, horror's reliance on the short cycle of films and the preponderance of sequels in the genre – a feature which has been maintained to the present day

– very much derives from this period and, arguably, is as much a key to understanding horror's identity as are any distinctive thematic or iconographical elements associated with the genre.

Some of the general features of the horror genre are discussed at greater length below. But it should already be clear that while there is undoubtedly a very close relationship between Gothic and horror, it does not follow that all Gothic texts are horror or, for that matter, that all horror films are Gothic. Focusing as this chapter does on the new monsters of contemporary horror cinema provides one means of considering the complicated and often tortuous relations between mode and genre. An apt starting point for such a project is what is in effect the 'birth' of one of these new monsters.

Gothic meets the serial killer

The date is 31 October 1978. The place is Haddonfield, a small town in Illinois. Laurie, a teenage babysitter, is about to have an eventful evening. It begins with the little boy she is looking after who, despite Laurie's assurances to the contrary, insists that the bogeyman is outside. It continues later in rather more dramatic vein with Laurie entering a neighbouring house in search of a friend only to discover three dead bodies. She herself is attacked by a masked figure but escapes. Returning to the house where her babysitting charges are waiting, she is attacked again by the man in the mask. This time she reacts more violently, stabbing him in the neck with a knitting needle and eventually, after a gruelling chase through the house, ramming the sharp end of a clothes hanger into one of his eyes and stabbing him in the chest with a carving knife. Finally, as the apparently indestructible attacker resumes his assault on her, a psychiatrist who has been roaming the streets of Haddonfield searching for an escaped lunatic runs into the house and shoots Laurie's assailant six times. The killer falls from the bedroom window and lands on the lawn. 'It was the bogeyman', says Laurie. 'As a matter of fact it was', says the psychiatrist. He goes to the window and sees that the killer has vanished.

This, in a nutshell, is the last forty-five minutes of John Carpenter's *Halloween* (1978), a film which has been seen by many critics as inaugurating a new type of horror, one which has subsequently acquired the labels 'slasher film', 'stalker film', and 'teenie-kill pic'. Again and again in horror cinema of the late 1970s and early 1980s, when the 'slasher' cycle was at its height, a series of teenagers are stalked and murdered by a male killer who himself is eventually defeated by a sole surviving female. There are variants on this formula – in *Halloween*, for example, Laurie requires the assistance of the psychiatrist in order to survive while in *Friday the 13th*

(1980) the killer turns out to be a woman – but generally the most discernible feature of this short cycle was its machine-like repetitiveness, a feature which it shared with those dispassionate killers who depopulate the small towns, schools, and campsites which provide these films' characteristic killing grounds.

Recently Carol Clover has provided a fascinating account of this area of horror cinema and especially its convoluted sexual politics.[1] What I want to do here is consider the 'slasher' format from a different perspective, namely the relation of its principal villain – the serial killer, the man who kills repeatedly, coldly, and with only minimal motivation – both to broader developments in the horror genre that are taking place throughout the 1980s and early 1990s and to earlier 'classic' movie monsters. One outcome of this is an enhanced awareness of the nature of horror's ongoing engagement with what can be seen as essentially Gothic preoccupations and concerns.

In an important sense, the serial killer is the 1980s movie monster *par excellence*. Certainly this figure in all his (and occasionally her) manifestations has provoked more discussion and debate than any other contemporary horror bogeyman. From the feminist-led protests against the slasher film, and in particular Brian DePalma's *Dressed to Kill* (1980), in the early 1980s, to the more recent concern expressed over the serial killer as 'hero' given us in films such as *Man Bites Dog* (1992), *Henry – Portrait of a Serial Killer* (1987), and, most notoriously, *The Silence of the Lambs* (1991), the popularity of the cinematic serial killer has frequently been seen as symptomatic of an increasingly violent, dehumanised, and alienated society. In the face of such activity, much of which locates the fictional serial killer alongside his/her real life counterparts within a modern mythology of evil, it is worth considering briefly the place of this figure within movie monsterdom generally.

The serial killer as he appears in the slasher film is clearly a late product of what Andrew Tudor has referred to as 'paranoid horror'.[2] Earlier forms of horror, dubbed 'secure' by Tudor, tended to locate their monsters at a safe distance from the everyday world – hence the European settings of many 1930s US horror films -and, largely because of this, were able to show the monster in question as eventually destroyed by the forces of good. In paranoid horror, by way of a contrast, the settings are more often than not present-day and the monster, of which the serial killer is an important example, is a more implacable and irresistible force than before. As Tudor notes, 'In the typical narratives of paranoid horror, the defences protecting this world from the other have long since disappeared. Van Helsing is in his grave, the old remedies do not work and the lurker has crossed the threshold for good.'[3]

Tudor is not alone in identifying Hitchcock's 1960 film *Psycho* as a key text in this shift from secure to paranoid horror. However, there are important differences between Norman Bates, *Psycho*'s serial killer, and the 'killing machines' that stalk through the likes of *Halloween*, *Friday the 13th*, and their various progeny. Most significantly, Bates is a monster with a disturbingly human face who, characteristically for Hitchcock, is presented to us with some sympathy and is granted a degree of psychological interiority. The slasher-killer is an altogether more anonymous, less individuated figure, his face – and by extension his mind – hidden by a mask. In Laurie's words, this particular bogeyman is not a 'He' but instead an 'It'. In this light, the slasher-killer appears as a peculiarly modern (or even postmodern) monster, one which, as Mark Jancovich has pointed out, seems very much to answer to contemporary fears and anxieties, notably 'the fear that subjectivity is now threatened by behaviour that obeys its own relentless and compulsive logic'.[4]

However, the ostensible modernity of the slasher-killer should not distract us from seeing important elements of continuity between this figure and his more obviously 'Gothic' predecessors. In part, this continuity derives from a general feature of the horror genre already discussed above, namely the genre's reliance on sequels and short cycles of films. Most of the 'star' movie monsters – which include Dracula, Frankenstein and his creations, the Wolfman, the Mummy – are stars because they recur across a body of films. It is usually the case that each of these monsters is destroyed at the end of the narrative in which he appears only to be resurrected at the beginning of the next film in the cycle. In a sense, all such monsters, regardless of their 'secure' or 'paranoid' status, are serial killers, if only because they all appear in series of films. Seeing horror in this way – in terms of its exploitative imperatives and the accompanying monster-centred approach – requires us to revise our understanding of the nature and function of horror monsters generally. For one thing, the openendedness associated by some critics with paranoid horror – for example, the monster left free to roam at the end of *Halloween* – begins to look like a property of the horror genre as a whole in as much as audiences have for decades confidently expected many of the 'star' horror monsters to return, regardless of their fate in any particular film. The innovation offered by late 1970s and 1980s horror, then, is that the potential return of the monster, rather than being lodged mainly in the expectations of audiences and film makers, is insistently and very explicitly written into the narrative so that either the monster is left undefeated (as in *Halloween*) or, more usually, there is a suggestion of a resurrection shortly to come (as in some of the *Nightmare on Elm Street* (1984–91) movies).

A further element of continuity which links the slasher film to a range of other horror films, and which is especially pertinent to the Gothic, derives from the fact that despite the modernity of the slasher killer and the world through which he moves, a sense of history, of a past that lurks behind the everyday present, is vital to the operations not only of *Halloween* but many of the variants on it. For example, in *Halloween*, the serial killer – who goes by the name of Michael Myers – begins his killing 'career' in the early sixties when, as a six year old boy living in Haddonfield, he murders his own sister. That is to say, Michael's crimes are not imposed on an idyllic Haddonfield from a hostile outside world but rather are inextricably bound up with the history of Haddonfield itself. The trace of Michael's original crime is still clearly present in the late 1970s, the film's present day, in the shape of the Myers house, which is now deserted and boarded up, the 'bad place' (to use Carol Clover's term) past which local children walk nervously. Importantly, these children – of which Laurie and her soon-to-be-murdered friends are but a few – are almost entirely ignorant of what actually happened in the house. One consequence of this lack of historical knowledge is that for these young people Michael's attacks on them are inexplicable; for Laurie in particular her assailant is not a fellow inhabitant of Haddonfield – although in reality he has certainly been that – but rather 'the bogeyman', and 'It', an object completely divorced from her experience of the world.

To a certain extent, it is the blissful lack of awareness of the not-so-distant past which renders the young people of Haddonfield so vulnerable and which the film itself identifies as a form of complacency that verges on the culpable. Because several of the killer's victims in *Halloween* (and for that matter in the slasher film generally) are either engaged in sexual activity or thinking about sex when they are dispatched, several critics have detected a highly moralistic tone, albeit a deeply hypocritical one, to the proceedings, with the killings functioning in this respect as punishments for moral transgressions. It does seem, however, that the culpability of the victims lies not in their engaging in extramarital sex but rather in doing this when they should be guarding themselves against the killer. Ignorance, not sex, is the 'sin' that is being punished here, and, accordingly, it is Laurie, 'watchful to the point of paranoia' (to use Clover's phrase), who survives the evening.

The general complacency and lack of curiosity displayed by the children has resulted in an unpleasant aspect of Haddonfield's past being conveniently forgotten. But in *Halloween* the past has a force and power of its own, and as the narrative progresses the shadows of the Myers house begin to reach out into and contaminate those houses around it, so that the familiar geography of Haddonfield is eventually transformed into something strange and threatening. One consequence of this is that the house in which Laurie is babysitting, which is initially a haven of light and warmth, suddenly becomes a potential killing ground: its furniture provides hiding places for the monster, a closet turns into a deathtrap and everyday household objects become lethal weapons. Certainly the killer is ejected violently from the house at the end of the film, but by this stage it is clear that, to all intents and purposes, Laurie's house has become Michael's house, and there can be no going back to a status quo characterised by complacency and ignorance.

Seen in this way *Halloween* and accompanying slasher films can readily be aligned with earlier Gothic fictions. While these modern horrors might lack the more obviously Gothic trappings of the period horror film, their presentation of the past as a barbaric force which interrupts and theatens a mundane, everyday world is a scenario which, in broad terms at least, they share with such diverse but undoubtedly Gothic works as Ann Radcliffe's *The Mysteries of Udolpho* (1794), Charles Maturin's *Melmoth the Wanderer* (1820), Bram Stoker's *Dracula* (1897), and Shirley Jackson's *The Haunting of Hill House* (1960). However, this by no means makes the serial killer in himself a traditional 'Gothic villain'. David Punter has identified three principal types of Gothic monster, the Wanderer, the vampire, and the seeker: 'all have desires which are socially insatiable; that is to say, their satiation would involve social disaster, as well as transgression of boundaries between the natural, the human and the divine'.[5] Clearly none of this applies to the slasher killer who, if anything, is characterised by an absence of desire and feeling (although his apparent indestructability does involve a blurring of boundaries between the human and the supernatural, a blurring positively encouraged by *Halloween*'s insistence that its serial killer is, quite literally, 'the bogeyman'). In this respect, this particular movie monster is more like the zombie, another movie monster which lacks any notable precursors in eighteenth- and nineteenth-century Gothic fiction.

It seems then that while *Halloween* and the cycle it was in large part responsible for inaugurating displayed a distinct affinity with the Gothic, the villains of these various films generally resisted such a categorisation. However, while the influence of the slasher film is apparent still in recent horror films, the slasher cycle itself was a relatively short-lived phenomenon and the serial killers that appear later in the 1980s – most notably Dr Hannibal Lecter in *The Silence of the Lambs* – are somewhat different from their 'killing machine' predecessors. Lecter will be discussed shortly, but as a way of understanding some of the important changes taking place in horror throughout the 1980s, and their relation to Gothic, it is worth considering here what turned out to be one of the major horror cycles of the 1980s.

Nightmares on Elm Street

Freddy Krueger is undoubtedly one of the star monsters of 1980s horror. Between 1984 and 1994 he appeared in seven feature films, *A Nightmare on Elm Street* (1984, d. Wes Craven), *A Nightmare on Elm Street 2: Freddy's Revenge* (1985, d. Jack Sholder), *A Nightmare on Elm Street 3: Dream Warriors* (1987, d. Chuck Russell), *A Nightmare on Elm Street 4: The Dream Master* (1988, d. Renny Harlin), *A Nightmare on Elm Street 5: The Dream Child* (1989, d. Stephen Hopkins) and *Freddy's Dead: The Final Nightmare* (1991, d. Rachel Talalay), and *Wes Craven's New Nightmare* (1994, d. Wes Craven).

Carol Clover has suggested that many of the sequels found in contemporary horror cinema are 'more remakes than sequels'. While this might be the case with certain films, her claim does the *Nightmare on Elm Street* cycle an injustice. Elements are repeated from one Elm Street film to another – the monster himself and particular settings – but one also finds a considerable amount of revision, elaboration, and addition as the cycle progresses. Most notably, the shifting of the child-killing monster Freddy Krueger from his relatively small role – in terms of screen-time at least – in the first Elm Street film to centre-stage in subsequent productions reveals certain facets of Freddy's 'monsterdom' that are not immediately apparent from an appraisal of the first film alone.

A comparison of the first Elm Street movie, Wes Craven's *A Nightmare in Elm Street* with *Halloween* reveals some obvious parallels between the two. In each a crime occurs within a particular community – Haddonfield in *Halloween*, Springwood in *A Nightmare on Elm Street* – the memory of which the community seeks to suppress, with the result that years later the children of that community are completely unaware of this particular aspect of the community's past and are therefore extremely vulnerable to attack when the person associated with the original crime returns to wreak destruction. In *Halloween* it is Michael Myers who comes home while in the Elm Street movies it is Freddy Krueger, an inhabitant of Springwood who murdered over twenty children, then escaped judicial punishment on a legal technicality, and was subsequently hunted down by vengeful parents and burned to death. As is also the case with *Halloween* those young people who go about their lives in a generally complacent way are ruthlessly killed while the watchful, paranoid woman – Laurie in *Halloween*, Nancy in *A Nightmare on Elm Street* – turns away from the mundane reality of her peers and, showing great resourcefulness and courage, confronts the monster and survives.

These parallels between the two movies have led Carol Clover to discuss *A Nightmare on Elm Street* as a slasher film. However, if one considers the Elm Street cycle as a whole, some important differences between it and the slasher film – differences that are largely implicit in the first film, increasingly visible in later productions – become apparent. For one thing, Freddy, unlike Michael Myers, comes to be associated with a number of traditional Gothic devices, figures, and conventions. For example, the elaboration of his origin in *Elm Street 3* involves both a ghostly nun (who turns out to be the spirit of Freddy's dead mother) and Bedlam-like asylum for the criminally insane within which Freddy is conceived as a result of his mother being gang-raped by the inmates (thereby earning Freddy the memorable epithet 'bastard son of a hundred maniacs'). In addition, Freddy's defeat in the film involves the judicious use of a crucifix and holy water, devices more conventionally associated with the destruction of vampires. Similarly, in the fourth Elm Street film, Freddy is destroyed in true vampire fashion with the aid of a mirror while in the fifth film the asylum and its resident ghostly nun reappear, although this time the asylum has been transformed visually into what looks very much like a Gothic castle. Finally, in a plot twist that suggests that the Elm Street monster is a Melmoth-like wanderer as well as a vampire, in the sixth film Freddy sells his soul to the dream demons.

These appeals to 'old-fashioned' Gothic are usually associated with the containment and defeat of Freddy, revealing weaknesses which can then be exploited by his opponents. That the defeat of Freddy is never final is, as suggested above, a general feature of popular horror cinema. However, the ineffectiveness of these traditional remedies is further underlined in most of the Elm Street films by conclusions which clearly indicate that Freddy is not dead really – so at the end of *Elm Street 3* a light still burns ominously in Freddy's house, in *Elm Street 4* Freddy's reflection is glimpsed briefly, and in *Elm Street 5* the ghostly children associated with Freddy appear in the film's final shot. In the context of this openendedness, what the references to Freddy as a vampire or Wanderer permit is the projection of the monster into a world of 'secure' horror where he becomes manageable, this in turn enabling the narratives in which he appears to be brought to satisfactory conclusions. Because on a very fundamental level Freddy is not actually a vampire or a Wanderer but instead much more a creature of paranoid horror, this ostensible solution to the threat he poses can never be totally effective. What this suggests is that the 'secure' traditional elements in the Elm Street films function as projections outwards of what are essentially introjected elements, most notably Freddy himself. This movement from internal to external is particularly visible in the importance accorded in a number of the films to the bringing of Freddy out of the world of dreams where he lives into the real world where he can more easily be defeated.

This in turn points to another crucial difference between Freddy and *Halloween*'s Michael Myers, namely that Michael, for all his credentials in Haddonfield as local boy made bad, is figured largely as an external threat while Freddy, quite explicitly, threatens from inside. In the Elm Street cycle's central conceit, Freddy stalks through the dreams of teenagers, and if the teenager in question is killed by Freddy in the dream then he or she will die in reality. This quality of Freddy, the way in which he lodges in the minds (and sometimes the bodies) of his victims, suggests that rather than seeing these films as 'slashers', it makes more sense to think of them as a variant of the 'possession' theme in horror. Hence the extraordinary scene in *A Nightmare on Elm Street* where Nancy falls asleep in the bath and Freddy's razor-fingered hand emerges from between her legs – Freddy is quite literally inside her – and the climactic scene of the film where Nancy absorbs Freddy back into her body; hence, too, the sequences in *Elm Street 2* where the male lead graphically gives birth to Freddy and in *Elm Street 5* where Alice travels into her own womb only to find Freddy waiting for her there. Carol Clover has argued that occult possession fantasies often present the experience of being open to possession as a feminine one: 'occult films code emotional openness as feminine, and figure those who indulge it, male and female, as physically opened, penetrated. The language and the imagery of the occult film is thus necessarily a language and imagery of bodily orifices and insides (or a once-removed but transparently related language of doors, gates, portals, channels, inner rooms).[6] Much of what Clover has to say here can be applied to the Elm Street films, especially their emphasis on the 'openness' of Freddy's teenage victims. Accordingly, the majority of Freddy's 'portals' are female while the one film in the cycle which boasts a male teenager as Freddy's principal portal – namely *Elm Street 2* – is characterised by what one critic has described as 'homosexual panic'.[7]

Not only does Freddy live inside his teenage victims, but he is also fully conversant with contemporary youth culture and teenage mores. This is most apparent in the six sequels to the original film, each of which is replete with references to rock music, popular TV shows, MTV, and computer games. At the same time, much of Freddy's behaviour, reliant as it is on vicious practical jokes and sick humour, is decidedly juvenile. This familiarity with and closeness to youth is often accompanied by Freddy's ruthless mocking of youthful aspirations and ideals (although again this is more apparent in the sequels, after Freddy has himself become the star of the cycle). In fact, most of his victims are, in the end, killed by twisted versions of their ambitions or interests. So, to give just three of the many examples available in the cycle, in *Elm Street 3* a girl who wants above all else to be a TV actress is attacked by a television – 'Welcome to prime time, bitch,' snarls Freddy as he smashes her head through the screen – and a boy whose hobby is making marionettes is himself turned into a puppet with veins and arteries ripped from his body to form the strings, while in *Elm Street 5* a youthful comic book artist is drawn into the pages of a comic book and then killed by one of his own creations.

As important as this to an understanding of Freddy is the fact that he and his victims are always placed in the context of dysfunctional families – usually families where one or other of the parents is missing and where the parents who are present do not understand their children. In many instances, these parents turn out to be as dangerous to their children as is Freddy: in the first Elm Street film, for example, Nancy's boyfriend dies because his parents won't let Nancy wake him up and Nancy's own mother constantly puts Nancy in danger from Freddy; while in *Elm Street 4* a parent drugs her own daughter in order to make her sleep, this inevitably resulting in the death of the child concerned. (On a broader level, of course, these parents are also responsible for inflicting Freddy on their children in the first place.) Freddy himself is frequently associated with these parents, not only because he is of their generation but also because on occasion he repeats lines delivered earlier by parents (in *Elm Street 3*, Freddy actually disguises himself as Nancy's father, while in *Elm Street 6* Freddy's own daughter dispatches him while delivering the line 'Happy Father's Day').

When seen in this way, as a force close to and intimately familiar with teenagers but at the same time distant from them, Freddy begins to look very much like a collective teenage superego, an internalised and in this case highly malevolent voice of parental authority which imperiously denies the feelings and perceptions of youth and which seeks to mock and destroy them. As Freddy himself puts it in *Elm Street 2* when he addresses teenage guests at a party: 'You're all my children now.' What this suggests is that the popularity of Freddy as monster with teenage audiences is of a deeply masochistic kind. It also points to the way in which certain elements apparent in *Halloween* have here been recast so that while we still find 'forgetful' communities peopled by bad parents and vulnerable teenagers, the interruption of the present by an unassimilated and ugly past operates much more explicitly in the Elm Street cycle on the level of the teenage psyche. What the crimes of Freddy and the Elm Street parents have resulted in, then, is essentially the deformation of the personal and collective consciousness of the young people of Elm Street.

The internalising impulse in Elm Street is reflected in the presentation of the 'bad place' in the cycle. In *Halloween*, the bad place was Michael's house, which operated in the film as an undeniable sign of a barbaric past. In Elm Street, this place is Nancy's house, which in subsequent films comes to be known as Freddy's house. This construction takes on an increasingly labyrinthine, unknowable quality as the cycle progresses, with bizarre corridors, doorways and other spaces opening up in unexpected places each time we return to it. In part, this relates to what was referred to earlier as the language of possession, but the house can also be seen as symbolising the infected and mutating teenage psyche which permeates all the films and which, in the end, renders all the teenagers' attempts to defeat Freddy ineffective. Freddy himself thus becomes a marker of a psychologically internalised transaction between the past and present, a struggle which has been formed by and feeds off the material conditions of the Springwood community – especially its attempt to repress the past – and which periodically erupts in violent form into the external world. For the teenagers in the cycle (and, presumably, the audiences for the films) the experience of Freddy involves feelings of loss of control over both self and environment and a deep-seated sense that even in the apparently familiar, domesticated, and comfortable setting that is Springwood one can never be fully at home. On a fundamental level, Nancy's house can only be Freddy's house because Nancy and all her friends are sick inside, with no hope of cure or redemption. In the self-lacerating teenage Gothic of Elm Street, Nancy/Freddy's house becomes a potent symbol not only of the terrible things that history and your parents do to you but also of the damage which you, inexplicably, inflict upon yourself.

Lecter, Pinhead, and Candyman

In the Elm Street movies, previously unperceived spaces continually open up within familiar domestic settings, spaces which do not represent in any escapist or Utopian sense the possibility of separate new worlds but rather figure as distortions in the fabric of everyday reality brought on by the persistence of memories and histories not immediately assimilable within society's 'official' version of itself. In this context, Freddy is simultaneously inside and outside this world, standing as he does at a point where the boundaries between the real, dreams, memories, fantasies, and desires have become infinitely permeable. Of course, it is true to say that stories which tell of the dead hand of the past lying on the present are hardly new in either the horror genre or, for that matter, in Gothic generally. However, it does seem that the peculiar qualities offered by Elm Street's monsterdom – the intertwining therein of paranoid and secure elements, and the sense given of an unhealthy past that produces what might be termed here an ongoing 'mutation' of the present – are qualities which inform a range of other horror films produced in the 1980s and early 1990s and which to a certain extent determine the nature of the monsters found within these.

Dr Hannibal Lecter, who appears both in *The Silence of the Lambs* (1991, d. Jonathan Demme) and the earlier *Manhunter* (1986, d. Michael Mann), is perhaps the most discussed of all 1980s monsters. Like Freddy Krueger, Lecter displays a certain affinity with traditional villains and monsters of the Gothic. For one thing, his combination of considerable charm with great brutality places him alongside such figures as Radcliffe's Montoni, LeFanu's Uncle Silas, and Collins' Fosco. His Gothic credentials also include his living in what is presented to us as a kind of dungeon, his Frankenstein-like status as a misguided and anti-social man of knowledge and the perceptions of him he produces in other characters in the film, most notably one of his guards who asks whether Lecter is a vampire.

Despite these Gothic elements, and all they imply in terms of film about the fixed types and categories of secure horror, the nature of *Lambs'* monster and its relation to the world through which it moves turns out to be rather less fixed than at first seems the case. At one point in *The Silence of the Lambs* the heroine is warned not to speak of personal matters with Dr Lecter because, as her boss puts it, 'You don't want Hannibal Lecter inside your head', and indeed Lecter, like Freddy and despite his existence as a 'real', independent character within a particular narrative, finds his true home in the disturbed, distorted psyche of individuals and/or of societies characterised by an inability to come to terms with their own history.

In *The Silence of the Lambs* the psyche in question belongs to FBI trainee Clarice Starling who is struggling to prove herself in a male-centred world – all her problems are intimately connected with the death of her own father when Clarice was still a child. Within such a context Lecter becomes one of Clarice's several father figures, a key point of reference in what is essentially her narrative, not by any means his. In this context, Lecter's reappearance at the end of the film disturbingly implies that the tensions accruing from Starling's fraught relationship to various patriarchal institutions and figures have not been laid to rest but are instead ongoing.

However, in the case of *The Silence of the Lambs* the glossy production values and realist *mise-en-scène* bestowed by a multi-million dollar budget tend to exclude the vivid stylised representations of the past as a living force in the present that one finds in the much lower budgeted Elm Street films. The bad place at the end of *The Silence of the Lambs* is serial killer Buffalo Bill's house – within which Clarice saves Bill's intended victim and in so doing saves herself – which, when all is said and done, is not 'alive' in the way that Freddy's amorphous, mutating house is. In its presentation of the bad house, *Lambs'* principal antecedents in the horror genre are *Psycho* and *The Texas Chainsaw Massacre* (1974), both of which offer realistically depicted houses which contain terrible secrets associated with the past but which themselves are as dead as the history which weighs so heavily on the houses' inhabitants (as opposed to Freddy's house which offers the unhealthy interpenetration of present and past as a process rather than as an accomplished fact). It follows from this that, while in *The Silence of the Lambs* much of the horror comes from within, the world in which this horror is played out is, for contemporary horror at least, a relatively stable one.

The same could not be said of the *Hellraiser* (1987–92)[8] films and *Candyman* (1992, d. Bernard Rose). It is true that, like both Freddy and Lecter, the monsters found in each display some traditionally Gothic features. For instance, beneath his sadomasochist's garb *Hellraiser*'s Pinhead (so called because of the nails driven into his head) is very much a composite of the archetypal Wanderer and Seeker figures. Inasmuch as he emerges from hell to answer to the dark desires of those who have summoned him, he also embodies attributes of the vampire. Candyman, too, has to be summoned – in his case by his victim-to-be looking into a mirror and saying the monster's name five times. Like the vampire and, to a certain extent, Maturin's Melmoth, Candyman is a tempter whose power is of an essentially seductive kind; hence his promise to the woman who has called him that if she becomes his victim, he will transform her into an immortal urban myth. But in both cases, the monsters are – in Elm Street style – associated with a disturbance of the contemporary world brought on by past events, the consequences of which have not been worked through by that world. This historical weight upon the present manifests itself in a cracking of the surface of reality – with, in both *Hellraiser* and *Candyman*, walls opening up to reveal previously unseen spaces, spaces which carry a historical charge and from which the monsters themselves emerge.

The second and third *Hellraiser* films reveal that Pinhead was originally a Captain Spencer, a disillusioned veteran of World War One whose search for new experiences transformed him into chief denizen of the film's version of Hell. In *Hellraiser III: Hell on Earth*, the space of this war – into which Joey, a 1990s TV reporter, enters via a window in her apartment – is mapped onto the space of the Vietnam war, or, to be more specific, Joey's dreams of her father's death in Vietnam. When in the film's conclusion Joey enters into this war space – which is a continuum of both World War One and Vietnam – while away from her apartment, it turns out that the window in her apartment is in some way equivalent to a window in her mind. At the same time, the scenes of warfare are clearly not meant to be seen as the illusory products of Joey's imagination – they exceed this, manifestations as they are of a history which, as is the case in all the *Hellraiser* films, offers only brutality and cannot satisfy the desires of its inhabitants for some form of transcendence. Importantly, the transcendence on offer in these 'new' spaces has a distinctly corporeal character to it, turning as it does on the inventive tearing apart of the human body, including Pinhead's own. The 'fleshiness' invoked here suggests that there can be no simple escape from the material world but only a rearrangement and contortion of its substance, with the body figuring as the principal site of this activity. (Hence Pinhead's threat in the first *Hellraiser* film that he will tear his victim's soul apart is essentially a physical threat.)

In *Candyman* the monster is the educated son of an ex-slave who has an affair with a white woman and is then tortured and killed at the command of the woman's father. Decades later, a housing project called Cabrini exists on the site of his destruction. For the black inhabitants of Cabrini, the stories they tell about Candyman function as a myth which binds them together and which, the film suggests, offers them, too, the possibility of transcendence, of a meaningfulness which is apart from but at the same time caught up in and expressive of the material constraints upon their lives. The attempts of the white middle class academic Helen to dispel the myth of Candyman through a process of rationalisation eventually provokes the appearance of Candyman himself who, like Freddy and Pinhead, causes the familiar geography of Helen's world to undergo a transformation. While at the site of a murder at Cabrini, she finds a space behind a mirror which leads into another room that functions as a shrine to Candyman; this discovery echoes an earlier moment in Helen's own apartment block – which turns out originally to have been planned as part of a Cabrini-like project – when Helen finds a gap in the wall behind her bathroom mirror. The opening up and entering into of these spaces – both the Cabrini space and Helen's own domestic space – in the course of Helen's investigation and the accompanying disruption of Helen's feeling of being at home in the world are inextricably linked in the film with issues to do with racial oppression, the slavery from which Candyman comes and the inner city ghetto of Cabrini mapped onto each other in the same way that the wars are interrelated in *Hellraiser III* in order to produce a historical destabilisation not only of particular ways of seeing and being in the world but also of that world itself.

Conclusion

The horror genre does not develop in any simple, unilinear fashion; at any point in its history it is characterised by a mixture of different formats and styles. In the case of contemporary horror, the silent killing machine of the first part of the 1980s makes several reappearances throughout that decade (in the *Maniac Cop* films, for example) in which period horror is also intermittently present (notably Coppola's 1992 version of *Dracula*). While acknowledging this diversity, this chapter has sought to identify certain key features of some of horror's newest monsters. In particular, it has focused upon the ways in which a number of traditional Gothic characteristics – types of monster and the theme of the past interrupting the present – are presented as, and to a certain extent transformed into, spatial deformations of contemporary reality which impinge upon and disrupt the psyche of the characters caught up in this process. Within such a situation, the monsters exist in a space where boundaries have become most permeable – where it is no longer clear where dreams, fantasies, and memories end and the real begins. This space is usually associated with a barbaric past which appears strange to the everyday world but which at the same time is always close to that world, hidden away in secret rooms in those domestic settings which provide the characteristic locales for contemporary horror, awaiting the initial breaching of boundaries from which the monsters and the horror will then emerge. In contemporary horror cinema, these monsters are never far away, are always close to home. As Freddy Krueger puts it in *Freddy's Dead: The Final Nightmare*, 'Every town has an Elm Street.'

Notes

1 C. J. Clover, *Men, Women and Chainsaws: Gender in the Modern Horror Film*, (London: British Film Institute, 1992).

2 A. Tudor, *Monsters and Mad Scientists: A Cultural History of the Horror Movie* (Oxford: Blackwell, 1989).

3 *Ibid.*, p. 184.

4 M. Jancovich, *Horror* (London: Batsford, 1992), p. 106.

5 D. Punter, *The Literature of Terror* (Harlow: Longman, 1980), p. 120.

6 Clover, *Men, Women and Chainsaws*, p. 101.

7 *Monthly Film Bulletin*, vol. 50, no. 633, October 1986, 313.

8 To date the *Hellraiser* films include *Hellraiser* (1987, d. Clive Barker), *Hellbound: Hellraiser II* (1988, d. Tony Randel) and *Hellraiser III: Hell on Earth* (1992, d. Anthony Hickox).

Gothic spaces: the political aesthetics of Toni Morrison's *Beloved*

There is a blue house that sits on this river between two bridges. One is the George Washington that my bus has just crossed from the Manhattan side, and the other is the Tappan Zee that it's heading toward. My destination is that blue house, my objective is to tape a dialogue between myself and another black American writer, and I stepped on this bus seven years ago when I opened a slim volume entitled *The Bluest Eye*. Where does the first line of any novel – like any journey – actually begin?

Gloria Naylor, 'A Conversation [with Toni Morrison]'

I

'Gothic' has its origin as an architectural term, applied to medieval buildings marked by pointed arches and vaults. Its first use dates to the early eighteenth century, when John Evelyn censored medieval buildings in favour of classical structures, those that 'were demolished by the Goths or Vandals, who introduced their own licentious style now called modern or Gothic'.[1] Modernity, thus invented with a backward glance, is defined as an architectural landscape built upon destruction, a vandalism against proper morals, taste, and the achievements of civilisation.

This invention of modernity as medieval destruction takes place at the time of the rise of the bourgeoisie. Housing structures changed. The term 'modern' was to accommodate concepts that excluded medieval vaults and arches, and which, indeed, relegated those features to a realm of exotic splendour. The word 'comfort', for example, was first applied to houses in the eighteenth century. The term shifted from the discourse of religious and legal studies to signify not simply satisfaction, but also to expand on the notion of convenience.[2] According to Witold Rybszynski, Walter Scott, a historicist dreamer of medieval times, was one of the first novelists to use the word in its newly acquired sense: 'Let it freeze without,' he wrote, 'we are comfortable within' (20). 'There is nothing like staying at home for real comfort', Jane Austen would soon write in *Emma*, as Rybszynski points out (101).

While Gothic architecture seemed to strive for an assimilation of the grandeur and vastness of nature and spirit, the bourgeois home, as invented in the eighteenth century, drew a clear line between the inside and the outside. Inside, one was able to find not only shelter but also thermal content; the inside provided protection against outside spaces filled with potentially hostile forces. In contrast to the bourgeois house, a medieval one offered fewer rooms; rooms were not yet designated for specific functions. The limited space did not acknowledge individual needs, and furniture was largely temporary. For the eighteenth-century bourgeois, the coldness and the emptiness of medieval spaces could signify discomfort only. With the separation of work and living quarters, rooms that allowed for privacy, the eighteenth-century bourgeois was, as an individual, able to construct an alternative life – the comfort of the 'inside'.

It was during the time of the redefinition of bourgeois private space that the medieval castle was rediscovered as a stage set for Gothic literature. Unlike the sheltering bourgeois home, but also unlike classical, symmetrical architecture, it does not represent the owner's control over its space. But the medieval castle clearly represents another class of owners as well. Compared to the bourgeois house, its aristocratic inhabitant was disowned of his authority over its structure even before a political movement would stress the difference in social positions, and the different avenues of the classes' development. In an aristocrat's house, the bourgeois owner would now suspect, anything could happen. Even ghosts could appear.

A Gothic building, as it survived in its representational form, and as it was represented in fiction, was simply unsuitable for the idea of home. Homes, however, were proper housing for the individuals of the eighteenth-century middle class. Not only comfort and privacy were promoted, but domesticity as well, which, in turn, became increasingly feminised. As work and living spaces separated, and work divided according to gender lines, the house became the woman's domain. 'Und drinnen waltet / Die züchtige Hausfrau', Friedrich Schiller was eager to explain what was already widely accepted as true.[3] In the Gothic novels of the eighteenth century, however, this power over the inside space, the authority of *walten*, was not given to women. Women rather suffered as the victims and captives of their male and often foreign persecutors. Ironically, this may have been a more precise account of the female social position and struggle for rights at that time than Schiller's idealisation, as the house's comforts were also established by a devaluation of women's work.

Compared to the money that buys comfort, comfort's maintenance is a secondary task. As Clara Reeves and Ann Radcliffe, but also as many male authors, knew, not just the novel, but precisely the Gothic novel became the fantasy space in which to explore women's roles and the feminine.[4]

The idea of modernity as related to bourgeois houses was not created by the backward glance, but by the idea of new acquisition and progress. Money, earned outside, bought comfort, and new objects contributed to the comfort and gave evidence of how a house could be put to the inhabitant's service. Privacy had to be protected, and the collection of objects, reified goods, provided such a protection as well. Instead of a person leaving the house, the world could symbolically enter. Because their presence itself would thus provide a usefulness of comfort, eighteenth-century collections encompassed objects of Gothic interiors as well, which, at the same time, seemed to have lost their meaning or sense of purpose in this context. The Gothic, once constructed, could be fragmented, imitated, fetishised. Indeed, Gothic elements were eclectically collected, and integrated into the new and more intimate space. The move to establish the uncanny was countered by the move to make it familiar in the bourgeois' own way: by economic appropriation.

II

The idea of the modern bourgeois home did not remain a European invention. It was imported to the American Colonies, and it has survived on either continent well into the twentieth century. A house as a home is, indeed, a recognisable commodity. It can be multiplied in the construction of neighborhood developments, or reduced to the outward simplicity of a child's drawing. In its deceptive simplicity, it can gain symbolic meaning and indicate the lifestyle of its dwellers. Introduced into a school primer, for example, a sketch of such a home would not only tell of the building's material and looks, but also of the individuals occupying it:

> Here is the house. It is green and white. It has a red door. It is very pretty. Here is the family. Mother, Father, Dick, and Jane live in the green-and-white house. They are very happy. See Jane. She has a red dress. She wants to play. Who will play with Jane?[5]

This house, built for the nuclear family, tells of the regular income of its adult inhabitants, their sense of order, and their acceptance of an American way of life as a celebration of middle-class values. The description is also generic enough to be recognised by young readers as a reference to their own home. Housing is translated into a familiar concept that would help to overcome the strangeness of the letters, and promote the learning of a new skill. This primer's modern house is both a lesson in reading, and a confirmation of values.

For those whose house does not resemble this picture, it is a lesson in acculturation. The description of Dick and Jane's house serves as the beginning of Toni Morrison's first novel, *The Bluest Eye*. Published in 1970, the novel turns to the 1940s to describe the life of Black families in the small town of Lorain, Ohio, struggling to come close to the bourgeois ideals that the primer promotes. These ideals, however, are defined by a society not only divided by class, but also by race. There is a jarring difference between the white-and-green house of the textbook, and the decaying storefront building on the southeast corner of Broadway and Thirty-fifth Street in which the Breedlove family lives. There is a jarring difference, too, between the ideal of beauty promoted by Greta Garbo or Ginger Rogers, and the looks of the little black girls who are compared with them (10). Drinking milk from her Shirley Temple cup, young Pecola Breedlove dreams of having blue eyes. The movie screen, the Shirley Temple cup, and Dick and Jane's house turn in Morrison's novel into facades that cover the social inequity, and translate the notion of home into a bourgeois concept that is part of a racially determined aesthetics. If you cannot change your looks, why try to change your house? We are told that the Breedloves accept their house and social standing because they admit to their ugliness (28).

The inside of the Breedlove's storefront residence resonates with an almost medieval one-room lifestyle:

> The plan of the living quarters was as unimaginative as a first-generation Greek landlord could contrive it to be. The large 'store' area was partitioned into two rooms by beaverboard planks that did not reach to the ceiling. There was a living room, which the family called the front room, and the bedroom, where all the living was done . . . In the center of the bedroom, for the even distribution of heat, stood a coal stove. Trunks, chairs, a small end table, and a cardboard 'wardrobe' closet were placed around the walls. The kitchen was in the back of this apartment, a separate room. There were no bath facilities. Only a toilet bowl, inaccessible to the eye, if not the ear, of the tenants. (25)

Clearly, this house does not offer any possibility of privacy. The distinction between inside and outside is, however, important nevertheless: to rent, or even to own, a house designates stability and social standing. To own or care for property is, moreover, central to the bourgeois ideal. While the green-and-white house may never be within reach, burning down the house in which one lived, as Pecola's father, Cholly Breedlove, does, is not just arson, but a crime of larger proportions:

> Outdoors, we knew, was the real terror of life. The threat of being out-
> doors surfaced frequently in those days. Every possibility of excess was
> curtailed with it. If somebody ate too much, he could end up outdoors.
> If somebody used too much coal, he could end up outdoors. People
> could gamble themselves outdoors, drink themselves outdoors . . .
> To be put outdoors by a landlord was one thing – unfortunate, but an
> aspect of life over which you had no control, since you could not
> control your income. But to be slack enough to put oneself outdoors,
> or heartless enough to put one's own kin outdoors – that was criminal.
> There is a difference between being put *out* and being put out*doors*. If
> you are put out, you go somewhere else; if you are outdoors, there is
> no place to go. The distinction was subtle but final. Outdoors was the
> end of something, an irrevocable, physical fact, defining and comple-
> menting our metaphysical condition. (11)

This transformation of a home by vandalism may have little to do with
the modernity of the Gothic; the Breedlove's home is hardly a classical
structure, nor is it replaced by a contemporary one. The ruin stands, confirming the difference between rich and poor, white and black, property
owner and renter, and the act of drunken protest.

Only seemingly, race provides a dividing line that cuts through class
distinctions. As the dominant model of beauty and the Breedlove's acceptance of their ugliness shows, the bourgeois ideals are defined for and by
white people. Indeed, part of the Breedlove's tragedy is their acceptance
of bourgeois values that leads to schizophrenia and self-annihilation. This
is shown, quite poignantly, already in the comparison of houses.

Morrison's novel *Beloved* begins with the description of a house as
well:

> 124 was spiteful. Full of a baby's venom. The women in the house
> knew it and so did the children. For years each put up with the spite
> in his own way, but by 1873 Sethe and her daughter Denver were its
> only victims. The grandmother, Baby Suggs, was dead, and the sons,
> Howard and Buglar, had run away by the time they were thirteen
> years old – as soon as merely looking in a mirror shattered it (that was
> the signal for Buglar); as soon as two tiny hand prints appeared in the
> cake (that was it for Howard).[6]

The house number, representing the building metonymically, acquires a
life of its own. Each of the three sections of the novel begins, moreover,
with a reference to 124 in which the house turns from being 'spiteful' to
'loud', and, finally, to 'quiet' (3, 169, 239). Morrison comments on the
beginning of her novel as a conscious effort to start in *medias res*:

> Snatched just as the slaves were from one place to another, without
> preparation and without defense. No lobby, no door, no entrance – a

gangplank, perhaps (but a very short one). And the house into which this snatching – this kidnapping – propels one, changes from spiteful to loud to quiet, as the sounds in the body of the ship itself may have changed. A few words have to be read before it is clear that 124 refers to a house (in most of the early drafts 'The women *in the house* knew it' was simply 'The Women knew it'. House was not mentioned for seventeen lines, and a few more have to be read to discover why it is spiteful, or rather the source of the spite.[7]

The reader is made to arrive at the house much as the protagonists do for whom 124 is, however, a dwelling of choice. '124' as a number constitutes an address, and therefore a desired property. But it contrasts sharply with Dick and Jane's house in the primer, too, reducing the description of a home to a series of ciphers that cannot, from the outset, refer to any comfort and intimacy. Preoccupied with the house's actions, the reader is not directed towards its looks. The 'posture of coziness' is,[8] indeed, suggested by another building's name in this novel, that of the Southern plantation 'Sweet Home'. The Garner family, owners of 'Sweet Home', insist that the members of their plantation live and work in a harmonious family setting, and that their slaves are treated as paid labourers. Indeed, the sweetness of their home seems to become their inhabitants' attributes: 'Mrs Garner put down her cooking spoon. Laughing a little, she touched Sethe on the head, saying, "You are one sweet child". And then no more' (26).

Sethe came to 'Sweet Home' as a young girl and she is the only female slave on the plantation. At 'Sweet Home', Sethe 'marries' Halle Suggs, and bears him two sons and a daughter. When Mr Garner dies, his brother, 'schoolteacher', and two nephews take over the plantation. Similar to the movies' false images in *The Bluest Eye*, the Garners' home reveals now the cruel character that it always had. Sethe realises her own role as a breeder and as an object without rights that would be available for the nephews' sexual assault. Trying to save her children from a similar fate, she sends them ahead to their freed grandmother Baby Suggs and flees herself, giving birth to her fourth child, Denver, during the escape. But the schoolteacher follows her, and finds her hiding place. Unwilling to send her children into slavery, Sethe decides to kill them, and indeed kills her older daughter, the 'crawling already?' child. While she is punished for her deed, she can also survive with her other three children and Baby Suggs in freedom and later move to 124. Halle, a traumatised witness of the nephews' sexual advances on Sethe, will never join her.

As the novel opens, 124 is already a house of women. Both sons have left. But it is the visit of Paul D., a freed 'Sweet Home' man, who provokes Sethe's memories of the past. These reflections centre again and again on the dead child. Perhaps it is also this child that turns 124 into a haunted house, which personifies this house, breaking the family further apart. This is 124's prehistory:

> Each one fled at once – the moment the house committed what was for him the one insult not to be borne or witnessed a second time. Within two months, in the dead of winter, leaving their grandmother, Baby Suggs; Sethe, their mother; and their little sister, Denver, all by themselves in the gray and white house on Bluestone Road. It didn't have a number then, because Cincinnati didn't stretch that far. In fact, Ohio had been calling itself a state only seventy years when first one brother and then the next stuffed quilt packing into his hat, snatched up his shoes, and crept away from the lively spite the house felt for them. (3–4)

124 continues to resist the move of the city to integrate houses into neighbourhoods and 'stretch out'. It thrives on its isolation, just as it is about to be geographically integrated into a community by receiving a number. Sethe, although in freedom, is shunned by her neighbours because of the murder of her child.

Combining references to the family history with American History, Morrison is able to give the house a life of its own. 124 is no green-and-white house, but one of the greyish color that corresponds to the Breedlove's storefront building. By being haunted by a child, and by acting like a child, 124 is both familiar and defamiliarised – an uncanny actor that rules over its inhabitants. With Paul D.'s arrival, there comes the hope that a semblance of family life could be restored, and that the ghost could be banned. But the past is not only resurrected by Paul D.'s arrival and in narratives. A new person appears, with the name Beloved:

> A fully dressed woman walked out of the water. She barely gained the dry bank of the stream before she sat down and leaned against a mulberry tree. All day and all night she sat there, her head resting on the trunk in a position abandoned enough to crack the brim in her straw hat . . . It took her the whole of the next morning to lift herself from the ground and make her way through the woods past a giant temple of boxwood to the field and then the yard of the slate-gray house. Exhausted again, she sat down on the first handy place – a stump not far from the steps of 124 . . .
>
> Women who drink champagne when there is nothing to celebrate can look like that: their straw hats with broken brims are often askew; they nod in public places; their shoes are undone. But their skin is not like that of the woman breathing near the steps of 124. She had new skin, lineless and smooth, including the knuckles of her hands. (50)

The newness of Beloved's skin is as puzzling as her curious mixture of wisdom and ignorance. There is the rumour that a black girl had been kept imprisoned in one of the nearby houses, and Beloved acts indeed like a prisoner freed. Her body, as well as her behaviour, give rise, however, to the suspicion that it is not only the name that connects this Beloved to Sethe's dead daughter. Indeed, 'Beloved' is the only word written on the 'crawling already?' baby's tomb stone, the only word Sethe was able to buy by selling her body to the engraver; the word became thus the baby's name.

After Beloved enters Sethe's house, the baby ghost and the building seem to commence separate existences. Gaining physical presence, however, Beloved can both recall and provide a link to a past that Sethe previously tried to suppress. Beloved, pushing Paul D. aside in Sethe's affection, but finally being sent away by him, turns the novel less into an investigation about her identity, but about Sethe's and her family's history. 'She was my best thing' (272) Sethe says after Beloved leaves, stressing the bond between her and the young woman. This bond is reflected again in her relationship to Baby Suggs, her stepmother Nan, and her mother of whom she only knows that she arrived from Africa.

In a conversation with Gloria Naylor, Morrison cites two sources for her novel.[9] One was a newspaper clipping from 1851 that referred to Margaret Garner, a slave from Kentucky who escaped and killed one of her children; Garner stated when interviewed that she did not want her children to return to slavery. Morrison had come across her story while collecting material for *The Black Book*, a collection of writings on Black history and culture that she edited in 1974.[10] Next to the story of this 'serene young woman',[11] Morrison claims to have been struck by the photographs in James Van Der Zee's collection, *The Harlem Book of the Dead*, for which she wrote the foreword.[12] Van Der Zee's pictures feature dead loved ones in peculiar poses: a dead baby in the arms of its parents, or a fully dressed person in a coffin. To give the dead a semblance of life has an artistic tradition that extends the use of photography in the Black community.[13] Van der Zee, however, found a special variation for this genre. He worked not only with touch-ups, but also with double exposures. In addition to floating lines of scripture and poetry, many of his pictures also show angels and the Christ image. Photography, as the art of shadows, develops with Van der Zee in the art of religious ghosts, reminding the viewer of the comforting presence of the otherwise invisible divine. Van Der Zee's angels, as well as the Christ figure, are, moreover, white and 'conventional' images of Christian religion. Van Der Zee articulates implicitly already a confrontation of white and black reality and religion that Morrison will rewrite and rephrase in her own work.

One of the photographs shows an eighteen-year-old girl who was shot by her jealous lover, and who chose to help him escape rather than save her own life.[14] Morrison explains:

> I had about fifteen or twenty questions that occurred to me with those two stories in terms of what it is that really compels a good woman to displace the self, her self. So what I started doing and thinking about for a year was to project the self not into the way we say 'yourself', but to put a space between those words, as though the self were really a *twin* or a thirst or a friend or something that sits right next to you and watches you, which is what I was talking about when I said 'the dead girl' . . . So I just imagined the life of a dead girl which was the girl that Margaret Garner killed, the baby girl that she killed.[15]

This space is also one of geographical distance. But the distance between Kentucky and Harlem, New York, parallels a temporal one. It is a distance of historical significance for Black people, that separates the plantation South from the abolitionist North. South to North is Sethe's route of escape, leading her from Kentucky's 'Sweet Home' to Cincinnati. It is not Van Der Zee's photograph but rather Margaret Garner's interview that renders a voice to the muted past. Garner's story is, first of all, a slave's history, framed by the newspaper text as the Breedlove's story is framed by quotations from the school primer, the words of which run together and form fragmented sentences, introducing every section of *The Bluest Eye*. *Beloved* reworks Garner's slave history in a collage of poetry, dreams, past and current stories, to reconstruct a memory that would lead beyond an individual's tale as a recovery of the Afro-American past. It is in this sense, that Samuels and Hudson-Weems called *Beloved* 'a ghost story about history' (135). In picturing the dead, Morrison constructs a language to make the past visible.

III

How is it possible, however, for a slave narrative and a Gothic tale to come together? Slave narratives, recorded since the late eighteenth century, were often dictated to white writers, and always edited and published by them. White editors vouched for their authenticity. Often very brief, these narratives are statements presenting a victim's point of view, a route of suffering that would lead from inhuman conditions to a better, if not always fully emancipated, way of life. Unlike confessions, these autobiographies do not describe a conversion due to an inner revelation. The slave's life and *Bildung* is entirely dependent on the economic conditions of his or her white surrounding, and his or her possibilities of protest and escape.

112

From J. van Der Zee, Owen Dodson, and Camille Bishop, *The Harlem Book of the Dead* (Dobbs Ferry, NY: Morgan & Morgan, 1978).

The genre of the document is based on the written word. Slave narratives strive to be documents. Though the slave's story is often told to the editor/writer rather than written, the narrative retains formulaic conventions that are familiar to the readers of literature. Part of the success of slave stories lies in the fact that they were recorded by white men for readers who came from a white tradition.[16] In her reworking of the slave narrative in *Beloved*, Morrison, in contrast, gives preference to the oral word. This is the tradition that she herself remembers as uniquely hers, but also as the tradition that the Black community can and should reclaim.[17]

According to Morrison, oral literature is open-ended, it asks for participation, and thrives on narratives of dreams, myths, and folkloric elements that can be traced back to African roots. This 'oral' literature may provide the voice of the slave that had been silenced in the slave narratives, turn Garner's story from a third-person into a first-person narrative. In changing perspectives, it may introduce an alternative tale that, as fiction, may bear more experiential truth.

For Morrison, this change focuses, above all, on the woman's voice. Although doubly silenced by the white Western tradition, black women emerge in Morrison's tale as persons of special strength. They are able to take action, and their government of the house finds its limitation not in black male power, but only in the white system. In a conversation with Rosemarie Lester, Morrison insists that black women, having always been mother and labourer at the same time, are better suited to feminist demands.[18] The ghost in *Beloved*, who is female, too, relates particularly well to the female members of the household. The novel proves that the supernatural is not truly alien, but that it takes the black women's side against white power. It represents Sethe's family and the historical past. In the novel, it also introduces with Sethe's story a history that may have been repressed by blacks, but that the white slaveholders and masters attempted to sever and obliterate.

For Walter Scott, history had been represented by the visual backdrop of British castles and Highland costumes; they provided a distance between the fictional world and that of his readers that provided the freedom and licence of the historicising effort. For novelists like Clara Reeve or Horace Walpole, the historicising was disrupted by supernatural elements that, introduced as accidental, established order by a denial of a continuum of events that would be shaped by their protagonists. Radcliffe's psychologising makes it clear to what extent the supernatural countered the historical. In Morrison, the supernatural is able to strengthen the position of the person who encounters it – the woman who encounters the female ghost. Fingerprints tell of the presence of unknown beings.

Furniture moved or any other action taken by invisible powers echo the Gothic tradition. These signs and actions disrupt the continuum of events and disturb the sense of comfort. Sethe's sons, Howard and Buglar, know of this and flee. For the women who stay on, however, the supernatural is, far from being ahistorical, a reintroduction of history, the sign of memory that takes physical shape with the appearance of Beloved. The women in 124 seem to realise that the figures add up to the magic number seven; they accept the ghost because the house is really theirs: 'It's a feminine concept – things happening in a room, a house. That's where we live, in houses. Men don't live in those houses, they really don't.'[19] Living in a space that is feminised, women do not only become the bearers of children but also the bearer of history through their memory, or, as Morrison calls it, rememory. Sethe explains to her daughter Denver:

> I was talking about time. It's so hard for me to believe in it. Some things go. Pass on. Some things just stay. I used to think it was my rememory. You know. Some things you forget. Other things you never do. But it's not. Places, places are still there. If a house burns down, it's gone, but the place – the picture of it – stays, and not just in my rememory, but out there, in the world. What I remember is a picture floating around out there outside my head. I mean even if I don't think it, even if I die, the picture of what I did, or knew, or saw is still out there. Right in the place where it happened. (35–6)

Elsewhere, Morrison writes that rememory designates 'a journey to a site to see what remains have been left behind and to reconstruct the world that these remains imply'.[20] Memory itself is understood as geographical space.

IV

One has only to compare recent novels by Stephen King with Toni Morrison's invocation of the supernatural to see a similarity of motifs; the dead come to life in both, and haunt the living. The ambiguity of the motif of a ghost's appearance cannot be denied. This may, on the one hand, prove the limitations of the study of motifs. On the other hand, however, it may also tell much about Morrison's craft and the attractiveness of her work for a wider audience of black as well as white readers. While Morrison insists on introducing Black voices, she has also been trained in British and American literature and wrote a master's thesis on Virginia Woolf and William Faulkner, the latter no stranger to the Gothic tradition. Introducing Beloved in *Beloved*, Morrison is, indeed, not only restoring Black history via Black folklore, but also reworking the white tradition of Gothic literature in writing the history of its ghosts. But Morrison's use of the Gothic does more than that. While treating slaves as invisible spirits, American plantation homes – like 'Sweet Home' – are described as Gothic settings that feature slaves as invisible Blacks. Ghosts, therefore, do not signify the limitations of a white man's power, but a social order that relies on their presence. Morrison's reframing is, therefore, a political one, and it has consequences not only for the contemporary Black novel, but also for a new evaluation of the British literature of the past.

In an essay on the place of the Afro-American experience within the literary canon, Morrison discusses white American literature and the Afro-American response. She argues for a rereading of texts by white authors to discover the 'unspeakable things unspoken', 'a search, in other words, for the ghost in the machine'.[21] In this essay, shattered mirrors or finger prints are not only signs of a Beloved, but also the signs of a different voice within American literature. This voice is, indeed, scarcely recorded yet, because it was deprived of the traditional letter, a claim to visibility that ghosts as well as oral literature cannot fulfil. Afro-American literature, moreover, is not simply housed within American literature, as the Breedlove family lives in the Greek landlord's house. Nor does it occupy a very separate realm, as Pecola's mother would suggest when she bars her daughter's entry into the kitchen of her white employers. Afro-American literature responds to the white tradition in and by subversion; by a re-naming and retelling of the story.

In *Beloved*, examples for this renaming are given by individual protagonists. Stamp Paid, who helps Sethe in her escape, has given himself his name after he had to offer his wife to their white master. Baby Suggs rejects the name Jenny, stated on her slave bill, and calls herself by the name her husband had given her. Naming the house by its number only, 124, resonates with the renaming of geographical places elsewhere in Morrison's novels. In *Sula* (1973), for example, the black community calls their neighbourhood on the hill 'Bottom', and knows about the 'No Mercy Hospital' and the 'Not Doctor Street'.[22]

In her interviews, Morrison describes her work as 'village literature',[23] consciously turning back from the city to a community many Blacks experienced before moving 'North'.[24] Her 'village' is dependent on a linguistic community, and this linguistic understanding relies on references to the ancestral past, common experiences, as well as verbal action. While the act of renaming and naming is achieved by the Black author, the white and the black reader may read differently. Morrison quotes an early paragraph from *The Bluest Eye* that follows the excerpt from the primer:

The Bluest Eye begins 'Quiet as it's kept, there were no marigolds in the fall of 1941.' The sentence, like the one that open each succeeding book, is simple, uncomplicated. Of all the sentences that begin all the books, only two of them have dependent clauses; the other three are simple sentences and two are stripped down to virtually subject, verb, modifier. Nothing fancy here. No words need looking up; they are ordinary, everyday words. Yet I hoped the simplicity was not simply-minded, but devious, even loaded. And that the process of selecting each word, for itself and its relationship to the others in the sentence, along with the rejection of others for their echoes, for what is determined and what is not determined, what is almost there and what must be gleaned, would not theatricalise itself, would not erect a proscenium – at least not a noticeable one.[25]

Morrison continues, however, to describe this beginning not just as a devious simplicity, but also as the indication of 'illicit gossip', 'whisper', 'oral language', 'comprehension as in-joke for some' (218–19) that defines for her Black literature. In her interviews, Morrison does not deny white critics the ability to read and interpret Black literature, in the same way as she herself insists on a reading of Faulkner or Emily Dickinson and an understanding of these authors' positions:

If I could understand Emily Dickinson – you know, she wasn't writing for a *Black* audience or a *white* audience; she was writing whatever she wrote! I think if you do that, if you hone in on what you write, it will *be* universal . . . not the other way around![26]

On the one hand, Morrison accepts the idea of universal literature. On the other hand, Morrison suggests, white readers may realise the devious-ness of her novel's first sentence, but not the whisper, smoothing over the differences to adjust to an ideal of universal literature. What Morrison is struggling with, and at times with contradictory statements, is the notion of a universal literature to be gained in the face of difference. The rela-tionship of the 'universal' to 'difference', the peculiarity of a different voice that tries to subvert what it responds to, remains unclear. Africans have many words for yam, Morrison repeats in her interviews, seemingly exposing the universal as a simplifying and unifying measure of a white invention.[27] In an interview with Elsie Washington, Morrison insists that 'black' is no longer something one is born as, but a choice, a 'mindset'.[28]

White readers, in an act of bleaching purification, may indeed be tempted to read Morrison's reworking of a British tradition as a deafen-ing act to prove that tradition's primacy. In the case of *Beloved*, Margaret Atwood may be such a reader in point. Her review of the book mentions neither the specificity of a Black novelistic tradition, nor does she refer to Morrison as a black woman author. Entitling her piece 'Haunted by their

Nightmares', Atwood evaluates the novel with a simple account and counting that supersedes that of 124:

> *Beloved* is Toni Morrison's fifth novel, and another triumph. Indeed, Ms Morrison's versatility and technical and emotional range appear to know no bounds. If there were any doubts about her stature as a pre-eminent American novelist, of her own or any other generation, *Beloved* will put them to rest. In three words or less, it's a hair-raiser.[29]

And Atwood continues: 'The supernatural element is treated, not in an 'Amityville Horror', watch-me-make-your-flesh-creep mode, but with magnificent practicality, like the ghost of Catherine Earnshaw in *Wuthering Heights*' (143), and she finally applauds: 'Students of the supernatural will admire the way this twist is handled' (146).[30] Sometimes, it seems, the Gothic may offer the more familiar house.

Notes

I would like to thank Morgan & Morgan Press for permission to reproduce James Van Der Zee's photograph, published in *The Harlem Book of the Dead*.

1 J. Evelyn, 1702; quoted in 'Gothic', *Encyclopedia Britannica*, 11th edn (1910).
2 Witold Rybczinski, *Home: A Short History of an Idea* (New York: Viking Penguin, 1986), p. 20.
3 'And the virtuous house wife rules inside.' Friedrich Schiller, 'Das Lied von der Glocke', stanza 8, 29–30.
4 In this context, I would like to refer to Nancy Armstrong and Leonard Tennenhouse's forthcoming study on American captivity tales and the 'origin' of the British novel. I believe that the Gothic novel in particular explores the captivity theme as a gendered one.
5 T. Morrison, *The Bluest Eye* (London: Chatto & Windus, 1979), p. 1.
6 T. Morrison, *Beloved* (New York: Knopf, 1987), p. 3.
7 T. Morrison, 'Unspeakable Things Unspoken: The Afro-American Presence in American Literature,' in Harold Bloom (ed.), *Toni Morrison* (ser.) *Modern Critical Views* (New York: Chelsea House, 1990), pp. 228–9.
8 Morrison, 'Unspeakable,' p. 228.
9 G. Naylor and T. Morrison: 'A Conversation', *The Southern Review* 21 (1985), pp. 583–5.
10 Published by Random House, Marylin Sanders Mobley points out rightly that a copy of the news article, entitled 'A Visit to the Slave Mother Who Killed Her Child', appears on p. 10 of Morrison's anthology; see Mobley, 'A Different Remembering: Memory, History and Meaning in Toni Morrison's *Beloved*', in Harold Bloom (ed.), *Toni Morrison* (ser.) *Modern Critical Views* (New York: Chelsea House, 1990), p. 190. Ironically, Wilfrid D. Samuels and Clenora Hudson-Weems insist that Garner's story was not included, but that Morrison 'saved' it for her novel; see Wilfrid D. Samuels and Clenora Hudson-Weems, *Toni Morrison* (Boston: Twayne, 1990), p. 95.
11 Morrison in Naylor, 'Conversation', p. 583.

12 J. Van Der Zee, Owen Dodson, and Camille Bishop, *The Harlem Book of the Dead* (Dobbs Ferry, NY: Morgan & Morgan, 1978).

13 See Stanley Burns, *Sleeping Beauty: Memorial Photography in America* (Altadena, CA: Twelvetrees Press, 1991).

14 Van Der Zee, *Harlem Book of the Dead*, p. 53; see illustration.

15 Morrison in Naylor, 'Conversation', p. 585.

16 This is, of course, played out in Morrison's citation of the school primer in *The Bluest Eye*, as Michael Awkward rightly observes. See his 'Roadblocks and Relatives: Critical Revision in Toni Morrison's *The Bluest Eye*', in Nelly McKey (ed.), *Critical Essays on Toni Morrison* (Boston: G. K. Hall, 1988), p. 59.

17 See Christina Davis, 'Interview with Toni Morrison', *Presence Africaine. New Bilingual Series* 145, 1 (1988), pp. 144–9.

18 R. K. Lester, 'An Interview with Toni Morrison, Hessian Radio Network, Frankfurt/M, West Germany', in Nellie Y. McKay (ed.), *Critical Essays on Toni Morrison* (Boston: G. K. Hall, 1988), pp. 48–9.

19 M. Watkins, 'Talk with Toni Morrison', *New York Times Book Review*, 11 September 1977 (New York: Arno Press, 1978), p. 50. In an interview with Robert B. Stepto, Morrison insists on 'a woman's strong sense of being in a room, a place, or in a house'; ' "Intimate Things in a Place": A Conversation with Toni Morrison', in Michael S. Harper, and Robert B. Stepto (eds.), *Chant of Saints: A Gathering of Afro-American Literature, Art, and Scholarship* (Urbana: University of Illinois Press, 1979), p. 212. See also the interview with Rosemarie Lester in regard to girls' and boys' different relationship to architecture and space (p. 47), and Morrison's own rearranging of space to save her writing in the presence of her own sons: Jane Bakerman, ' "The Seams Can't Show": An Interview with Toni Morrison', *Black American Literature Forum* 12, 2 (1978), p. 57.

20 Morrison, 'The Site of Memory,' in William Zinsser (ed.), *Inventing the Truth: The Art and Craft of Memoir* (Boston: Houghton Mifflin, 1987), p. 113. See also Ashraf H. A. Rushdy, ' "Rememory": Primal Scenes and Constructions in Toni Morrison's Novels', *Contemporary Literature* 31, 3 (1990), pp. 300–23, and Susan Willis, 'Eruptions of Funk: Historicising Toni Morrison', *Black American Literature Forum* 16, 1 (1982), pp. 34–42. In an interview with Elizabeth Kastor, 'Toni Morrison's "Beloved" Country', *The Washington Post*, 5 October 1987, B 12, Morrison defines 'speculation' as the novelist's task; he/she does what the (professional) historian, concentrating on 'ages', 'issues', and 'great men' is unable to do. 'Rememory' is, quite obviously, such a speculation.

21 Morrison, 'Unspeakable', p. 210.

22 C. A. Davis discusses Morrison's use of names and naming in her essay 'Self, Society, and Myth in Toni Morrison's Fiction', in Harold Bloom (ed.), *Toni Morrison, Modern Critical Views* (New York: Chelsea House, 1990), pp. 7–8.

23 See, for example, Tom LeClair, 'An Interview with Toni Morrison', *Anything Can Happen: Interviews with Contemporary American Novelists* (Urbana: University of Illinois Press, 1983), p. 253; and Ntozake Shange with Steve Connon, 'Interview with Toni Morrison', *American Rag*, November 1978, p. 52. See also Morrison's essay 'Rootedness: The Ancestor as Foundation', in Mari Evans (ed.), *Black Women Writers (1950–1980): A Critical Evaluation* (Garden City, NY: Anchor Books, 1984), pp. 339–45.

24 See the discussion in Houston Baker, Jr, *Workings of the Spirit: The Poetics of*

Afro-American Women's Writing (University of Chicago Press, 1991), p. 137, and Morrison's essay 'City Limits, Village Values', in Michael C. Jaye and Ann Chalmers Watts (eds.), *Literature and the Urban Experience* (New Brunswick: Rutgers University Press, 1981), pp. 35–43.

25 Morrison, 'Unspeakable', p. 218.

26 J. Bakerman, 'The Seams Can't Show', p. 59.

27 See Tom LeClair, 'An Interview with Toni Morrison', p. 259; and Claudia Tate, 'Toni Morrison', in Claudia Tate (ed.), *Black Women Writers at Work* (New York: Continuum, 1983), pp. 123–4.

28 E. Washington, interview with Morrison, *Essence* (October 1987), p. 136.

29 M. Atwood, 'Haunted by Their Nightmares', in Harold Bloom (ed.), *Toni Morrison* (ser.) *Modern Critical Views* (New York: Chelsea House, 1990), p. 143; the review appeared first in the *New York Times Book Review*, 13 September 1987, 1, pp. 49–50.

30 See also Judith Thurman's description of *Beloved* as a 'ghost story,' in 'A House Divided', *The New Yorker*, 2 November 1987, 175, or Thomas R. Edwards, 'Ghost Story', *The New York Review of Books*, 5 November 1987, p. 18.

Problems of recollection and construction: Stephen King

In his immensely long fiction *The Tommy-Knockers*[1] Stephen King offers his readers a highly conventional scenario for horror. An alien spacecraft is discovered buried in the ground; from it there come forces which turn the inhabitants of a small town variably odd or murderous. This creeping evil spreads, seeming to sweep all before it, until the town is cut off from the outside world and its inhabitants have become the servants or hosts of those who control – or used to control – the spacecraft. The lone survivors of an untransformed humanity are picked off one by one, until it seems there is no hope of survival.

But then the scenario changes. What has been happening in the small town comes to the attention of the outside world. Greater forces, forces of the US state, are mustered; and then the whole illusion crumbles. The power which the aliens appeared to have is revealed as not so very great after all, certainly incapable of withstanding the mass of human weaponry. The 'tommy-knockers', who have appeared impregnable, are revealed for what they are: not the rulers of the universe but a long-dead gang of space gypsies whose weapons are ineffective and fall apart in their hands. Victory goes conclusively to the home side.

This, I believe, is an Ur-plot of King's, a hidden master-narrative, although it is rarely so fully or so lengthily articulated. It hinges psychologically on a swing between two different world-views, which we can conveniently assign as the views of the child and the adult. Those apparently alien forces which swamp the child in terror are revealed to the adult as things of mystery no longer: the power which keeps the child transfixed is at best a concocted affair, and only seems omnipotent because of the shortage of vision – the psychic analogy of King's archetypal US small town – typical of early experience.

What psychic end is served by this plot? Reassurance, certainly: an assertion that powerlessness will in the end be overcome and we shall all – or almost all – come into our very own and golden city. Or, to put it another way, King puts forward a particular version of communal values, whereby the childish squabbling which makes us weak will be transcended by a stronger power of organisation vested in the state and designed to relegate the power of the Other to its proper place. The analogy with gypsies is no accident: cut off from lines of communication back to wherever their original home might have been, and cut off further by the fact that we are seeing only an *aftermath* of their activities rather than the activities themselves, these interplanetary dealers in space junk are swept aside, sent back to the death on which they have battened.

Or, to put it another way, the text enacts the construction of a 'we', produces a readership which is at all points coterminous with US norms. And this is obviously a major root of King's enormous popularity: feelings of loss in childhood, and also feelings of adolescent separation, are eventually overcome in a perfected version of adulthood. We might see King's project as an overcoming of mourning: the loss of faith in the good parent which is the psychic equivalent of the intrusion of the alien is revealed as available for compensation. A price, of course, is exacted: plenty of other people die so that 'we' may survive, leaner, fitter, and apparently more experienced, to take our just place in society.

Of course, to say that this is King's master-narrative is to oversimplify: there are examples where the narrative stops short at a point where resolution does not fully occur.[2] But where this happens, there is often a further device which reassures us that all will come well in the end, namely the presence of the writer. The 'presence' of the writer in King's texts is doubled in a complicated rebus. In *Misery*, for example, the protagonist is a writer, captured by a crazed fan and forced, under pain of mutilation, to produce for her the narrative she wishes to read. The protagonist of *The Shining* is again a writer, and here his weakness comes about as a susceptibility to the writings of others, the writings, perhaps of the hotel itself, which fill up the empty space afforded by writer's block.[3]

These writers, then, the writers-in-the-text, offer a range of subject positions; but only in company with the 'presence' of King-the-writer himself, the King who announces himself on every title page, the writer in Maine who is in constant touch with his legions of fans and who is dedicated to supplying them with the product they want. Does anybody ever reread King? Are his texts susceptible to rereading? We might reasonably suspect not: what we have instead is a manic proliferation of texts, texts about texts, further texts spun from side-hints and ideas, texts designed to fill an endless vacuum.[4] And if there is such a vacuum, then on the psychological model of maturation it is clear where it must be: in the latency period, in that phase of development where nature runs counter to nature, where development is in abeyance and we are at the mercy of uncomprehended forces.[5] King's works form a vast triumphal arch over latency: below we can see the devils and monsters reaching up for us, but we are not confused, for there is a writer at our elbow, a narrative to fill the void where there are no narratives, a figure invisibly saying that in the beginning was the word, and that the word is still with us and will not let us down.

In the beginning. But to speak of the beginning, to speak of the time 'before', to extend and promulgate a series of narrative acts on the supposition that we can reach back through time and memory, is immediately to feel the psychological polemic within the texts, and at the same time to glimpse the deeper nature of the problem which King's work encounters and attacks, and it is the same problem as the one which besets all psychoanalysis, just as it is now proving the lodestar of literary theory; for these are texts which grapple directly with the question of origin. They constitute a series of encounters with our recollection of the primal scene.[6]

We might say, for example, that King offers his reader a series of opportunities to re-experience scenarios of childhood anxiety under conditions of relative safety; the super-fiction *behind* King's fictions is that potential childhood traumas are laid out before us, and we avidly revisit the forbidden places of past periods of our maturation. But there are, of course, no guarantees of the accuracy of these recollections. Although psychoanalysis, at least in its earlier forms, claimed to hinge on the possibility of rememorating a primal scene, emblematically in Freud's case history of Little Hans, it can offer us no epistemological guarantee of the validity of these supposed 'memories' – a point, of course, which the Wolf-Man himself took up during the course of his own analysis.[7]

Ned Lukacher develops this point of undecidability: 'What Freud recognises', he writes, 'in *From the History of an Infantile Neurosis* [the case history of the Wolf-Man] is that the finitude of temporality demands that the origin be sought not in the past, buried by forgetfulness, but in the future, in the projective repetition of the origin as it is elaborated through the transference.'[8] Or again, comparing Freud with Heidegger:

> Freud and Heidegger demand that we understand the relation between forgetting and remembering in a new way. The patient has forgotten the primal scene, and the history of metaphysics has forgotten the history of Being. The remembrance of that forgotten history and of that forgotten scene does not occur within the mode of subjective or personal recollection; it occurs as an act of interpretation, as a construction, as reading.[9]

In other words, are we to treat these primal scenes as memories – memories beyond screen memory, as it were – or as constructions which we build, textually or analytically, to cover over the vertiginous abyss of the forgotten? In what sense is the relation we as reader or patient establish with text or analyst a recapitulation of previous relations or the immediate projection of a desire, a component of the future, a pre-statement of a wish as to how we would like the world to be? We might, on the one hand, ask what other loves we can ever form than those which are built upon the hidden foundations of the past; or, on the other, what feasible imaginings we can have of the quality of our past loves except in terms of the present, *but* a present which is dominated by projection towards an imaginal future.

Either way what we would see is that the present itself is what now figures as the vacuum, as latency: however closely King's narratives may affect us, there is always another sense in which they *pass us by*: we need the guide at our elbow, the *psychopompos*, because we are ourselves blind and deaf, lost in a world where forces move in ways which we do not understand. The trouble which King persistently traces is powerful because, looked at from the underside, as it were, it is *real* trouble: it is the anguish of establishing a foothold of presence when we are haunted by absences, when we sense that the arch on which we stand, as in one of John Martin's paintings, is held there only by the power of the Other. King's 'power', according to the repetitive aphorism which has come to dominate his book jackets, is indeed in his 'words'; but they are also *his* words, and we have no guarantee that the conventional morality into which he draws us has anything in common with the imaginal lines which we draw between past and future and on which we hang suspended.

If we look at matters in this way, then many of King's devices fall into place; for I would say that there is a sense in which his fictions strike at the heart of all loneliness. We can now say, however, that this loneliness, the fearful isolation of his struggling protagonists, always on the brink of being swamped in unidentifiable and unnamable material, is not in itself a recollection of childhood loneliness; rather, it is precisely a restatement of the Ur-loneliness, which arises from our ontologically peculiar knowledge of having forgotten the past the moment after it has happened.

One of the texts in which King approaches this most closely is 'The Langoliers'.[10] The name of these creatures, who roll up the myth of being as night comes and replace it with nothingness, conjoins the languor of sleep and unconsciousness with the doubled notion of lying: 'lying', in the first place, as our prone position, in sleep, the expression of our powerlessness and of our ignorance; 'lying' also as the untruth of our apparent recollection. The langoliers neatly sum up the lapse, the gap, the hiatus which structures all 'memory': they figure as all our doubts as to what goes on in the outer world while we are absorbed in the inner; they suggest the crucial question of what *else* there is other than dream-time, of what it is which might guarantee continuity despite the manifest discontinuities suggested by dreaming, waking, and the archetypal difference which is encapsulated in the 'recapture' of dream material.

The popularity of King is evidence that the textual psyche he constructs is one which in some sense 'matches' the cultural psyche of the late twentieth century in the West; and here again we have to deal with the paradoxical problematic of latency, for child abuse stands as a key motif, not only in King's texts, nor even in the West's contemporary preoccupations, but also in precisely the problem of epistemological validation which, after all, haunts not only psychoanalysis but all psychology and all history, and which is further emblematised in the deconstructions of postmodernism. Nobody knows what happened; we may know, as in the symptomatic title of Joseph Heller's novel, that *something* happened, but our only way of negotiating the detail of past event is precisely through the telling of story;[11] and thus, of course, King's narrators emerge as story-tellers supreme, hovering on the enticing, langorous, infantile borderline between the voice which lulls us to sleep and the voice which whispers of terrors in the dark.

In this realm, for example, we find the novella 'The Sun Dog', which I would like to deal with at some length. The principal structures of the text are easily stated. There is a camera, and it is a gift to a boy. It is dropped, and this event opens in its viewfinder a hairline crack. Or, to put it more mythically, we might say that it 'falls'; and it is important at this point to underline that we have to deal in mythic discourses, for as we have hinted it is only through these suspensions of temporality that the structure of the primal scene can be approached. But *both before and after* the 'fall', no matter in which direction the camera is pointed, it shows one 'scene' only (and this sense of the obsessive scene, the obsessed dark-adapted eye, should not fail to remind us of the transfixed stare of the child, the inability in latency to escape from prefiguration and repetition, all the ingredients of the 'primal scene', no matter how we figure their temporal status): a stretch of white fencing, and in front of it, a dog. But although the 'frame' of the scene is always the same, the stance of the dog and its 'aspect' changes. To begin with it seems a harmless enough animal. Gradually, as the boy, becoming mesmerised, transfixed by the process, takes more and more pictures, first in the hope of shaking the camera's own transferred transfixation and then in the service of the burgeoning wish to know what will happen with the dog next, it turns more and more towards the camera and as it does so it grows ever larger, ever closer, ever more menacing until it becomes evident that it 'wasn't any dog God had ever made'.[12]

The camera falls into somebody else's hands, the hands of a *bricoleur*, a 'tommy-knocker' whom we need only know as 'Pop', a 'father' such as God never intended, who takes more pictures, which the boy, the original owner, experiences in the shape of a sense of growing certainty that the terror is about to break into his life, into this world and destroy it for ever; for the dog is becoming a figure of pure hate. The new owner, however, eventually realises something of what is happening and decides to desist from further photography. But it is in this moment that the present is passed over in, as it were, an unseen flash; or, to put it in the cognate terms of Poe when he deals with the suspension of life and death, that the will yields utterly.[13] It is, as we are told in a savage parody of the flash of the photograph, as if a white light explodes inside Pop's head; and 'as in a dream' he takes the camera, not seeing it but mistaking it for something else, and continues to take more photographs, thereby bringing the dog closer and closer to the barrier represented by the hairline crack in the real.

This hairline crack can be seen also in other contexts. It is mentioned, for example, by Elisabeth Bronfen in *Over her Dead Body*, in the course of her extended discussion of the connections between death and femininity in Western culture. She speaks of 'the breaks that puncture the imaginary and the symbolic register, the crack that disrupts both orders so that, momentarily, the real emerges', and goes on to outline the 'central question' of 'whether the crack of sexuality/death can be closed, with representation solving the enigma by virtue of disclosure'.[14] It may seem at first glance as though this is to put the argument about registers the other way round, but this is to underestimate the trickiness of textuality, whereby the crack itself opens us to a world where the registers fuse, where competing claims for the status of the real, all such claims bracketed by the role of the semiotic, are the very substance of which text is woven. It is interesting, too, how this notion of the crack is connected by Bronfen with the complex issues of repetition and mourning, and here, as I have done above, she takes Poe's 'Ligeia' as an essential component of a guide to the underworld.[15]

The denouement of 'The Sun Dog' need not concern us here; what is interesting in terms of the problems of recollection and construction is the moment when the will yields. Pop has decided that the trouble coming must be averted at all costs; he is on his way to get a sledge-hammer to destroy the camera.

And as he neared the door to the back shed, a shutterflash, huge and white and soundless, went off not in front of his eyes but behind them, in his brain.

He turned back, and now his eyes were as empty as the eyes of a man who has been temporarily blinded by some bright light. He walked past the worktable with the camera now held in his hands at chest level, as one might carry a votive urn or some other sort of religious offering or relic.[16]

Yielding, emptying, what we have here is the consummation devoutly to be desired, the takeover, the 'per-vasion' by some force perceived as outside the self, the single bright white light at the back of the mind to guide us, the illusion of an origin, and in the process of recognising this external force we are introduced also to the bearing of the votive chalice, the very emblem of the pure symbol. Pop is no longer in need of the myriad stratagems which have been his hallmark: he has moved beyond them into a purer and more unified realm, whose own alternative hallmark is an unwitting, an unconscious destruction. Its agency is, of course, animal; but not animal in any sense of a real perception of the beast, or of the human as an 'ancient animal full of grace', rather he has been taken over, overtaken by the dog.

Or not. Perhaps we should rather say that what has 'taken over' at this point is precisely the force of the threshold, the undecidable gift and withholding of presence, the god who lives, facing both ways, in the hairline crack, whose function is to obliterate the divisions of class, status, gender which comprise the frame through which we see (view-find) the world, and from which we manage to structure the simulacrum of recollection; this god has found himself fortuitously located in a 'visible' crack (as the forces of malevolence which crowd onto the child, emanations of the will to damage within the child's own self, make themselves visible through the curious interlocking of that which cannot be remembered with that which can never be forgotten, which is the stamp of dream) and able to peer out. A single glance from 'earth's wide eye' is enough to overwhelm consciousness;[17] it figures as the long-awaited bright light of knowledge (of the imaginal past) before which the will must yield utterly. We should not underestimate the pleasure in this experience.

We should also not underestimate the complexity of levels which we enter, along the path controlled and revealed by this hairline crack. Some of these are relatively obvious. For example, the world of the camera inevitably introduces us to the gaze, to scopophilia, thus from a specifically reticulated angle to the whole realm of 'penetration', to a set of mechanical complexes rooted in the evolution of a 'tool', a handle sufficiently strong to rebut or disguise the feared and denied penetrative capacity of the mother, that which has been psychologically (and porno-graphically) imaged in the equation of nipple and penis,[18] which in turn represents the early silencing of the (male-)child by a force of fascination and nurturance which at the same time stoppers the mouth, violates precisely the *will*, the will to select alternative pleasures which cannot even be 'seen' around the mountainous, necessary presence of the breast. In this realm, what might the crack in the viewfinder signify, apart from but also through maternal genitalia? Presumably the possibility of a new entrance, the mooted presence of a world which is not under the control of mother, which is not at all within the confines and boundaries of 'creation' even when this maternal creativity is displaced and fed back, as it constantly is in the 'real present' of 'monotheistic' conflict, as an allegi-ance to the one (male) god.[19] The pleasure in yielding to this absolute Other is simultaneously the pleasure of supplanting, replacing the 'nat-ural', removing the hieratic power of the summation of the matriarchal law which the dog does not recognise, which the dog comes with an atrocious permission to savage. To achieve this proffered liberation no price is too high to pay; or rather, our knowledge of the price will be willingly yielded in the moment of the one bright light which comes to wipe out the whole web of ties, of conditionings which we resent from birth, even while we falsely recast them as the chains of our mortality.

That this liberation can only be into death goes without saying, as does death itself; for here what we need to sense in the terms of the master-myth is that Eros is present but *entwined*; although – and because – Eros represents the possibility of *not* being enwrapped by birth trauma, he is the force which holds the end of, or limit on, answerable questions.

> Some argue that Eros, hatched from the world-egg, was the first of the gods since, without him, none of the rest could have been born; they make him coeval with Mother Earth and Tartarus, and deny that he had any mother or father, unless it were Eileithyia, Goddess of Childbirth.
>
> Others hold that he was Aphrodite's son by Hermes, or by Ares, or by her own father, Zeus; or the son of Iris by the West Wind. He was a wild boy, who showed no respect for age or station but flew about on golden wings, shooting barbed arrows at random or wantonly set-ting hearts on fire with his dreadful torches.[20]

Eros, I suggest, is a crucial figure for our dealings with the problem of recollection and reconstruction; and incest and child abuse, the fatal undecidability – and indecision – of the father (which is the root of all undecidability) are all present here in the myth suggested by the Sun Dog, who is in himself the ironic inversion of the hounds of hell. The Eros of horror is held in stasis, yet at the same time he approaches, encroaches with an irresistible force, not yet to be tamed by the false realisations of adulthood which in themselves amount only to the nervous suppression of the dream. If the primal scene is a refraction of a fear of future powerlessness (in itself the image of the encroachment of death) then the way in which King recounts it has a certain accuracy; for this is not a fear which announces itself along the trajectories and dimensions of the real, rather it is a refraction through the ever-present hairline crack which will always prevent the real from assuming the robes of its own omnipotence, will always assure the dog its own space while building the most complex and sophisticated of defences to prevent its (recurring, imagined) intrusion.

We can see here nonetheless the liberatory potential of the 'dog beyond the world'; we can also sense that 'entwined' in this set of Eros myths there is a major doubt, a root of much myth-making; we sense that we are here on the cusp of a historic realisation (which will also always be the root of misrecognition) of the masculine participation in conception, and thus we remain locked (in terror) on the site of the primal scene. If it was not incest, then perhaps it was Ares or Zeus; or perhaps it was really the West Wind, a non-human force which might blow through the hairline crack. In the world of fascination evidenced in and by the camera, and for which Eros is a psychic name, anything is believable because all the barriers are down, or potentially so, no force can withstand or fail to yield; the enjoyment of powerlessness is laid bare for all to see and thus becomes the site of the endless recapitulations and reconstructions which become necessary after latency in the name of disembarrassment, or disentwining from the (un)natural proximity of the dangerous mother.

It seems necessary to read the psychological 'level' down the gentle slope towards myth; and there we might find ourselves also encountering a previously suggested etymological level, in terms of the notion of 'per-vasion', the incipient takeover of the vulnerable flesh by a force which is without control or explanation. This per-vasion is again re-contained within, reconstructed in the glare of, the single bright white light which is beyond the world, beyond at least the human-shaped world and thus beyond will or Nous: what happens here happens under the guise of an irresistible mastery, and is also thereby signed, as Lukacher suggests, as a type of transference. For the image makes itself clear: it is an image of a kind of event which has been 'known before', the photo-flash, and thus it fits neatly into the chain of such events which is unfolding (before or behind our eyes); but it is also in itself precisely the unassimilable, the irremediable break, the momentary vacuum – and here it needs to be said that the clinical evidence for latency is not what is textually at stake, for the very image of latency becomes transformed, before our eyes as it were, into the problem of the langoliers, the question of how, in the absence of a history of Being, we might connect one moment to another or surpass the alternative, lake-bed arch constructed by dream not over but under the very site of presence which, in our imaginations only, could effect, succour, and cement such a connection.[21]

We see here the point at which there is always an absolute qualitative break in the signifying chain, and perhaps this is indeed the inner heart of the primal scene: it is that which we hold most closely to ourselves, unremembered, unforgotten – indeed, unforgiven – as a counterbalance to the ineffectualities and incapacities of the tommy-knocker world: while in the apparent present we may fumble about in an absence of convincing narratives, at least we can hold to a notion that there was a cause, an explanation for why all this went wrong, a hairline crack in the past through which seeped an impossibly contaminating matter, such that all our experience is now of the impossible.[22]

We are speaking here of thresholds, and this seems to me apt both in terms of King's work as a whole and also in terms of the problem of the primal scene; for what may be held in the liminal area before remembering and forgetting is surely a threshold, and perhaps this is the best image our recollection has to offer us. Beyond this threshold, 'The Sun Dog' tells us, there is only pervasion: there is only the lack of individuation, the absence of separable event, we are instead now in a different 'presence', sacred, perhaps, holy, such that its agent needs to be carried like a chalice, like an unintelligible precious object, like an artefact which has been made by neither god nor man.

The camera, of course, is well known as the agent of soul stealing, as the surrogate organ which will drain power, or soul, from any living body which it confronts. If we think in some of the terms offered by Deleuze and Guattari, we might say that the camera is the organ without a body, the result of an appalling separation, a deflection of and within the gaze such that we no longer know what is our 'own' and we can no longer find anything of our (point of) view; or rather, perhaps, that it is that 'inorganic organ' which attaches itself to and pervades any body with which it has to do.[23] The text here grasps, it seems to me, that *this* process of pervasion is dialectical: it is not a matter of power flowing *through* the camera from object to subject but rather a representation of a process of dehumanisation which is perhaps also a fabricated memory of non-humanisation, in which precisely the link of relationship which would alone guarantee humanity to either or both sides of the equation is placed in brackets, and those brackets are again summarised in the frame of the viewfinder. Again, then, and now at the level of soul or spirit, we have to ask ourselves: what of the hairline crack? And here, perhaps, we find ourselves on firmer ground: for it takes only a brief discursive sidestep for us to see, and indeed announce, that the crack *is* soul. It has to be: if the process of photography is an apt image for de-souling, for stealing soulstuff and funnelling it from both sides into a 'black hole' where it disappears (inside the camera, never to emerge despite the even more disquieting implications of Polaroid), then a crack in the fake completeness of this process, a spot of tarnish on the armour of the larcenous ego, has to be seen in terms of a gesture of letting soul out again, of letting it live in the only way it can, which is in a world of its own devising, engaged in gradual and slow activities which move to the beat of a different drum, the reverberations of which enjoin us to construct the primal scene as a means of rendering intelligible that which cannot be brought under control. The shape this world might take, which is here composed of the attributes of abjection in Kristeva's sense,[24] cannot, of course, be estimated in advance because the only way to approach them any more closely would be by transiting over an impossible threshold; nevertheless, this crack is here the only promise of soul, and the plotline, the master-narrative which repudiates it and colours it with the deeper shade of black which we associate not with the 'darkened' world of Hades but with the absence of colouration of the void or vacuum can be read only in terms of the depths to which the historically real – here a thoroughly etched picture of a regime of contemporary US society – will go to avoid the possibility of that which is – to put it at its very least – beyond the confines of the conventional, that which smacks of the excesses, transgressions, and transfixations of the primal scene.

This, at least, is something of what the text appears to tell us; but perhaps we should rather say that it is *there* that the text appears to lead us. We might further say that 'it' – and in putting it that way we are now speaking of the Ananke component of the text[25] – leads us into the heart of a blocked and static impasse which we might cast in terms of the primal scene; or we might – and the connection is crucial – cast it in terms of colonisation. Where, as we have to ask in every textual context and very particularly not only in relation to those scenarios which abut onto an overt historical 'presence', is the colonial agency here? Is it to be apprehended in some relationship, always burgeoning, always disappearing, between the forms of invasion and pervasion? How can we discriminate between them when their basic terms cannot be mutually translatable? Or, to put it another way again, how shall we start to quantify or qualify the exact relationship between the violence of the dog and the violence of the social formation within which it is locked in the common premonition of a mutual doom? Or – and perhaps the rhetoric of 'levels' becomes exhausted at this point – what does dream replicate, at what point are its static images revealed as, although freestanding in *shape*, nevertheless composed of *materials* which are, after all, always and everywhere day-residues, the compacted and sedimented forms of the dayworld, its shaping politics and its own particular violences and imperialisms?[26]

The Sun Dog. If we want to turn this trope of exhaustion further, then we can do it by playing about with these words . . . endlessly? For instance: by whom is the son dogged? Why, by Pop, of course: the bad father, the wicked uncle, also Coca-Cola and the invasion by ghastly plastic juices of the innocent bloodstream. Sun God, Sun King, sunspot: the blindness which cannot see for brightness, the dazzled obliteration of difference in the face of the blinding presence of the One God, the Sun God, which is also oedipal blindness but yet again the blindness we feel in our ecstasies before the throne of, indeed, who else but the sun god, who is the god of the masculine, the primary force, presiding (and usurping) deity in the primal scene, the force endlessly claiming primacy, seeking to usurp the West Wind and thus demonstrating the inseparability of ego-based monarchy and usurpation, the force in whose face we find ourselves bending as we experience revelation, seeking the obliteration of multiplicity in the form of woman, the great replacer of lunar matriarchy, the force which will, in fact, not permit lunacy because the multifariousness of the shapes of madness will destabilise and upset the Sun King's throne.

With this particular god, to continue to spin out the tropes, the *son* feels profound sympathy: he wishes to yield because the alternative is continued humiliation. To yield at the altar of macho, to internalise the images of masculine hunting-and-shooting normalcy (smalltown ethos) which (sun/son)King's texts proffer might now seem precisely the solution to being haunted; and naturally the promise of release from such birth-directed haunting comes through an extreme exacerbation of the hauntings which have first driven us to the brink, to the threshold.

At this threshold we find the figure whom we might call the 'god-son', the blessed youth who will have a firm white light to guide him through the perils of a dog-infested or even dog-embodied universe, a world where Sirius reigns and the dog comes to end our days; the faithful friend is precisely he who, in the world envisaged as small town USA, is the only one who can really betray us, the one dog who will in the end round on us and proffer a new life if we will accompany him through the gates of Hell, through the hairline crack (which is also Alice's looking-glass) beyond which all the registers will be rearranged through a process akin to the constant mistaking of the concrete for the symbolic which is the hallmark of psychosis.[27] He is there in the inverted form of the sun-dog, the only sure guise through the morass, the tearer-out of throats; we can see here the further traces of an inversion of the great goddess in her subjugated, abject role of assuming the vestments we wish her to, those with which we want to clothe her – although here again we are on a terrain of ambivalence, for we want always to see her both hieratic-ally arrayed and stripped bare, the holder and betrayer of her own and our secrets. In this array of imagery we also see the ambiguous form of desire itself, the distortion of the soul with which we have to work if we are to get further in the effort to comprehend the aporias which under-line and undermine our lives, and we thus glimpse some of the ways in which we seek to transform these incompatibilities into an acceptable textuality.

I would contend, then, that in 'The Sun Dog' we see a clutch of projects struggling within the text, centred on a wish to develop a primal scene. We look back at the protagonist in the textual past; but what we find is a project for maturation, ideologically coloured, and the construc-tion of an explanation for the fatal flaw, the hairline, the crack of mortality which is *at the same time* the only evidence of our continuing connection with death, and thus with mortality and life itself. What the white light comes to do is to 'remind' us of the rebus-like intertwining of memory and forgetting: within that white light there is no past at all, only the naked terror of an unimaginable future which we need to populate with figures resurrected from the dead, from the void which provides memory with all the structure it has.

If we turn briefly to another of King's texts, Misery, we can see a similar set of projections. On the surface we have here a text which concerns the primal horror of the all-encompassing mother; the writer's deranged female fan has all the power, the protagonist is sick and motion-less, imprisoned, oppressed unto death by the overwhelming presence of her large, rigid, unyielding body, in which is also transparently coded the withholding of the breast. He is all too literally transfixed, all the more so as 'mother' starts to cut off parts of his body. But this apparent primal scene serves only as, precisely, a 'pre-text': the narrative is centred not on the 'facts' of imprisonment but on the possibilities of escape, and one of the principal pieces of evidence for this occurs in a scene near the end where the protagonist, free at last, walks into his own living room to discover 'mother' there, bloody and axe-wielding, only then immediately to realise that this is a trick of the imagination, an after-effect or after-image which can be disposed of in the same way as the tommy-knockers.[28]

Misery itself, then, becomes an after-image, in this case perhaps a means of explaining and justifying male violence. For in *Misery* what the protagonist has experienced is a prolonged and extreme form of child abuse; or rather, that is the (obviously uncorroborated) claim advanced by the text. The psychic uses to which this fictive primal scene might be put are manifold: it might be developed as an excuse for stasis, for an inability to progress beyond the rememoration of trauma; or it might be used as a justification for a process of maturation consisting of emerging into the world unscathed and unscatheable, as an imaginal perfect male body which grows back over the literal and emotional scars which the text would have us believe have been inflicted – among other things, as a punishment for the precocity of the masculine writer.

We face here a discursive crux of extreme danger, which has an obvious bearing on current debates about the therapeutic effectivity as well as the epistemological validity of the analytic process. For the construction of a primal scene becomes itself, seen in these terms, the perfection of the alibi: the ever-present status of discourse as other than what it is, as that which stands in for and, as Lacan says, 'murders' the real through excess of the symbolic,[29] becomes foregrounded and highlighted through the subjection of the past and, naturally, through the equally difficult subjection of the analyst to the (unnaturally) strengthened will of the patient. The primal scene becomes the triumphal site at which the body of truth lies prone, whereupon we find that we have converted the revelatory potential of analysis into the most abject complicity.

But, of course, we do not 'find' this: who, indeed, could the 'we' or 'I' even be on a scene where all has been converted into an apparently present alibi for projection? What we have to deal with here is a vanishing, a disappearance of the self which is simultaneously the vaunting of the perfecting of the psyche which we faultily and hesitantly describe as the 'cure'.

In *The Library Policeman*[30] the matter becomes even more clear in a variant of the master-narrative which is rare in King, for here the apparently supernatural events of the text are in the end pinned directly and closely to early experience of child abuse and of betrayal of the child by an adult. There are many other aspects of the text: what is interesting is that only an incomplete attempt is made to fit them into the structure, with one of the figures of terror ending up rather resembling a very small piece of chewing-gum. Shades of *The Tommy-Knockers*; but more significantly the occurrence of this scene of abuse is, precisely, a library, the site where the writer learns his trade, perhaps, or the point where the hairline crack through which knowledge of sexuality comes to the child is opened but within the order of the symbolic, through books, through the text. Again we might say that as in psychosis the symbolic is rendered directly into the concrete, with the abuser, the man who calls himself a 'library policeman' in order to assault the child protagonist, figuring as a direct and unmediated representation of a knowledge too unsettling to bear.

The summoning up of powerful countervailing forces of defence within the psyche and their projection onto concrete objects in the outer world receives a further incarnation in *Christine*, with its adolescent section headings: 'Teenage Car-Songs', 'Teenage Love-Songs', 'Teenage Death-Songs'. Here the plot hinges on a car which in some way funnels the evil and resentment of its previous owner and transforms this into a power of malevolent self-regeneration which appears impregnable until one of the protagonists – the one who survives – thinks of the obvious solution, which is to find a motor vehicle, not possessed of supernatural powers but vast, violent, and explicitly female, which has the power to crush all 'memory' of Christine. Whether this attempt is entirely success-ful is left open: by the end of the narrative it appears that Christine's powers of regeneration have increased, and that it is possible that she can recreate the whole of herself if even one small fragment of her material body is left. It does not take much insight to see here a crushing out of existence of early memories of humiliation, alongside the realisation that this act of crushing, of 'forgetting', can only be complete *if we succeed in remembering the past as it never was*, a past in which there was no Christine at all; neither is it a very long step from this to see the text itself as self-immolating. Thus the preservation of a fragment of Christine becomes both a source of terror and the only means of salvation of a sense of self: without the possibility of her return there remains no stock of images, no repository of the forms of love which might in time be transmuted into a mature psyche.

Another way of putting what is going on in these narratives is by thinking in terms of animation and disanimation. If the primal scene is constructed rather than recollected, then we have to face also the possib-ility that all vestiges of the animate, the organic, the spirited face trans-formation into their mechanical equivalents, that the freedom, the exorbitancy, the unspeakable *excess* of love which is the maternal heritage and which is too inexplicable to be borne, rather than being cathected onto further love objects, is instead reduced, remade as a thing of bits and pieces, reassembled as a lifeless *bricolage*. True it is that many of King's protagonists conclude their stories by leaving us with a sense that there is nowhere very much to go from here: the sheer strength required in the struggle to suppress the problem of the past means that nothing is left over, and thus we can take the notion of desire through a further twist. For the desire enshrined here is not merely for a kind of maturity which has dealt with, to the point of expunging, any possibility of memory of the real; it is also a desire to have done everything forever, a desire to equate maturity with death. This incarnation of the death drive is very strong in *Salem's Lot*, where the effort of ridding the small town of its vampires drains the energies of the protagonists (or we might say the split protagonist, man and boy, 'father' and 'son') but at the same time suggests that the rest of life is going to be a vast disappointment.[31] But the desire for disappointment is a very strong one: once one has anticipated the future under this sign, then there is no further damage that can be inflicted upon us. We have prefigured all potential loss, we have extinguished hope, we have engaged in, and continue to engage in, a prolonged work of surrogate mourning which occurs *before the fact*.

And this takes us back again to what Lukacher has to say about the reversal of remembering and forgetting. 'The projective repetition of the origin as it is elaborated through the transference': *The Sun Dog* is obviously predicated on repetition, the repetitions of photography, the repetition of an inescapable scene, but a scene which, although always the same, is nevertheless one in which, uncannily, something is also always happening, a work of transmutation from familiarity to terror is always going on. Does it go on only when we take a photograph, or lie on the couch, or attend to the promptings of love? Or does the other world, the world behind the crack, have a mode of continuity, perhaps of a non-temporal nature, of its own? To put the question in a different but related way: what is it that we do to dream when we claim to figure it as an alternative, discontinuous mode of discourse, relegate it to the world of sleep? What is it that we forget in waking life, not about the events of the night before, but about the dark background which remains with us – 'behind our eyes' – all the time?

As Bronfen says, we have indeed to attend all the time to the *aporias*, the incompatibilities: the real and the symbolic refuse separation, the semiotic and the somatic will not stay in their appointed places, and the name of this set of refusals is death. To take Lukacher's argument one stage further, we can also say that the series of attempts we make to 'stage' the primal scene is also a series of attempts to stage our own death, in that it serves us as explanation of our own mortality. But at the same time it provides us with an alibi; because the construction of the primal scene simultaneously abolishes truth (as do the langoliers), then we remain consummately free to regard death itself as a lie; and this is what enables us to continue to live.

What, then, do we find in King's texts when we try to read them against this background, to see them as a series of elaborations of desire? What we find, not surprisingly, is a circle, and it is a circle heavily in-scribed with writing, a circle in which text proliferates and is consumed as an emblem of the body which proliferates and is consumed. We can turn, for example, to 'Secret Window, Secret Garden';[32] here again the protagonist is a writer, and he is persecuted by a mysterious figure who seems to know much more about him than he should and clearly has murderous impulses, impulses which he vents not only on the writer himself but also on those around him. The text builds up an elaborate structure of suspense in which we are constantly hovering on the brink of the realisation that this 'second figure' is a double, that he is perhaps a figure from one of the writer's fictions made incarnate, that he is the writer himself during those increasingly frequent times when he finds himself overcome with lassitude and forgets where he has been.

But this forgetting is indeed a remembering, an unconscious and uncontrollable recollection of the death drive: one of the minor characters hypothesises that the murderous and murderously named John Shooter may have been in some sense a character from one of Morton Rainey's fictions (482), but the hovering alternative version would have things the other way round: that Rainey is in the service of Shooter, that the desire for obliteration, only slightly postponed by the entanglements of textuality, works its way through the use of Rainey's increasingly recumbent body. But other explanations are also possible. For there is no desire for fusion here, no will towards the reintrojection of separate psychic functions: instead there is a peculiar refraction of the impulse I have mentioned before, to be, in Kurt Vonnegut's phrase, 'lonesome no more'.[33] The conjuring of the dark Other thus becomes the ambiguous counterpoint to the problems of community and proximity which are encoded in small town USA: in a world where everybody knows everybody else, then the only way of protecting a 'secret', of holding onto whatever is in the crypt, is through a structured proliferation of the self.

But this reminds us, too, of the extent to which King's very settings have to do with defences, the way in which small town USA marks itself off as a remembered, imagined past, in stark contrast to the intrusion of the real at the end of *The Tommy-Knockers*. King deals in the vicissitudes of community, but in a way which reminds us constantly of the interchangeability of openness and closure: openness to the behaviour of others, knowledge of their whereabouts and of their daily habits, is a simultaneous closure to the possibility of change. Psychologically, we are speaking here of an intertwining of transparency and opacity, such that certain kinds of 'knowledge' serve only to reinforce the stereotypical. Or we might say that two kinds of knowledge are opposed in the texts: knowledge of 'what is', what Hegel referred to as the quintessence of positivity, which has its own certainty but is immune to difference, and knowledge of what surrounds this island of certainty, a knowledge which opens up the richness of the imagination but simultaneously produces the hair-line crack through which uncorroborated versions of past and future flow.

If we turn to reflect on the Gothic in general, by way of conclusion, than one key we have to the essence of the Gothic can now be seen to lie in the dual nature of the imagination. We may speak – as did the Romantics – of the bright imagination and the dark imagination, but we can also ally these to highly specific childhood formations.[34] The bright imagination, we might say, is born of security, of a sense of apt containment, of a sense of freedom within boundaries which allows the safe space in which one can withdraw always knowing at a deeper level that one can return and find the essential coordinates of security still in place. The dark imagination, on the other hand, is born of the absence of boundaries, of insecurity which produces fear, of a sense of danger which, unconsciously, requires the elaboration of fantasies of further damage, projected onto the outer, in order to survive.

Thus, probably, utopias and dystopias: because the imagination always remains rooted in childhood and because these two formations of the imagination bifurcate sharply, the more difficult imagining of the future would strike between these two poles. But thus also two different approaches to the construction of the primal scene and, although this has yet to be theorised, two different versions of the transference. Explained and unexplained supernatural, survival and obliteration, these tangles are worked and reworked in Gothic: the dispelling of the supernatural achieves nothing because the rational view of the past is as riven with hiatus, as unavailable for corroboration, as its alternative.

The 'memory' of loneliness is the fear of future loneliness: the strategies, textual and psychic, with which we seek to evade or populate this loneliness constitute also an attempt to provide an array of figures beside the deathbed – which is also the bed of the writer in *Misery*, or the bed of misery in the writer. The scenario in which 'mother', in the uniform of a nurse, hangs over our bed bearing a cleaver or a chainsaw is a reticulation of the cultural conflation of the image of the maternal body, the matrix, with the image of undifferentiation. What the writer in *Misery* loses to this composite Fate is a foot and a thumb: he suffers attacks on his mobility in the real world and on his mobility, his authorship, in the world of text.

But around this 'primal scene' in King there are also other figures moving, figures which remind us of something we have forgotten, sometimes of things we continue to forget. In *The Shining*, for example, there are the mysterious forms of the 'topiary animals', which on occasions appear to move, to menace, on others remain firmly, innocently in place.[35]

They are animated avatars of the sundog, they occupy a dimension beyond the human, they are the limit of what the Hotel Overlook can 'overlook'; or, to use a different meaning of the word, they are symbols for what has always been overlooked, that which has been omitted from the equation, that which reminds us that no equation is possible because when we are 'subjected' to love we are subjected to excess, to embarrassments and humiliations, and conversion into terror is the only way that we can escape from this sense of unworthiness. There is a sense in which the protagonists in King achieve their 'worth' through grappling with these terrors, these dangers; but there is also a sense in which this can only be done through massive reincorporation, through forming a perfected body, whether of the state or of the individual, which is built on lies, which lies through clenched teeth, which seeks to reject the sense of *aporia* and replace it with a web of narrative strained to breaking point, the evolution of a clenched and resistant body which will suffer – and be lonesome – no more.

Notes

1 King, *The Tommy-Knockers* (New York: 1988).
2 For example, King, *Christine* (New York, 1983).
3 King, *Misery* (New York: 1987); *The Shining* (New York, 1977), e.g. pp. 152–66.
4 For example, the hinted character connections which link 'Rita Hayworth and Shawshank Redemption' and 'Apt Pupil', both in King, *Different Seasons* (New York, 1982).
5 Freud, for example, 'The Dissolution of the Oedipus Complex' (1924), in *The Standard Edition of the Complete Psychological Works of Sigmund Freud*, ed. J. Strachey *et al.* (24 vols., London, 1953–74), XIX, pp. 173–9.
6 Freud, *From the History of an Infantile Neurosis* (1918), in *Standard Edition*, XVII, pp. 48–60.
7 Freud, *Analysis of a Phobia in a Five-Year-Old Boy* (1909), in *Standard Edition*, X, esp. pp. 135–6; and *From the History of an Infantile Neurosis*, XVII, pp. 29ff.
8 N. Lukacher, *Primal Scenes: Literature, Philosophy, Psychoanalysis* (New York, 1986), p. 42.
9 *Ibid.*, pp. 42–3.
10 King, 'The Langoliers', in *Four Past Midnight* (New York, 1990).
11 The reference is to Joseph Heller, *Something Happened* (New York, 1966).
12 King, 'The Sun Dog', in *Four Past Midnight* (New York, 1990), p. 905.
13 The reference is to Poe, 'Ligeia' (1838), in *Collected Works of Edgar Allan Poe* (3 vols., Cambridge, MA: Harvard University Press, 1969–78), II, p. 310.
14 E. Bronfen, *Over her Dead Body: Death, Femininity and the Aesthetic* (Manchester University Press, 1992), p. 256.
15 Bronfen, *Over her Dead Body*, p. 326.
16 King, 'The Sun Dog', p. 871.

17 The reference is to Roy Fisher, 'The Hill Behind the Town', in *Poems 1955–1980* (Oxford University Press, 1980), pp. 23–4.

18 Freud, *Leonardo da Vinci and a Memory of his Childhood* (1910), in *Standard Edition*, XI, pp. 86–7.

19 J. Hillman, *The Dream and the Underworld* (New York, 1979), e.g. pp. 59–64.

20 R. Graves, *The Greek Myths* (2 vols., Harmondsworth: Penguin Books, 1955), I, p. 58.

21 I am thinking here of the imagery at the beginning and end of Poe, 'The Fall of the House of Usher' (1839), in *Collected Works*, II, pp. 397–8 and 417.

22 I am thinking here not only of the notion of the unconscious but also of the Derridean 'experience of the impossible'; see, for example, *Experiencing the Impossible*, ed. T. Clark and N. Royle (Stirling, 1993), p. 2 and *passim*.

23 The references are to Gilles Deleuze and Felix Guattari, *A Thousand Plateaus: Capitalism and Schizophrenia*, trans. B. Massumi (London, 1988).

24 J. Kristeva, *Powers of Horror: An Essay on Abjection*, trans. L. S. Roudiez (New York, 1982).

25 Hillman, *Re-Visioning Psychology* (New York, 1975), pp. 159–61.

26 Freud, *The Interpretation of Dreams* (1900), in *Standard Edition*, V, pp. 554–64.

27 For example, D. W. Winnicott, 'Transitional Objects and Transitional Phenomena' (1953), in *Essential Papers on Object Relations*, ed. P. Buckley (New York, 1986), esp. pp. 259–60.

28 King, *Misery*, p. 364.

29 Lacan, 'The Function and Field of Speech and Language in Psychoanalysis' (1953), in *Ecrits: A Selection*, trans. A. Sheridan (London, 1977), pp. 30–107.

30 King, 'The Library Policeman', in *Four Past Midnight* (New York, 1990).

31 King, *Salem's Lot* (New York: Double day and Co. Inc., 1975), pp. 3–12, 470–83.

32 King, 'Secret Window, Secret Garden', in *Four Past Midnight* (New York, 1990).

33 K. Vonnegut, *Slapstick: Or, Lonesome No More!* (New York, 1976).

34 For example, Paul L. Harris, *Children and Emotion: The Development of Psychological Understanding* (Oxford University Press, 1989), pp. 51–80.

35 King, *The Shining*, e.g. pp. 283–91.

Postmodern Gothic: desire and reality in Angela Carter's writing

According to Angela Carter 'we live in Gothic times',[1] where the marginalised subgenres of the past have necessarily become the appropriate and dominant modes of our present discourse. This view corresponds with the more general recent discussions of the development of the literary fantastic from the emergence of the Gothic mode in the eighteenth century to the contemporary practice of postmodernism. Neil Cornwell, among others, claims that 'the fantastic has itself become the dominant mode in the modern novel'. It is part of what he terms the '"portmanteau novel" . . . to designate the complex, multi-levelled or multi-layered novel', characterised by irony, parody, intertextuality, and metafiction.[2] Leslie Fiedler, quoted by Angela Carter in an epigraph to her novel *Heroes and Villains*, sees the Gothic mode as 'a form of parody, assailing clichés by exaggerating them to the limit of grotesqueness'.[3] Emphasising the importance of this tradition for her own writing, Angela Carter characterises Gothicism as a genre ignoring 'the value systems of our institutions', and dealing 'entirely with the profane'. Its 'characters and events are exaggerated beyond reality, to become symbols, ideas, passions . . . style will tend to be ornate, unnatural – and thus operate against the perennial human desire to believe the word as fact . . . [The Gothic] retains a singular moral function – that of provoking unease.'[4] Gothicism in this sense is placed in opposition to mimetic art, to realism, and situated within the realm of non-mimetic art, of fantasy and the fantastic, areas which have always been associated with imagination and desire.

Images and symbols of 'infernal desire' which trace the forbidden paths of cultural taboos are the particular domain of fantastic literature, the acknowledged literature of the unreal, in which the questions discussed in this essay by necessity arise: namely the questions of the nature of desire and of reality. Angela Carter's novels and tales provide superb examples of a literary and theoretical exploration of these features.[5]

Eros and Thanatos: the subject as battle-ground

In her novel *The Infernal Desire Machines of Dr Hoffman*, Angela Carter engages the hero/narrator and her readers in what she makes him call a veritable 'Reality War' (27). In this war reality is linked to order, reason, and rationality as opposed to fantasy, imagination, chaos, and desire. The unnamed Minister of State and Dr Hoffman respectively figure as representatives of Super Ego and Id, reality principle and pleasure principle, as the narrator informs us. So we are presented with what seems to be a paradigmatic Freudian drama by its own definition, a text which writes its own interpretation as it goes along. Whereas earlier Gothic/fantastic texts had to be interpreted in psychoanalytic terms by readers and critics, this text provides its own reading.

But, of course, there is more to it than meets the eye/I of the hero/ narrator whose vision is questioned and whose I-dentity is at stake. First of all, the figurehead of reality and rationality, the Minister, remains conspicuously absent throughout the novel (apart from a recorded conversation between the Minister and Dr Hoffman's ambassador at the outset of the novel). Likewise, his counterpart Dr Hoffman, the representative of infernal desire, appears only at the very end, although he (and possibly the Minister?) seems to have been present throughout the novel in various disguises (e.g. as peep show proprietor, as Sadeian Count). Hence Carter's 'Reality War' seems to be displaced onto the level of actions involving the narrator/hero, Desiderio, and Hoffman's daughter, Albertina. Desiderio, working for the Minister, is sent on a quest to save mankind, a mission which can only be accomplished by destroying Dr Hoffman. Appointed to the position of an 'Inspector of Veracity' (40) Desiderio visits a town fair, meets a peep show proprietor in whose tent he is supposed to marvel at wax models of the 'Seven Wonders of the World' (42) – a veritable catalogue of the fragmented human body (womb, eyes, breasts, head, penis, mutilated body, culminating in the representation of copulating bodies) and its interpretation in images of desire (and fear). Another tent reveals a series of pictures of 'A Young Girl's Most Significant Experience' (58), which turns out to be the proverbial Sleeping Beauty being kissed by a Prince who is transformed into Death. These images (wax models, pictures) bear strange resemblances to persons and events in Desiderio's past and future: one of the women depicted in the 'Seven Wonders of the World' resembles the beautiful and enigmatic Albertina, who had earlier appeared in the shapes of a black swan and that of Dr Hoffman's male ambassador. The castle represented inside the wax model womb reappears at the end of the novel as Hoffman's Gothic abode. The paintings of the Sleeping Beauty resemble Desiderio's past amorous encounter with the town mayor's daughter Mary Anne (the night before) and her future death (the next morning). After this fatal event Desiderio has to flee from the Police who charge him with seduction, murder, and necrophily performed on a minor as well as with impersonation of a government inspector (62). During the course of the novel he lives as an Indian among the River People, travels as nephew of the peep show proprietor from fair to fair, accompanies a Sadeian Count to the perversions of the 'House of Anonymity' (128), falls into the hands of a cannibalistic tribe, is received in the land of the Centaurs, until he finally reaches the castle of his opponent Dr Hoffman.

The dialectic and reversibility of the pattern of flight and persecution, of the figures of victim and persecutor as known from classical Gothic/fantastic novels like *Frankenstein* and *Dracula* is thematised throughout in association with the quest motif. Desiderio's mission is death: the destruction of Dr Hoffman. Yet almost from the start this mortal mission is accompanied and sometimes replaced by the quest for love of Albertina, Hoffman's daughter, an unmistakable hint at the Freudian tenet of the inseparability of Eros and Thanatos. Desiderio pursues and saves Albertina who in turn rescues him and in fact is his constant companion, most significantly in the disguise of Lafleur, the servant of the notorious Sadeian Count. Here the link between the ambivalence of the structural pattern and the figural pattern in Gothic/fantastic literature is made obvious. The technique of using various disguises, of changing identities, of splitting/multiplying personalities is taken to an ironic extreme. It seems only logical that after having been presented consecutively as a government inspector, an Indian, a nephew of a peepshow proprietor, and a guest of a Sadeian count, Desiderio finally realises himself in a mirror in Hoffman's castle as 'entirely Albertina in the male aspect' (199). If Albertina, as she claims, has been 'maintained in [her] various appearances only by the power of [Desiderio's] desire' (204), then the identification of the Minister and Dr Hoffman with rationality and desire respectively, also has to be questioned. All 'the roles are interchangeable' (39), as the doctor's ambassador explicitly points out. The neat borderline between reality and pleasure principle has become more and more blurred.

The described pattern of similarities between the images presented at the travelling fair and the experiences of the hero recurs throughout the novel. Image and experience constantly reflect each other, or rather appear as inseparable. Aptly, the peep show proprietor lectures the hero that the models and slides shown at the fair once belonged to Hoffman's museum of 'symbolic constituents of representations of the basic constituents of the universe' from which all possible situations of the world can be deduced. Consequently the symbols can be interpreted as 'patterns from which real events may be evolved' (95). So the novel identifies this set of samples as what could be called the constituents of a grammar of desire 'derived from Freud' (108). Furthermore, the constituents of this grammar, as they are translated into Desiderio's experiences, can be directly connected to Todorov's distinction between themes of perception (e.g. metamorphoses) and themes of discourse (desire) in fantastic literature: in Carter's novel themes of perception appear as metamorphoses between the human and the animal aspect (Centaurs), between animate and inanimate (animal furniture in the 'House of Anonymity'), between object and subject (acrobats dissolving, transformations of personalities). Among the catalogue of themes of desire figure allusions to necrophily (Sleeping Beauty, embalmed Mrs Hoffman) and incest (River People), homosexual rape (Acrobats of Desire), rape by Centaurs (Albertina), torture (tattooing), sadism and blasphemy ('House of Anonymity'), and cannibalism (River people, Black tribe, Centaurs). Moreover the ancestry of the Doctor himself is firmly rooted in the Gothic tradition of Dracula, whereas the Count is explicitly linked to de Sade: names representing perceptions of the world governed by infernal desires.

Throughout the novel Desiderio is confronted with Gothic transformations of self and desire without ever reaching the consummation of his own single desire, Albertina. When their union finally is about to take place, he kills her in order to escape from being literally reduced to a – in Deleuze's and Guattari's terms – 'desiring machine'.[6] For the fate prepared for him and Albertina by the Doctor is to permanently become part of 'a pictorial lexicon of all the things a man and a woman might do together within the confines of a bed of wire six feet long by three feet wide' (214). In recent criticism this murder has received diverse readings. On the one hand, David Punter reads it as an example of 'the defeat of the political aspirations of the 1960s, and in particular of the father-figures of liberation, Reich and Marcuse' as well as a result of Desiderio's having been 'formed by the Minister's society, by the society of apparent institutional order and totalitarian conformism'.[7] On the other hand, Ricarda Schmidt sees it as a result of Carter's attempt to show 'that the absolute rule of desire would make life just as repressive, sterile and static as the absolute rule of reason', and argues that the author supposedly 'examines the promise of desire completely and always fulfilled and finds that it does not guarantee happiness and freedom'.[8] Both readings seem to presuppose the attainability of a realm of desire without its vocabulary and grammar, presenting desire mostly in the Gothic forms of the return of the repressed, mixed with pain. The course of the whole novel, however, reveals the inseparability of desire from the projectionist's sample of images. Images, symbols, and myths are structuring the unconscious as much as the conscious. Pleasure principle and reality principle cannot be kept apart. In this sense Carter's novel can also be read as a parody on psychoanalytic attempts to pen 'desire in a cage' (208), to define it as the Other of rationality and reason. Carter's Dr Hoffman thus aptly appears to combine aspects of the father-figures of psychoanalysis (Freud) and of Gothicism (namely E. T. A. Hoffmann, E. A. Poe, and de Sade) respectively, thus reminding the reader in various ways of the inseparability of the fantastic and its Freudian interpretations: first, the reader, of course, remembers the fact that Freud developed his theory of the uncanny in relation to a story by E. T. A. Hoffmann. Secondly, the appearance of the doctor in the novel is presented as a mock analytic situation, where the doctor is sitting on a stool holding the hand of a woman on a couch, who, however, in a Poe-like Gothic twist of the scene, turns out to be the embalmed corpse of the doctor's dead wife. Desire remains a zero unit, a pure absence like death. So Desiderio's erotic quest necessarily implies at the same time an entropic pull. Desire as a vacant term, defined as a lack, has to be given an object and thereby filled with meaning. Death by necessity remains an imaginary space, a space of non-reality, which gains its meaning solely in relation to reality as difference, as other, as realm after life. In that respect the (nondescript) space of death and the (non-directional) movement of desire both point towards a void or an absolute zero point. But because absence cannot be represented, we are ironically left with embalmed corpses and the futile killing of desire (as represented by Albertina's death) and its inevitable return as a narrative of memory – in yet another kind of representation.

Reality and fantasy: the confusion of image and object

This notion of the inseparability of desire (and death) from its representations, its cultural constructions (images, symbols, myths), has decisive consequences for the notions of reality and fantasy/the fantastic with regard to their fictional representations. Most definitions of the fantastic and its related areas have centred on its correlative opposition to the real. This implies a definition of the real as governed by the principles of order and rationality. The fantastic then – as its counterpart – is viewed as an expression of reality's constraints, giving space to the unreal, the unseen, and unsaid. The representational forms of the fantastic are by necessity historically bound and thus vary according to the changing value systems (and thus reality concepts) of the society to which they relate. Following Todorov's familiar and often applied terminology,[9] the unreal or the Other is explained as supernatural within religious societies and is thus contained within the realm of the marvellous, the unhistoric; within secular societies the unreal is naturalised, e.g. in terms of a subjective perception, and thus can be contained as uncanny within the realm of the mimetic. The historical development of naming the unaccountable other as evil has consequently been traced as a gradual process of internalisation ranging from the devil (Lewis, *The Monk*; Maturin, *Melmoth*), to demons (villain/heroes of Ann Radcliffe and the Brontës) to the self as Other (Stevenson, *Dr Jekyll and Mr Hyde*; Hitchcock, *Psycho*). Today, critics like Rosemary Jackson see the fantastic as 'confounding the marvellous and the mimetic', as an aspect of instability and uncertainty, as that which lies beyond interpretation. Thus the fantastic in her words fundamentally 'traces the limits of [culture's] epistemological and ontological frame' by problematising vision (eye) and language (I) as reliable constituents of reality.[10] The fantastic, Rosemary Jackson goes on to explain, 'plays upon difficulties of interpreting events/things as objects or as images, thus disorienting the reader's categorisation of the "real" to such an extent that reason and reality appear as arbitrary shifting constructs'.[11] Applying these ideas to the tradition of Gothic literature, the decisive difference between earlier examples and contemporary texts of the fantastic becomes clear. While Frankenstein's monster and Stoker's vampires materialise as product of self and invasion of self respectively and become real, Angela Carter's creatures never become real in that sense. Angela Carter actualises images as objects and events, just as Mary Shelley and Bram Stoker did in the nineteenth century, but she insists on the process of actualisation rather than on the actualisation itself, creating a constant limbo between object as image, and image as object. Her fictions express Rosemary Jackson's theoretical persuasion that 'things slide away from the powerful eye/I which seeks to possess them'.[12] The travelling heroes of several of her novels, particularly those of *The Infernal Desire Machines of Dr Hoffman* and *Nights at the Circus*, are confronted with recurring clusters of images commonly identified as representations of the relational/oppositional other: namely, the unknown country, the travelling fair or circus, and – of course – the Gothic mansion and its inhabitants.

The unknown country recalls the fictional tradition of *Robinson Crusoe* and *Gulliver's Travels* respectively as two complementary ways of naturalisation (familiarisation as appropriation) of the unknown on the one hand and estrangement (defamiliarisation as satire) of the known on the other hand. Carter explicitly and ironically takes up both traditions by referring to Yahoos and Houyhnhnms in *The Infernal Desire Machines of Dr Hoffman* and in *Nights at the Circus*, and to Friday in the story 'Master' in *Fireworks*. Her heroes' experiences in unknown countries among unknown people provide ample opportunities to ridicule Western civilisation and its attempts at defining the Other in its own terms. Thus their wonder at the absurd nature of unknown mores, magic rituals, and languages only refers back to their/our own societies: in *Nights at the Circus* Jack Walser's explanation of the way the Siberian natives deal with foreigners can thus be related directly to the above-mentioned explanation of the history of Gothic/fantastic literature: 'Since they did not have a word for "foreigner", they used the word for "devil" instead and began to get used to it' (253). Similarly Walser's observation of the natives' tendency to confound object and image only reflects his and our own: 'The Siberian natives cannot distinguish between a bear as a household pet and as a "minor deity," "a transcendental kind of meta-bear" in the narrator's diction' (257). Furthermore, Walser himself (and the reader) cannot distinguish between the heroine Fevvers as a bird woman and Fevvers as a symbol of Victory, Death, Freedom or whatever other associations are evoked throughout the novel. In comparison and contrast to Swiftian satire Angela Carter not only uses the motif of the unknown country to criticise contemporary society, but eventually rather to represent ironically the process of signification and its arbitrariness and thus unreliability, a process which is all-encompassing and thus without conceivable alternative.

The travelling fair and the circus recall literary traditions associated with aspects of inversion and/or imitation of the known world. The world of the fair and the circus is the everyday world upside down: the abnormal becomes the norm within its confines, yet it always remains exotic with regard to the outside world. Angela Carter is interested in precisely this ambivalence: the other as a norm and as a monstrosity on display. In *The Infernal Desire Machines of Dr Hoffman* the observer/hero is tempted to explain the art of the Acrobats of Desire, such as juggling their own eyes or dismembering themselves, as that of tricksters who play with the human perception (perhaps using mirrors to create their effects). But this reassuring interpretation of the unreal as real (uncanny) is destroyed later on: the acrobats clearly do transcend the possible; (thus they seem to belong to the realm of the marvellous). But at the same time, the narrator reminds us of the fact that 'often, the whole fair seemed only another kind of set of samples' (110), of images displayed in the tent of the peep show proprietor. The fantastic double vision or rather oscillation between the different interpretations remains unresolved. In *Nights at the Circus* the heroine Fevvers, the bird woman, is celebrated as the world's 'Greatest Aerialiste'. But eventually her admirer and biographer Walser hits upon the paradox of meaning when he ponders: 'if she were indeed a *lusus naturae*, a prodigy, then – she was no longer a wonder . . . but – a freak . . . As a symbolic woman, she has a meaning, as an anomaly, none' (161). This not only applies to the attitude of others towards her, but also to her vision of self. The threat of being 'no Venus, or Helen, or Angel of the Apocalypse, not Izrael or Isfahel . . . [but] only a poor freak', throws her into a crisis which, however, is prevented by the gaze of her onlookers: 'the eyes fixed upon her with astonishment, with awe, the eyes that told her who she was' (290). In order to signify the birdwoman has to believe in herself as an image and a symbol. Meaning and representation are by necessity symbolic constructions, artefacts.

The issue of gender: ontology v. iconography

The analysis so far has shown that Angela Carter's fictional exercises in Gothicism are very effective renditions of her theoretical statements on the nature of the genre which deals in exaggeration, distortion, in cliché images and symbols. An additional attraction of the Gothic genre for Carter is its potential of integration insofar as it allows her to link fairy tale and pornography in her novels and many of her short stories. Since, according to Carter, both are derived from myth, both exhibit 'a fantasy relation to reality', depicting wo / man as 'invariable' and denying his / her 'social context'.[13] Thus in *The Infernal Desire Machines of Dr Hoffman* the vampiric Sadeian Count is described in utterly theatrical terms as 'connoisseur of catastrophe' (122) whose 'rigorous discipline of stylisation' (123) forces him to remain 'iconoclast, even when the icons were already cast down': 'As if from habit he pissed on the altar [of a ruined chapel] while the valet set out the meal' (125). During their visit to the 'House of Anonymity' the Count and Desiderio change into hooded costumes which according to the narrator 'were unaesthetic, priapic and totally obliterated our faces and our self-respect; the garb grossly emphasised our manhoods while utterly denying our humanity. And the costumes were of no time or place' (130). Consequently they are confronted not with women, but with variations of 'ideational femaleness', which turn out to be 'sinister, abominable, inverted mutations, part clockwork, part vegetable and part brute' (132). In a climactic scene the Count as 'the Pope of the Profane, officiating at an ultimate sacrament . . . snatched a candle . . . and used it to ignite the rosy plumage of a winged girl' (133), who, however, – as the reader is informed subsequently – far from being real 'had only been a life-like construction of papier mâché on a wicker frame' (134). In *Nights at the Circus* the winged girl has materialised, and after having been displayed in Mme Schreck's museum of woman monsters, has to escape first from being bled to death by the quasi-vampiric Christian Rosencreutz and later from being diminished to a miniature artefact by a demonic collector of toys and other rarities. The airs of omnipotence displayed by these Gothic villains are, however, counter-acted not only by their theatricality, but also by their 'quivering pusil-lanimity' (*Infernal Desire Machines*, 145) which shows itself as soon as they are faced with resistance.

The artificiality of Gothicism and its machinery is further revealed in Angela Carter's short story 'The Lady of the House of Love' (from her collection *The Bloody Chamber*),[14] where the vampire queen is likened by the hero to a doll, to a clockwork wound up years ago, to an automaton (102), and her mythical midnight mansion is stripped of all horror and fascination by the morning light: 'now you could see how tawdry it all was, how thin and cheap the satin, the catafalque not ebony at all but blackpainted paper stretched on ruts of wood, as in the theatre' (106). Similarly, when Desiderio reaches Dr Hoffman's castle, he realises: 'I was not in the domain of the marvellous at all. I had gone far beyond that and at last I had reached the power house of the marvellous, where all its clanking, dull, stage machinery was kept' (*Infernal Desire Machines*, 201).

A final twist in Carter's use of Gothicism is thus related to the idea of gender. Whereas earlier Gothic fiction shows the materialisation of ideas (Frankenstein's monster, Dracula), Angela Carter uses Gothicism to reveal the process of transformation of human beings, particularly women into symbols and ideas by the process of gender construction. Gothicism as a blend of fairy tale and pornography most obviously shows the replacement of the ontological by the iconographic. In her analysis of de Sade, *The Sadeian Woman*, Angela Carter links pornography to the stylisation of graffiti:

> In the stylisation of graffiti, the prick is always presented as erect, in an alert attitude of enquiry or curiosity or affirmation; it points upwards, it asserts. The hole is open, an inert space, like a mouth waiting to be filled. From this elementary iconography may be derived the whole metaphysic of sexual differences – man aspires; woman has no other function but to exist, waiting. The male is positive, an exclamation mark. Woman is negative. Between her legs lies nothing but zero, the sign for nothing, that only becomes something when the male prin-ciple fills it with meaning.[15]

In her novel *The Passion of New Eve* Angela Carter uses Gothicism (among other genres) in this sense to reveal the process of gender con-struction as a process which places the hero turned heroine Eve/lyn 'outside history' (125), because it is a process of being transformed by 'the false universals of myth' (136). But how can wo/man be situated in his-tory, in the real world, if this world, too, is a symbolic construction? The answer to this question given by the narrator/hero(ine) of the novel, 'a critique of these symbols is a critique of our lives' (6), indicates that Carter intends to move from the symbolic level of her texts to the symbolic representation of our reality.

Conclusion

As pointed out above, Angela Carter's fantastic creatures never become real in the way Frankenstein's monster or Dracula do. They necessarily must stop short, because the real only exists as absence, as vanishing zero point in a world constructed by images, symbols, and myths. If the fantastic is defined as tracing the limits of our cultural frame, as that which lies beyond interpretation, then the real as that which cannot be represented has become the 'real' topic of the postmodern fantastic. Yet this topic can never be grasped but can only be encircled (via parody, intertextuality, metafiction, and irony) in an endless process of de-mystification which, however, always acknowledges its own futility. The fantastic has not been replaced by Freud's psychoanalysis, as Todorov suggested, but has rather been reinvigorated by Lacan's revision of Freud. Rather than rendering the reader/critic unnecessary, Angela Carter provides him with the concrete textual illustrations of current literary theory.

Notes

1 A. Carter, Afterword to *Fireworks: Nine Profane Pieces* (London: Quartet Books, 1974), p. 122.
2 N. Cornwell, *The Literary Fantastic: From Gothic to Postmodernism* (Hempstead: Harvester, 1990), pp. 145, 154.
3 A. Carter, *Heroes and Villains* (Harmondsworth: Penguin Books (1969) 1981).
4 Afterword to *Fireworks*.
5 The following texts are used: *The Infernal Desire Machines of Dr Hoffman* (Harmondsworth: Penguin Books (1972) 1982); *Nights at the Circus* (London: Picador (1984) 1984); *The Bloody Chamber* (Harmondsworth: Penguin Books (1979) 1987); *The Passion of New Eve* (London: Virago Press (1977) 1982).
6 G. Deleuze and F. Guattari, *Anti-Oedipus* (New York: Viking, (1972) 1977), Chapter 1.
7 D. Punter, 'Angela Carter: Supersessions of the Masculine', *Critique* 25:4 (1984), pp. 209–22; 211, 213.
8 R. Schmidt, 'The Journey of the Subject in Angela Carter's Fiction', *Textual Practice* 3:1 (1989), pp. 56–7; 61.
9 See Tzvetan Todorov, *The Fantastic: A Structural Approach to a Literary Genre*, trans. Richard Howard (Ittace, NY: Cronell Univeristy Press (1970) 1973).
10 R. Jackson, *Fantasy: The Literature of Subversion* (London: Methuen, 1981), pp. 12, 30.

11 *Ibid.*, pp. 20, 21.
12 *Ibid.*, p. 46.
13 A. Carter, *The Sadeian Woman: An Exercise in Cultural History* (London: Virago Press, 1979), pp. 6, 16.
14 On Gothicism in Angela Carter's tales see Patricia Duncker, 'Re-Imagining the Fairy Tales: Angela Carter's Bloody Chambers', *Literature and History* 10:1 (spring 1984), pp. 3–14.
15 *The Sadeian Woman*, p. 4.

Alien invasions by body snatchers and related creatures

At the beginning of Philip K. Dick's 1954 story *The Father-Thing* a mother is gathering her family for dinner. The father has been sharpening his shears in the garage. The son is sent to call him in for the meal. It seems the very image of routine domesticity until, that is, the son Charles says that his father is talking to himself – literally talking to a double. Father Ted enters the dining room and sets to work on his lamb stew, but Charles shrieks in horror that it is the 'other one', rushing out to the garage where he finds discarded traces of his father. It turns out that the substitute is controlled by a mysterious insect which is preparing to take over Charles' mother and himself. The substitute for the former is described as follows:

> A shape, a silent, unmoving shape that grew up from the mound of filth like some nocturnal mushroom. A white column, a pulpy mass that glistened moistly in the moonlight. Webs covered it, a mouldy cocoon, it had vague arms and legs. An indistinct half-shaped head. As yet, the features hadn't formed. But he could tell what it was.[1]

Slight as the story is, here we can already see the opposition taking shape which informs other narratives of alien invasion. Dick does not give himself room here to explain the origin of the mysterious insect; it is just from outside, from the realm of the unknown. The safe domestic interior is startlingly disrupted by creatures which take shape in filth and corruption. Defamiliarisation in the most literal sense takes place as the father's mask slips: 'in the brief instant Ted Walton's face lost all familiarity. Something alien and cold gleamed out, a twisting, wriggling mass.'[2]

The key effect signalled by the cue word 'alien' is loss, an erasure of human qualities. Here Ted's human facade metaphorically opens to reveal a non-human interior. It is as if one species has subverted another in a process of invasion which starts with domestic space and which culminates in the usurpation of the very citadel of the self – the human body. Dick's hyphenated title appropriately captures the neutering change where 'he' becomes an 'it'. In the grammar of English nominalisations 'father' functions as an aspect of 'thing'. The two terms are not paired equally. Similarly in John W. Campbell's story 'Who Goes There?', which was used as the basis of the 1951 movie *The Thing* and then given this title, the members of an Arctic expedition are put at the mercy of a creature thawed out of the ice. In a scene which had already become a cliché by the fifties this creature is unveiled on a table as possessing three eyes and wriggling worms 'where hair should grow', yet the real power of the story lies in Campbell's handling of uncertainty. Once again the key word emerges within the local context of a disparity. All the smells of the Arctic station are familiar except one: 'It was a queer neck-ruffling thing, a faintest suggestion of an odour alien among the smells of industry and life.'[3] The story attempts to define this 'thing', the least specific noun in the language, and progresses from smell to physical shape. A temporary and misleading relief is created by the apparent death of the creature but the team then discover that it can take on any form using the other's blood as a kind of catalyst. One scientist declares: 'It can imitate anything – that is, become anything.' Paranoia now surges through the team, increased by the claustrophobic Arctic setting, as each member begins to suspect that his neighbour is an anthropoid. Here another general motif of alien invasions emerges. The crude horror of physical abnormality is as nothing to the fear that human appearances cannot be trusted. So a character might suddenly shift from showing conventional behaviour to a 'suddenly feral, red-eyed, dissolving imitation'.[4]

Such changes enact a loss of self which Mark Rose has described as being characteristic of the Science Fiction genre: 'feelings of self-alienation typically express themselves as narratives of metamorphosis, stories of the transformation of men into something less than or more than human'.[5] The alienation, the change from self into other, can sometimes be traced in the progression of individual sentences, as, for instance, when one member of the team in *The Thing* reverts to the animalistic after death. The human subject blurs into an indeterminate other species: 'Kianer's arms had developed a queer scaly fur, and the flesh had twisted. The fingers had shortened, the hand rounded, the finger nails become three-inch long things of dull red horn, keened to steel-hard, razor-sharp talons.'[6] The description relies on its specifics not cohering into any recognisable shape. So we move through suggestions of fish or lizard (scales), animal, freak (distortion), or bird of prey. Human proportions of nail to limb are lost as the former expands and the latter contracts; and there are even suggestions of the limb as a technological weapon. It therefore seems to be the case that the alien is powerfully represented as an unspecified Other which is articulated through negatives, or through discontinuities like the passage just quoted. Singular identity becomes questioned by duplication with a resultant paranoid fear that the appearance of familiar benign figures might be masking an inner malignity.

The revival of interest in Science Fiction in the fifties coincided with the early peak of the Cold War which goes some way towards explaining the popularity of invasion fantasies. These narratives revolve around takeovers by alien forces, sometimes specified, sometimes not. They also frequently involve the estrangement of different members of a community from each other. In all cases, however, the narratives carry within themselves traces of the Gothic tradition. In the 1953 movie *Invaders from Mars* the aliens are finally confronted and destroyed in tunnels located symbolically beneath the town. In *The Thing* the narrative implicitly alludes to the werewolf and vampire legends, and even glances back to *Frankenstein* in its use of the Arctic setting for its struggle between adversaries. One of the most famous 'take-over' narratives of the decade was *Invasion of the Body Snatchers* (1956) based on a novel by Jack Finney. The latter's shorter title (*The Body Snatchers*) draws on the motif of violating the taboo of death. The phrase 'body snatcher' became current in the 1820s when the trade in stolen corpses to supply the medical profession became rampant. It then supplied the title of R. L. Stevenson's 1884 story which evokes a total dissociation between public life and secret criminality. The focaliser for most of the narrative is one Fettes, an assistant in the Edinburgh anatomy theatres who has the responsibility for receiving the corpses. The story enacts a reluctance to identify the explicit nature of his activities.

> Here, after a night of turbulent pleasures, his hand still tottering, his sight still misty and confused, he would be called out of bed in the black hours before the winter dawn by the unclean and desperate interlopers who supplied the table. He would open the door to these men, since infamous throughout the land. He would help them with their tragic brethren, pay them their sordid price, and remain alone, when they were gone, with the unfriendly relics of humanity.[7]

Fettes is the physical link in a chain which society conspires to suppress, a link between body-snatching and even murder, and the respectable practice of medicine. The circumlocutions and euphemisms in the passage above function melodramatically as the stylistic features of an attempt to maintain clear opposition between day and night, good and evil, respectability and criminality which gradually collapse as the story progresses. The echoes of the Gothic in Finney's title would have been further strengthened by the release in 1945 of a movie adaptation of Stevenson's story, and indeed the question of a title for the 1956 movie became complicated for that very reason.[8]

Finney focuses his narrative of extraterrestrial pods taking over a small Texas town on the developing relationship between the town doctor Miles Bennell (the narrator) and his former teenage sweetheart Becky Driscoll. *The Body Snatchers* opens with the return home of Becky after completing her divorce. Although she is erotically available to Miles, much of the action centres on his struggle against her obvious attractions.

Above all Mike relishes her continuity with the past, unconsciously expressing his fascination in self-contradictory terms:

> For the first time I really saw her face again. I saw it was the same nice face, the bones prominent and well-shaped under the skin; the same kind and intelligent eyes, the rims a little red just now . . . She'd changed, of course, she wasn't eighteen now, but well into her twenties, and looked it, no more and no less. But she was also still the same girl I'd known in High School.[9]

Becky's reappearance makes it possible for Miles to recover a lost routine of dating, until, that is, the pods cause complications. He records his attraction to her but qualifies virtually every statement with justificatory self-censoring counter-statements, either denials or typifying deflections of his own experience onto the projected (male) reader: 'Put a nice-looking girl you're fond of in your arms . . . have her weep a little, and you're a cinch to feel pretty tender and protective.'[10] It could happen to anyone, he protests, and then muffles the sexual nature of his reactions by casting himself in the role of guardian.

The progression of events in the novel brings that sexual dimension to the surface, without Miles ever quite admitting it to himself. The equivalent in Finney's novel of Stevenson's suppression of criminality is a sexual prohibition, relaxed by the arrival of the pods. The first body they see is a nude male figure unveiled by Miles before Becky's eyes. The second is a female nude, this time a version of Becky herself. These figures, and the sightings of the pods, all occur in symbolically meaningful locations. If the house can represent the 'organism as a whole' we should note that these figures are found in basements and within closed containers – trunk, cupboard, car boot. They are seen at night initially in Jack's house which is outside the town, and then progressively nearer and nearer to the main subject – Miles himself. When Miles suddenly realises that Becky may be in danger he initiates an episode which reads like a flawed seduction and which is packed with sexually charged detail. After the sexual rhythm of running to her house he enters her home by breaking a basement window, suggestive of guilt and also of bodily entry. When he gazes at Becky's double sexual arousal is dispersed through all his limbs 'I came to life once more, my heart swelling and contracting gigantically, the blood congesting in my veins and behind my eyes, in a panic of fright and excitement, and I got to my feet, my legs stiff.'[11]' The current of sexual excitement, not unpleasantly offset by fright, leads from the eyes not to the penis but to the more 'acceptable' seat of the emotions which is nevertheless given a primarily physical activity here. Freud has repeatedly glossed climbing stairs, ladders, etc. in dreams as a symbolic representation of sexual intercourse and here Miles' breathless ascent from basement to bedroom enacts the sexual preliminaries to a congress which never takes place.[12]

The 'romance' between Miles and Becky thus plays a more important part in the novel than merely shadowing the story of the pods. Clearly the two are interwoven in a remarkably consistent subtext, a psychosexual drama within Miles' consciousness. Both characters joke about the resemblance of events to a seduction but Miles' jokes function as a means of defence. His facetious admissions of sexual intent ('I have some wicked sinful plans in mind') are defused (but never quite erased) as a kind of game which he even pursues as a dialogue between proper and improper selves while contemplating himself in the shaving mirror. For all these tactics, however, the sexual temperature slowly but surely rises until he experiences an orgasmic kiss with Becky: 'suddenly it was more than pleasant, it was a silent explosion in my mind, and through every nerve and vein in my body'.[13] Just at this peak of pleasure (in which Becky seems to play no active part at all) Miles suddenly hears his name hissed, it seems, out of thin air and both descend once again into the basement with Jack, this time to watch giant seed pods exude a whitish-grey lava which takes on human form. One opposition which Finney dramatises in the novel is that between mind and feeling, head and body; and Miles' difficulties arise when trying to negotiate between the two. In this episode he tries various rationalising analogies with tumbleweed and South American dolls, but the comparisons collapse before the unavoidably visceral nature of the pods. By transforming their contents from plasma to human shapes they threaten the observers' complacency of species and specifically force on Miles' consciousness a physicality he has been suppressing. When he discovers two pods in his car boot he loses his mind completely and yields to physical frenzy: 'then I was trampling them, smashing and crushing them under my plunging feet and legs, not even knowing that I was uttering a sort of hoarse, meaningless cry – "Unhh! Unhh! Unhh!" – of fright, animal disgust, and rage'.[14] This image marks the farthest extreme from the calm rational observation on which Miles prides himself.

Finney suggests that Miles' social status and self-esteem depend to a large extent on his father, the town doctor before him. Whereas Becky denies her father and leaves his house, Miles keeps *his* house as a virtual shrine to his dead parents. Becky attracts him as a kind of living memento to his school days, but a fear comes over him, sexually analogous to the pods' transformation process: 'It seemed to me that I was turning into some sort of puppet who had no control over what was happening to him.'[15] The change into a sexual marionette is expressed through a slippage of subject pronouns from first to third person, a shift from self to Other. Nancy Steffen-Fluhr has discussed a similar process in the 1956 movie:

> The come-close/go-away pulse of Miles's emotions is the heartbeat of the film. It is the burgeoning intimacy with Becky, not the burgeoning pods, which is the hidden source of his fear . . . the pod plot is, at least in part, simply a surrealistic projection of these unacknowledged anxieties, of a man's terror of falling helplessly in love.[16]

This love motif reaches a bizarre culmination in Miles' surgery. He saves himself and Becky from transformation by deflecting the pods' forces on to his two skeletons (a male and a female). Having declared their love for each other, Miles and Becky enact their betrothal by smearing their blood on the skeletons. This macabre act smacks of corresponding events in vampire narratives, rituals to stave off evil forces. Indeed, *The Body Snatchers* does present a kind of vampirism where figures are 'occupied' rather than 'consumed'. In *Dracula* such a change releases sexual activity in the females and responsiveness in the males; in the 1956 movie *Invasion of the Body Snatchers*, however, it is Becky's lack of sexual response that tells Miles she has been transformed. The 1978 remake reverses this image completely by having the equivalent Becky-figure stand naked in undergrowth beckoning the protagonist to her. Whatever the permutation, sexuality becomes closely linked to predation and therefore to the loss of individual autonomy.

There are a number of problems in taking Finney's novel and 1956 movie as a Freudian psychodrama. First of all, both works are extremely self-conscious about psychological explanation. While no expert, Miles nevertheless has a smattering of Freudian jargon to hand and even analyses himself as a 'Don Juan personality. A pseudo- . . .' The last phrase is cut off before he can identify a specific lack of authenticity. More importantly, when he meets Wilma, the first 'patient', he reassures her: 'the trouble is inside you'. This line is repeated and reinforced by the town psychiatrist Mannie who cites examples of 'mass hysteria, auto-suggestion', thereby extending the notion of neurosis to the whole community. In fact, the novel introduces three commentators on the action, each one with his own explanation: Mannie's theory of collective delusion; Professor Budlong's (a professor of botany and biology) view that the pods are simply an unusual form of organic life which might conceivably – as compare Lord Kelvin's speculations on the origin of life – have come from outer space; and the writer Jack Belicec's attitude. The latter is not so much an explanation as a frame of mind. Jack keeps a file of newspaper cuttings. These stories revolve around 'things in direct contradiction to what we know to be true', and imply that our sense of real should be resilient enough to leave room for the inexplicable.

In pursing this strategy of internal commentary Finney is following on the tradition of late Victorian Gothic where the irruption of the strange figures not only as drama but also as an issue to be analysed, understood, and thereby brought under control. The inscription of analysis into these narratives explains the recurrence of experts, whether they are ghost-hunters, vampirologists, or psychologists. The appearance of the latter two figures in *Dracula* signals two historically determined alternative modes of explanation. The presence of a scientist and a psychiatrist in *The Body Snatchers* seems to point to similar alternatives. But Jack raises a third possibility in his collection of newspaper stories. Their source naturalises the alien into the odd and the cuttings act as a synecdoche of the novel as a whole in containing an apparently clear narrative with no explanation. In that respect they recall Miles' opening lines which explicitly forewarn the reader that explanatory strands will not be tied together. There is yet another complicating factor to this internal commentary. Marnie and Professor Budlong refuse the possibility of the pods' existence, the one by internalising experience, the other on biological grounds. But both figures have suffered the change and are therefore trying to put Miles off the scent of what is at that stage a mystery. It is ironically appropriate to the novel's reversals that Marnie and Budlong should reappear later as the justifiers of the pods. They are after all, the latter insists, only performing 'their simple and natural function', namely to survive. Why do they grow? There is no answer needed to this question because all forms of life fulfil themselves. As in John Wyndham's *Midwich Cuckoos* (1957), where extraterrestrial beings impregate the women of an isolated village, the biological imperative at one and the same time justifies the alien and situates it within other forms of life. By this point in *The Body Snatchers*, however, the so-called 'scientific attitude' has itself become parodied as inhuman detachment.

It should have become clear by now that Finney devotes far less attention to the pods themselves than to their consequences. His novel shows two transformations taking place: pod into humanoid, and human into humanoid. The first challenges presumptions of species definition, the second radically alters the community. It is therefore important that the action should take place in a small town because the novel opens with a situation of social familiarity. Being a doctor Miles is specially placed to know virtually everyone, whereas the 1978 movie awkwardly shifts the narrative to San Francisco, thereby excluding Finney's stark reversal of familiarity into its opposite. The very nature of the small town offers possibilities of horror not available in the same way in the city. Thus Philip K. Dick's *The Cosmic Puppets* describes the protagonist's return to the Virginian town of his birth assuming that it will be 'sleepy and ordinary', but in fact 'nothing was familiar. All strange, Alien.'[17] This rhetoric of opposites, as we shall see, is also used in *The Body Snatchers*. The shocks to Dick's Ted Barton come from place, people, and even records (the local newspaper lists his death while a child). In Frederick Pohl's story from 1954 'The Tunnel under the World', however, shocks are smaller and come more gradually. Here the business executive protagonist discovers that, following an industrial accident, a corporation has rebuilt a miniaturised replica of his town. In *The Cosmic Puppets* the town has been altered by a destructive deity. Whatever the specific explanations, all these narratives exploit a stark contrast between the known and the unknown, between internally familiar social processes and external threatening forces. Undoubtedly the Cold War sharpened these contrasts although the device of isolating the action and thereby creating an internal atmosphere of claustrophobia, has a pedigree stretching back into Gothic fiction. Invisible barriers are erected around the communities in *The Cosmic Puppets* and *The Midwich Cuckoos*. In *The Body Snatchers* the barrier is more psychological. Attempts to communicate with or escape to the outside collapse before the incredible nature of the story and the main characters' sense of obligation to family.

The first and most sustained impact of the pods in Finney's word is the division of family units; then, like Stevenson's paragon of apparent respectability, Dr Wolfe Macfarlane, Miles is gradually shifted by events from a position of social centrality and respectability to that of a burglar and ultimately of an outcast. Finney is dramatising a nightmare expressed by Philip Rieff in the following terms: 'suppose there occurred some disorder so fundamental in nature as to destroy the therapeutic function of the community *per se*'.[18] The pods literally produce such a disorder in both senses, triggering off what appears to be an epidemic and a disruption to town life. A descriptive motif runs through the novel of Miles looking at the town as a whole initially with the pride of belonging, and then with horror. Walking along a street he figures estrangement in painterly terms: 'I think I'd distort the windows of the houses we passed. I'd show them with half-drawn shades, the bottom edge of each shade curving downwards, so that the windows looked like heavy-lidded, watchful eyes, quietly and terribly aware of us as we passed through that silent street.'[19] Here the houses function as the personified facades of their concealed inhabitants and such a scene indicates the shift in the novel from a 'we-group' to a 'they-group'. Miles registers this change again when he overhears changed characters mimicking social pleasantries. Where we have earlier seen the house signifying sexual space it now connotes a social area from which Miles is excluded as he brings home this change powerfully. In the novel the participants in the know wear badges and strangers are removed by the police. In the 1956 movie Don Siegel depicts the event as a travesty civic gathering with all the towns-folk converging on the central square. To the watching Miles and Becky it is an event which horrifyingly excludes them and which paves the way for the final pursuit when they become fugitives from their own community. Michael Beard has argued that in this novel 'Finney's real focus is on community reaction to deviant behaviour', but without adding that social norms get reversed.[20] Where Miles was initially offering therapy to others, by the end he is being offered transformation as a rest, as nothing more than a painless treatment. This reversal builds up to a nightmare climax where Miles and Becky are surrounded by the towns-folk. Then Finney suddenly dissipates that tension through the *deus ex machina* of the pods leaving the Earth. The result is, as one reviewer remarked, a 'not entirely convincing denouement'.[21] One reason for this may have been Finney's evident desire to restore the town, to halt its entropic drift towards death, an issue which was largely ignored by the movie adaptations.

The question of whether *The Body Snatchers* has political reference cannot be answered in isolation from its context and an important precursor in that context was Robert Heinlein's *The Puppet Masters* (1951). Like Finney's novel and like Dick's *The Cosmic Puppets*, it dramatises a fear of loss of self, this time in explicitly futuristic terms. The time of the action is unspecified beyond taking place after a nuclear war between the USA and the Soviet Union. The narrator is an intelligence operative called in by his father/boss, the 'Old Man', to deal with a flying saucer. Heinlein acknowledges his approach to cliché (some of the early scenes describing the saucer are very reminiscent of Wells' *War of the Worlds*) by having Sam dismiss the latter as 'mass hallucinations'. In fact, the saucer in question has brought creatures from another planet in the form of slugs which attach themselves to humans' backs and transform them into zombies. Heinlein plays on feelings of disgust: 'the thing was uncovered. Greyish faintly translucent, and shot through with darker structure, shapeless – but it was clearly alive.'[22] Thematically he anticipates a number of details which recur in *The Body Snatchers*. The slugs are parasites and consume their hosts, transforming them into mindless slaves. When he is briefly taken over Sam recalls: 'I had no more to do with words spoken by me for my master than has a telephone. I was a communication instrument, nothing more.'[23] The novel also anticipates Finney's Marnie in its reference to flying saucers and demonic possession. Thus the term 'hagridden' is used by Heinlein to denote the physical position of the slugs (giving their carriers the appearance of hunchbacks) and to recall ancient fears of evil spirits. The slugs claim a genuine purpose ('we come to bring you . . . peace') and operate on a 'drive to survive' which biologically glosses a purpose to take over America and then the whole world.

The Puppet Masters, however, frames its action within the conventions and even the language of the spy adventure with the result that events are very quickly given a political dimension. The arrival of the slugs combines invasion and subversion and Heinlein directs considerable irony against the President's slowness to act because of his dependence on Congress. Once a national emergency has been declared, the terminology of warfare ('capture', 'occupation', etc.) gets stronger and stronger. H. Bruce Franklin is therefore amply justified in reading the novel as a 'Cold War allegory' against the 'insidious Communist menace' since 'the slugs are not distinct individuals but unfeeling members of a communal mind dedicated to the enslavement of all other societies'.[24] Apart from the consistency of the analogy Heinlein throws out intermittent references to Russia as an environment well suited to the parasites who even, again by analogy, make use of fifth columnists in their plot. The Russians for their part dismiss reports as an 'American Imperialist fantasy'. Ironically, that is exactly what Heinlein's novel is – a fantasy of invasion. Despite the ostensible posture of defence, the novel ends on a sabre-rattling moral: 'Whether we make it or not, the human race has got to keep up its well-earned reputation for ferocity. The price of freedom is the willingness to do sudden battle, anywhere, any time, and with utter recklessness.'[25]

The existence of a work like The Puppet Masters helps to explain the prevailing critical orthodoxy with respect to the film Invasion of the Body Snatchers, which is now generally regarded as a 'masterful piece of political allegory'.[26] Jack Finney has, however, categorically denied any such intent in his novel: 'It is not true that my book, The Bodysnatchers (sic), was intended as an allegory of any kind. When I wrote this book I was not thinking of McCarthy, or Communism, fascism, or of anything but writing pure entertainment . . . I don't write allegories.'[27] Nothing could be clearer. The question then remains how the allegorical interpretation of movie and novel could have reached such prominence. Undoubtedly the main answer must lie in their Cold War context and secondly in the new emphases which emerged as the novel was adapted to the cinema. Taking context first, we have already noted that Heinlein and Finney use the analogy of the witch-hunt in their fiction, a comparison which itself had become politically charged by the 1950s. Marion Starkey introduced her 1949 study *The Devil in Massachusetts* as no mere historical exercise, but as a warning to contemporary Americans:

> although this particular delusion . . . has vanished from the western world, the urge to hunt 'witches' has done nothing of the kind. It has been revived on a colossal scale by replacing the medieval idea of malefic witchcraft by pseudo-scientific concepts like 'race', 'nationality', and by substituting for theological dissension as whole complex of warring ideologies. Accordingly the story of 1692 is of far more than antiquarian interest; it is a allegory of our times.[28]

Secondly, the notion of the pods approached Cold War metaphors of Communism as a virus and its agents as germs. Then, as we have seen, the perception of change induces in Miles a paranoid sense of hidden forces similar in nature if not scale to those recognised by the ex-Communist Whittaker Chambers as 'working behind and below the historical surface'.[29] Finally, the master trope of war emerges towards the end of *The Body Snatchers* when Miles remembers Churchill's speech 'we shall fight them in the fields'.

These details suggest coincidental or oblique links between Finney's novel and contemporary ideological metaphors. Michael Beard has rightly addressed the level of political reference by stating that the reaction to the transformations 'functions as a generalised social anxiety rather than a specifically political one'.[30] In the 1956 movie the first modification to make the narrative more explicit was the change of title. As we have seen, Finney's title carries Gothic echoes, but this combination of theft and sacrilege assumed new proportions when prefaced by 'invasion'. The main precursor text now stands out as Wells' *War of the Worlds* (1898), a novel which straddles the horror, future wars, and alien invasion genres. As in all versions of *The Body Snatchers*, Wells gained his main shock-effects by having human figures confront some distorted version of themselves, in this case creatures which retained the semblance of a head with an atrophied body and octopus-like tentacles. They thus function as an evolutionary warning rather than the direct species threat posed by later narratives of alien invasion. The *The War of the Worlds* was first transposed on to the American scene by the popular press in 1897, then again by Orson Welles' famous radio adaptation of 1938 and, presumably to repeat quasi-documentary effects, producer Walter Wanger originally planned to have Welles read a prologue to *Invasion*.[31] The relation of Wells' narrative to contemporary America was further strengthened by George Pal's

1954 movie version of *The War of the Worlds* which places the action in California.

Invasion further built on Finney's similar location of a California small town by adding a frame to its main narrative. Partly this functions like the introduction to the 1950 crime movie *DOA* where the protagonist reports his own murder to the police. The dissolve into the past, here and in *Invasion*, where Miles reports his story to the authorities of a city hospital, initiates a looping narrative which will eventually explain how such things can be. Don Siegel's frame also sets a characteristic tone for the movie by introducing the interlocking themes of urgency, speed, time, and illness. The hospital in the opening shot carries no less than three 'emergency' signs and this is a term which echoes throughout the movie, reinforced by the recurring sound of police sirens. Secondly, clocks appear again and again, always related to the anxiety that characters will be too late. Hence the crucial importance of speed as we shall see in a moment. Finally, there is the question of illness and the irony of a doctor being treated by other doctors. The scene introduces and to a certain extent naturalises the incredible nature of the narrative to come and Miles' subsequent voice-over comments on the action serve a related purpose. They warn the audience not to make the same mistakes as he did in missing the significant implications of events at the time. In other words, the intermittent commentary speeds up the audience's process of recognition. The opening of the narrative proper has also telescoped events which take several chapters to develop in the novel. Miles returns home from a medical convention to find a fully formed situation. From the very first 'something evil' has taken over Santa Mira, which the opening episodes will reveal.

The simplest and most effective means of showing urgency in the movie is by having characters run from place to place, as some critics have noted, but Jack P. Rawlins tries to impose a psychological restriction on this device by confining it to the main two characters: Miles 'runs up endless, surrealistic flights of steps; he fights to save Becky from symbolic rape; he runs, she falls, they run to exhaustion but keep on running'.[32] We saw in the novel that Finney did indeed set up an intermittent psychodrama of Miles' ambivalent attraction to Becky, but the movie introduces running through a new scene which identifies it as a general social sympton. A boy runs out from Grimaldi's closed vegetable stand almost under the wheels of Miles' car. The choice of a boy is in line with a general pattern of fifties Science Fiction movies where, according to Nora Sayre, 'the child's role . . . is to alert others to the perils that prowl among us'.[33] This happens at the beginning of *Them!* (1954) where a traumatised girl is found wandering across the New Mexico desert. Here the film gradually unravels the pathos of the child's plight; in *Invasion* the child's sincerity is exploited to make the first case of changed identity make its maximum impact. Running gradually changes its nature, in the film, from protective purpose (running to save someone or to find out) to flight. As in most horror stories, the action alternates between areas of safety and of danger but gradually the former become so suspect that the whole environment becomes one of threat. The main street which Miles and Becky cross near the beginning emerges as a familiar social space but by the end of the film has become an avenue for escape. Hence the mounting claustrophobia of scenes in narrow alleys and corridors with blocked access. The cars in the film function as extensions of the social space, characteristically as vulnerable as anywhere else to invasion when two pods are placed in Miles' boot. The final chase brings this motif to its visual climax as the whole town pursues Miles and Becky up seemingly endless stairs into the hills. Running would predictably be linked to panic but in a nice reversal of *The War of the Worlds* the movie depicts the *absence* of panic as a source of fear in itself. Indeed Miles' panic takes on a special importance at the end of the film as he tries to snap drivers on the highway (and the viewer) out of their apathy.

The second major thematic device to be used in *Invasion* is scenic repetition with variations, a method which arises logically from a spatially limited setting within a community where everyone knows everyone else. One example of this can be seen in the use of Miles' surgery. The Grimaldi boy is brought in panic-stricken so Miles gives him a sedative pill. In the next appearance the change has taken place so the boy is calm. The surgery is not only a place of therapy but also for Becky a refuge ('we're safe here'). Miles gives them pills, but this time to keep them awake. Finally they are trapped in the surgery and forced to await the 'therapy' of transformation. This sequence is typical of the repetitions in taking a mundane situation and then reversing it so that doctor becomes the patient. Peter Biskind notes such reversals rather starkly by commenting: 'the docs are sick and the cops are criminals'.[34] The main source of power in this film is not revulsion to the physically grotesque pod reproductions, but rather a steady estrangement of the viewer from a whole series of ordinary social events which gradually become charged with sinister potential. Recurrence, for example, raises the question of similarity. Is Wilma's uncle as reassuring a figure as Jack simply because he too smokes a pipe? Does the daytime repetition of the scene in Becky's cellar turn into anticlimax because it is only the gasman, or is the anticlimax a prelude to fresh panic because the gasman might be in on the plot? Repetition thus induces in us a paranoid suspicion of everything and anyone, while at the same time dramatising the difficulty of knowing with certainty.[35]

If modified repetition destabilises characters' relation to each other and to the community, this effect is further increased by the movie's alternation of perspectives. A traditional use of shot-reverse shots is to show what is seen and then the observer's reaction. In *Invasion*, however, the object of vision is usually either human or humanoid. The opening frame episode explicitly confronts this question of seeing and being seen as a facet of credibility. Alternation of perspective thereby fills out the dialogues about meaning in the film and once again bears on issues of community. The interplay between 'us' and 'them' problematises the observer's (usually in practice Miles') relation to his social group. So in the last episode in Miles' surgery the discussion with Danny combines threat and a prediction of belonging ('Tomorrow you'll be one of us').[36] The camera alternates between the two main speakers as representatives of opposing ideologies. The ultimate issue is whether Miles and Becky will join the group, a question which has been raised visually when they crouch in Miles' closet. The grill on the door window suggests the analogy of a cell, the camera initially showing a guard's face framed in the window from within. This shot then reverses to one of the prisoners' faces framed from the surgery. Such reversals complicate distinctions between inside and outside which the film has any way rendered suspect by playing on the notion of human bodies acting as 'hosts' to their possessors.

The difficulties of seeing are compounded by the movie's last major device, its exploitation of chiaroscuro effects. In the Gothic tradition darkness has always combined suggestions of evil with perceptual difficulty. As Edmund Burke pointed out at the beginning of the Gothic movement, 'to make anything very terrible, obscurity seems in general to be necessary'.[37] Darkness regularly connotes lack of knowledge and both Finney's novel and the movie adaptations draw on this traditional association to create mounting suspense. So when Miles creeps into Becky's basement his only means of seeing is with matches (not even a fountain-pen torch, as he carries in the novel). This limits visibility to a small pool of light in front of his face whereas Danny carries a powerful torch on their second visit. The increase in light reflects the pervasive force of his explanation which is further reinforced – spuriously, as it turns out – in full light by the presence of Becky's father and the police chief. Or, to take an example not in the novel, the episode set on Miles' patio starts again as an ordinary domestic event – a barbecue. When Miles enters the greenhouse, however, the shot is skewed at an angle to suggest a disruption to the real. The lighting then becomes limited to barred and spotted effects (from the roof and the pod-creatures), anticipating the motif of confinement and the creatures' resemblance to sweat droplets. The general use of half-lighting and the gradual prevalence of nighttime over daytime settings ominously suggests the triumph of hostile forces, but darkness in the movie has a second, equally important part to play. Many shots are lit from below so that characters project huge shadows. They emerge as double entities at some points; at others back-lighting reduces them to silhouettes, emphasising the pods' function of duplication and erasure respectively. And once again this effect is written into the script as a collective social change.

All these modifications tie in consistently with Al La Valley's argument that the three key figures in making the movie sharpened its engagement with social issues. The scriptwriter Daniel Mainwaring introduced Becky's change, thereby excluding romantic redemption, and also strengthened Miles' role as a commentator by giving him key lines such as: 'In my practice I see how people have allowed their humanity to drain away.'[38] Don Siegel's main preoccupation was a resistance to systems and the producer Walter Wanger declared in a letter that the movie was to be a 'plea against conformity'.[39] Not only was the social urgency of the novel's plot strikingly increased in the 1956 movie; the latter also became more overtly political. In the novel the action of the pods is explained in some detail using the analogy of cell plasma. The necessary reduction of these lines to a bald statement by the psychiatrist in the movie puts a strikingly different slant on things: 'They're taking you over cell for cell, atom for atom.' As Nora Sayre recognised, the coincidence of biological and political meaning in the term 'cell' (and the possible glance – again through running – at the arms race) charges the statement with added connotations of subversion.[40] Even more important were the antithetical oppositions noted in the discussion so far. Peter Biskind rightly argues that 'the idea of the alien was profoundly influenced by the Manichean Us/Them habit of thought that was an occupational hazard of the cold war battle of ideas'.[41] For that reason when dealing with the fantasy fiction and films of the fifties at any rate, Thomas H. Keeling was mistaken in trying to keep the Gothic and Science Fiction genres apart while at the same time identifying characteristics common to both modes, in particular the notion that characters are driven by external forces and the view of the alien as evil.[42]

The evocation of the alien, as we have seen, depends for much of its effect on an interplay between extremes of familiarity and strangeness, an uncertainty in the focalisers of scenes, and on the gradual erosion of any safe areas, whether emotional or geographical. That is why the transformation of Becky adds so much to the bleakness of Siegel's movie. Although the narratives raise questions about human identity, and the nature of the body, they also have a crucial political dimension in depicting the individual's estrangement from a group which becomes transformed into a mindless production line for the pods. The general anxieties of Finney's novel grow, for Richard Gid Powers, out of the former's romantic traditionalism. He argues convincingly that Finney belongs in a line of nostalgic fantasists who express their misgivings about social and industrial expansion as the loss of cherished values such as the sense of a local community.[43] In contrast the 1978 movie of *The Invasion* shows a San Francisco which has been described as a 'catalogue of images of contemporary urban anxiety'.[44] The many street and corridor scenes underline the routine lack of contact between the citizens, so that the pods' effect simply increases what is already there rather than bringing about a reversal. Secondly, the pods are given an increased physical presence. The roof garden scene (equivalent to the greenhouse episode in the first version) is much more explicit in showing a travesty birth where the figures move and make sounds. Despite these changes the result is not necessarily to bring about a corresponding increase in horror.

The main problem with Philip Kaufman's 1978 remake can be exemplified through two scenes. At an early point in the film the protagonist Michael, a city health inspector played by Donald Sutherland, looks out of his window and sees a row of cars parked neatly along the kerb. The scene is more characteristic of Santa Mira and so it is as if Michael (and the viewer) is looking out of the film's diegetic frame on to mid-fifties small-town America. Again early in the film Michael is driving through San Francisco with his assistant when a man rushes in front of the car shouting 'Help! Help! they're coming . . . You're next . . . They're already here!' The man is none other than Kevin McCarthy who played Miles in the 1956 version. Accordingly when he is knocked down and killed the event carries no emotional plausibility because it signals the conclusion of the first movie and the point of departure for the second. We are thus placed in a position which has been summarised by Fredric Jameson as follows:

> our awareness of the pre-existence of other versions . . . is now a constitutive and essential part of the film's structure; we are now . . . in 'intertextuality' as a deliberate, built-in feature of the aesthetic effect and as the operator of a new connotation of 'pastness' and pseudohistorical depth.[45]

The awareness which Jameson locates is constantly heightened by the countless cinematic allusions in the 1978 movie. The reviewer Pauline Kael noted as much when she stated that 'for the opening third of the picture, almost every scene has a verbal or visual gag built into it'.[46] The general result is not quite as humorous she suggests. Rather it creates an overall effect of pastiche and formal introversion. Hence the film delights at toying with different levels of illusion. The psychiatrist is now played by Leonard Nimoy, who played the role of Mr Spock in *Star Trek*; a poster of Spock adorns the wall of the bookshop where Nimoy first appears. The action at many points thus degenerates into the familiar game of spot the allusion and even the ending becomes not so much a matter of suspense as curiosity: how will the transformation of Michael's lover be shown and who has survived the process? Theoretically the film goes one step further than Siegel in showing the protagonist as a humanoid; the last scene being a close-up on Michael's (Donald Sutherland) mouth as he shrieks inhumanly. But there have been so many allusions to science fiction and horror films that the shock of the alien becomes dissipated into a practical problem of presentation.

As we have seen, the narratives of alien invasions repeatedly enact a process of transformation. Wells' *War of the Worlds* sets the pattern by evoking an initial situation of suburban order which is rudely disrupted by the Martians' landings. Disorder then gradually extends outwards until it looks as if it might engulf Britain and the whole world. *The Body Snatchers* weaves a powerful variation on the pattern by making aliens indistinguishable visually from familiar human beings. The narrator / protagonist's estrangement is given a panicky edge by sheer uncertainty. Don Siegel then tightened up the political implications of the action and heightened the panic even further as an explicit warning to the audience. The 1978 movie version starts from a premise of urban alienation which undermines the theme by excluding the transformations from known to unknown whereby the protagonist becomes displaced from a familiar environment. Abel Ferrara's 1993 *Body Snatchers* returns to the use of a confined setting in an Alabama military base and, as a post-Cold War narrative, avoids political specifics. Thus Mark Kermode declares: 'Here, the fear is amorphous, shapeless and ultimately undefinable . . . This is paranoia in its purest form, a kind of free-floating existentialist panic.'[47] Now threat is no longer limited to town, city or country, but is dispersed across the whole natural environment. In all these cases, however, the alien is narrated as coming from outside the boundaries of the known and threatening the familiar by becoming unnervingly indistinguishable from it.

Notes

1 P. K. Dick, *The Father-Thing* (London: Victor Gollancz, 1989), p. 109.
2 *Ibid.*, p. 102.
3 J. W. Campbell, Jr, *The Thing* (London: Tandem, 1966), p. 11.
4 *Ibid.*, pp. 36, 69.

5 M. Rose, *Alien Encounters: Anatomy of Science Fiction* (Cambridge, MA: Harvard University Press, 1981), p. 179.

6 Campbell, *The Thing*, p. 64.

7 R. L. Stevenson, *The Wrong Box: The Body-Snatcher*, Tusitala edition (London: Heinemann, n.d.), p. 189.

8 During filming the project was known as *The Body Snatchers*. Other titles considered were *Better Off Dead*, *Sleep No More*, *Evil in the Night*, and *World in Danger*. The final title was chosen by United Artists (Al La Valley, ed., *Invasion of the Body Snatchers* (New Brunswick and London: Rutgers University Press, 1989), p. 26. A helpful survey of American invasion fantasies is given in Eric Mottram's 'Out of Sight but Never Out of Mind' in his *Blood on the Nash Ambassador* (London: Hutchinson Radius, 1989), pp. 138–80. J. P. Telotte gives a valuable analysis of the 1945 movie *The Body Snatchers* in 'A Photogenic Horror: Lewton does Robert Louis Stevenson', *Literature Fiction Quarterly* 10.1 (1982), pp. 25–37.

9 J. Finney, *The Body Snatchers* (London: Eyre and Spottiswoode, 1955), p. 9. The novel was next published by Award Books under the title *Invasion of the Body Snatchers*, probably as a movie tie-in.

10 *Ibid.*, p. 43.

11 *Ibid.*, p. 55.

12 The symbolism of the house as body is discussed in Chapter 1 (G) of Freud's *Interpretation of Dreams*, and within the Gothic context in Chapter 1 of Victor Sage's *Horror Fiction in the Protestant Tradition* (London: Macmillan, 1988). The analogies between windows and bodily orifices, and the sexual symbolism of stairs are discussed in Freud's *Introductory Lectures on Psychoanalysis*, Chapter 10.

13 *The Body Snatchers*, p. 84.

14 *Ibid.*, pp. 100–1.

15 *Ibid.*, p. 103.

16 N. Steffen-Fluhr, 'Women and the Inner Game of Don Siegel's *Invasion of the Body Snatchers*' in Al La Valley, ed., *Invasion of the Body Snatchers* (New Brunswick and London: Rutgers University Press, 1989), p. 208 (article orginally published in *Science-Fiction Studies* 11 (July 1984), pp. 139–51.

17 P. K. Dick, *The Cosmic Puppets* (London: Grafton, 1986), pp. 8, 11.

18 P. Rieff, *The Triumph of the Therapeutic* (Harmondsworth: Penguin, 1973), p. 59.

19 *The Body Snatchers*, p. 108.

20 M. Beard, 'Jack Finney', in David Coward and Thomas L. Wymer, eds., *Twentieth-Century American Science Fiction Writers* (Detroit: Gale, 1981), vol. I, p. 183.

21 *Astounding Science Fiction* (September 1955) p. 152. Glen M. Johnson usefully discusses the different endings to the serial and novel versions of Finney's narrative and to the 1956 movie in his article 'We'd Fight . . . We Had To: *The Body Snatchers* as Novel and Film', *Journal of Popular Culture* 13.1 (1979) 5–14.

22 R. A. Heinlein, *The Puppet Masters* (Boston: Gregg Press, 1979), pp. 19–20.

23 *Ibid.*, p. 53.

24 H. Bruce Franklin, *Robert A. Heinlein: America as Science Fiction* (New York and Oxford: Oxford University Press, 1980), pp. 99, 98.

25 *The Puppet Masters*, p. 218.

26 J. Brosnan, *Future Tense: The Cinema of Science Fiction* (London: Macdonald and Jane's, 1978), p. 127.

27 Letter from Jack Finney, 7 July 1993. Despite such insistence from Finney,

Arthur Le Gracy argues that novel and movie dramatise the fear of imposture in the period ('*Invasion of the Body Snatchers*: A Metaphor for the Fifties', *Literature Film Quarterly* 6.3 (1978), pp. 285–92).

28 M. Starkey, *The Devil in Massachusetts: A Modern Enquiry into the Salem Witch Trials* (London: Robert Hales, 1952), p. 11. It was this work which inspired Arthur Miller's oblique condemnation of the anti-Communist witch-hunts in *The Crucible*.

29 W. Chambers, *Witness* (South Bend: Regnery, 1979), p. 331.

30 Beard, 'Jack Finney', p. 183.

31 One such foreword drew explicit connections with the earlier: 'A few years ago, people were frightened by my "War of the Worlds" broadcast, which, I must say, seems pretty tame considering what has happened to our world since. When I think of the A-bombs, the H-bombs, the fall-outs . . . surely even Nature is behaving strangely, and no phenomenon seems impossible today' (La Valley, *Invasion*, p. 134).

32 J. P. Rawlins, 'Confronting the Alien: Fantasy and Anti-Fantasy in Science Fiction Film and Literature', in George E. Slusser, Eric S. Rabkin and Robert Scholes, eds., *Bridges to Fantasy* (Carbondale: Southern Illinois University Press, 1982), p. 161.

33 N. Sayre, *Running Time: Films of the Cold War* (New York: Dial Press, 1982), p. 199.

34 P. Biskind, *Seeing is Believing: How Hollywood Taught Us to Stop Worrying and Love the Fifties* (New York: Pantheon, 1983), p. 138.

35 See. D. Peary, *Cult Movies: A Hundred Ways to Find the Reel Thing* (London: Vermilian, 1982), p. 155.

36 La Valley, *Invasion*, p. 88.

37 E. Burke, *A Philosophical Enquiry into the Origin of our Ideas of the Sublime and the Beautiful*, ed. J. T. Boulton (London: Routledge and Kegan Paul, 1958), p. 58 (Part 2, Section III).

38 La Valley, *Invasion*, p. 82.

39 Ibid., p. 163. This Motif in Siegel's films has been discussed by Charles T. Gregory ('The Pod Society Versus the Rugged Individuals', *Journals of Popular Film* 1.1 (1972), pp. 3–14).

40 La Valley, *Invasion*, p. 88; Sayre, *Running Time*, p. 201.

41 Biskind, *Seeing is Believing*, p. 111.

42 T. H. Keeling, 'Science Fiction and the Gothic', in George E. Slusser, George R. Guffey, and Mark Rose, eds., *Bridges to Science Fiction* (Carbondale: Southern Illinois University Press, 1980), pp. 109, 113.

43 R. Gid Powers, Introduction, *The Body Snatchers* (Boston: G. K. Hall, 1976), pp. viii–ix. Powers' argument helps to explain the special value carried by the past in Finney's other fiction.

44 G. M. Johnson, 'A Note on *Invasion of the Body Snatchers*, 1978 Version', *Journal of Popular Culture* 13.1 (1979), p. 15.

45 F. Jameson, *Postmodernism: Or, the Cultural Logic of Late Capitalism* (London and New York: Verso, 1991), p. 20. Jameson is discussing a version of James M. Cain's *Double Indemnity* (1944) but his comments could apply to any remake.

46 P. Kael, 'Pods', in *When the Lights Go Down* (London: Marion Boyars, 1980).

47 M. Kermode, 'Review: *Body Snatchers*', *Fangoria* 128 (1993), p. 73.

Postcolonial Gothic: Ruth Prawer Jhabvala and the Sobhraj case

Gothic motifs are exceptionally prevalent in postcolonial fiction, even from very different locations.[1] Classic postcolonial transformations of Gothic emanate from the Caribbean (Jean Rhys's *Wide Sargasso Sea*), Africa (Bessie Head's *A Question of Power*) and India (Ruth Prawer Jhabvala's *Heat and Dust*). In Canada, Gothic is almost the norm: whether in Margaret Atwood's comic *Lady Oracle*, or Anne Hébert's *Héloïse* (the Quebecois tale of a vampire who haunts the Paris Métro), or Bharati Mukherjee's Asian-Canadian *Jasmine*. Unsurprisingly, when the heroine of Alice Munro's *Lives of Girls and Women* thinks of writing about Jubilee, Ontario, she promptly chooses to begin a Gothic novel. Nearer home, ghosts wander the pages of Paul Scott's *Raj Quartet*, and J. G. Farrell begins *Troubles*, the first volume in his *Empire Trilogy*, in a decaying Great House, complete with mysteriously fading heroine, demonic cats, and ever-widening crack in the external wall. Further afield, what is Isak Dinesen doing on a coffee farm in Kenya in 1931 – but writing *Seven Gothic Tales*?

It is Dinesen's activity which first raises the question of the ideological consequences of the transfer of a European genre to a colonial environment. As Eric O. Johannesson was swift to note, Dinesen creates a fictional Africa which is the counterpart of the eighteenth-century European feudal world of her tales. Setting out into an African forest, she writes: 'You ride out into the depths of an old tapestry, in places faded and in others darkened with age, but marvellously rich in green shades.'[2] (One suspects the Kikuyu did not share her view of a leopard as 'a tapestry animal'.[3]) In a more self-conscious vein, V. S. Naipaul, telling a tale of horrid murder in the Caribbean in *Guerrillas*, deliberately sets out to argue that life imitates art, in the postcolonial subject's awareness that 'reality' is defined elsewhere, and that postcolonial existence is scripted according to Western paradigms. *Guerrillas* opens in thoroughly Eurocentric fashion: 'After lunch Jane and Roche left their house on the Ridge to drive to Thrushcross Grange.'[4] As readers we are therefore immediately invited to consider whether we are dealing with 'real' people, or with characters in a novel – Jane Eyre and Rochester – and, as the pair descend from the 'Heights' of the Ridge to the Grange, whether they are moving across a physical reality (here, an unnamed Caribbean island) or from one Gothic text to another – from *Jane Eyre* to *Wuthering Heights*. Naipaul highlights here the tendency of the West to textualise the colonial, to transform the Other into a set of codes and discourses which can be recuperated into its own system of recognition, as hegemonic discourse accomplishes its project of endlessly replicating itself. In this particular Gothic, Jane supplies the liberal, sadomasochistic victim to the occupants of the Grange (now a revolutionary commune). At the close (following rape, sodomy, mutilation, and murder) the men write Jane out of the story, denying her very existence on the island. As a transplanted Eyre, this particular Jane's return to the Caribbean to exorcise her colonial guilts leads to the total annulling of her story, a revenge on the part of the silenced postcolonial which positions him, uncomfortably, in the role of the villain.

As this example demonstrates, the notion of generic transfer commonly intersects with questions of intertextuality.[5] Postcolonial writers frequently begin from a self-conscious project to revise the ideological assumptions created by Eurocentric domination of their culture, to rewrite the fiction of influential predecessors and therefore to deconstruct conventional images of the colonial situation. Intertextual strategies may work by repositioning the text in relation to its point of origin, or by providing revisions of canonical texts. Such rewritings can, of course, give the impression that non-metropolitan culture can only rework, has no creativity of its own, and is dependent for its materials on the 'centre'. Jean Rhys adroitly counters this charge of parasitism on a so-called 'original' by positioning the events of *Wide Sargasso Sea* before those of *Jane Eyre*, as a 'post-dated prequel'[6] rather than a sequel. She therefore enjoins future readers of Brontë to envisage nineteenth-century Britain as parasitic on its colonies, just as Bronte's heroine depends on both a colonial inheritance, *and* the warning example of her predecessor in the negotiation of her own independence.

Nonetheless, the problem which confronts the reader of *Wide Sargasso Sea*, as of *Guerrillas*, is that of revision as redemonisation, as the clock turns back to horror stories of 'barbarism' rather than forward to confront the legacies of Imperialism in the present. In producing the untold story of the first Mrs Rochester, Rhys deliberately exacerbates the Gothic mode of her predecessor, supplying a conjure woman, descriptions of obeah, ghosts, omens, zombi-lore, and poisonous potions, as part of the process of reclaiming the first wife for West Indian culture. The description of Antoinette (Bertha) Mason *may* transform her from Jane

Eyre's 'Foul German spectre – the Vampyre',[7] but it merely substitutes the unblinking gaze, enslaved will, and loss of memory of the zombi in its place. Despite Rhys' attempt to reverse the Imperialist assumptions of the original, so that the first Mrs Rochester's tale is no longer silenced, her story becomes not so much 'untold' as 'unspeakable'.

The consequences of generic transfer in the 'naturalisation' of Gothic suggest the difficulty implicit in any counter-discourse – the danger of rein-scribing the norms of the dominant discourse within its own apparent con-testation, as (to quote Richard Terdiman): 'the contesters discover that the authority they sought to undermine is reinforced by the very fact of its having been chosen, as dominant discourse, for opposition'.[8] Rewritings, counter-texts, run the risk of slippage from oppositional to surreptitiously collusive positions. The most recent version of *Jane Eyre*, for example, Robbie Kidd's *The Quiet Stranger*, is so concerned to centre on the black revolutionary wife of Richard Mason, Antoinette's brother, that it trans-forms Jane Eyre herself into a witch, and Antoinette into a 'tomboy' with an equine fixation.[9]

In less narrowly intertextual style, Margaret Atwood's *Lady Oracle* features a heroine who writes Costume Gothics, exploiting the socially conditioned and manipulative nature of a genre which provides socially sanctioned stories for unliberated women. Atwood's project – to argue that the premises of Gothic are true, that men are out to kill women – rebounds, however, into historical Gothic as the parody spiritualism of her opening suddenly produces the ghost of the heroine's mother, as presage of danger. The process is uncomfortably reminiscent of that use of occultism which Patrick Brantlinger has termed 'Imperial Gothic', in which the ghosts of Empire come home to roost, following the protag-onist back from some 'farther shore' which may equally be construed as Empire or spirit world.[10] As a result, Atwood's parody of the norms of popular Gothic reinscribes some of the original conventions within its apparent contestation. Toni Morrison runs some of the same risks in *Beloved*, conflating Africa with the 'other side', though her amiguity is more productive. Under slavery the disembodied are a political reality. Those who do not own their own bodies will constitute space, time, and the future quite differently.[11] Under these circumstances, who is not a ghost?

Postcolonial Gothic is therefore Janus-faced. At its heart lies the unresolved conflict between the Imperial power and the former colony, which the mystery at the centre of its plot both figures and conceals. Its discourse therefore establishes a dynamic between the unspoken and the 'spoken for' – on the one hand, the silenced colonial subject rendered inadmissible to discourse, on the other, that discouse itself which keeps telling the story again and again on its own terms. As a European genre,

Gothic cannot unbind all its historical ties to the West. Conversely, its ability to retrace the unseen and unsaid of culture renders it peculiarly well adapted to articulating the untold stories of the colonial experience. Eve Kosofsky Sedgwick has analysed the Gothic emphasis on the 'unspeakable', both in the intensificatory sense of 'nameless horrors', and in the play of the narrative structure itself, with its illegible manuscripts, stories within stories, secret confessions, and general difficulty in getting the story told at all. As Sedgwick puts it, Gothic novels are 'like Watergate transcripts. The story does get through, but in a muffled form, with a distorted time sense, and accompanied by a kind of despair about any direct use of language.'[12] In her analysis a central privation of Gothic is that of language. When the linguistic safety valve between inside and outside is closed off, all knowledge becomes solitary, furtive, and explosive. As a result dire knowledge may be shared, but it cannot be acknowledged to be shared, and is therefore 'shared separately', as the barrier of unspeakableness separates those who know the same thing. This Gothic apartheid is almost a classic definition of Imperialism's hidden discourse – the collaboration in a surreptitious relationship, never openly articulated, which is that of coloniser and colonised. Again in Sedgwick's account, Gothic offers an image of language as live burial. The notion that one's life is a text in an incomprehensible language opens the possibility that one is being placed in another's text, interpreted as the figural realisation of another's consciousness, a figure in somebody else's dream. Naipaul's *Guerrillas* exploits this aspect of textualisation, of being 'spoken for', whereas *Wide Sargasso Sea* concentrates its attention on the unspeakable and the silenced.

It is possible, however, for a novel to exploit both strategies – to politicise Gothic by overcoming the taboo on speaking, without slippage into the dominant discourse. A symptomatic reading of Ruth Prawer Jhabvala's *Three Continents* is instructive. *Three Continents* is situated at the sharp end of the Gothic generic transfer, not least because of its Indian subject matter, and is also explicitly related to one of the West's more recent horror stories.

A strong strain of Gothic has been identified in the works of Jhabvala which feature demon lovers, mysterious Indian palaces with intricately concealed secrets, ruined forts, poison, willing victims, plus the eroticisation of spirituality, with gurus standing in for sinister monks, and ashrams for convents.[13] Jhabvala is, of course, influenced by eighteenth-century European literature. Her London University MA thesis concerned 'The Short-Story in England 1700–1753', and among other topics discussed the Oriental tale and the falseness of its 'East' which was based on preconceived literary notions. Jhabvala also lamented the prevalence of the tale of the 'unfortunate maiden fallen into the hands of a dusky seducer'.[14] This is nonetheless precisely the plot of *Three Continents*, in which Harriet Wishwell, the scion of a wealthy, if now declining, American clan, stands to inherit a fortune with her twin, Michael, on their twenty-first birthday. When the pair fall under the spell of the mysterious Rawul, one of Jhabvala's ambivalent guru figures, the horrible possibility looms that their legacy will pass swiftly through his hands and into those of his charismatic second-in-command, Crishi, Harriet's husband, whose sexual favours she shares with homosexual Michael and the Rawul's mistress, Rani. Like Atwood, Jhabvala conflates historical Gothic with the plot of modern Gothic. As defined by Joanna Russ,[15] the latter involves a young, shy, passive heroine, with absent or ineffectual parents and a friend or ally in the pale, bloodless 'Shadow Male'. She travels to an exotic setting, forms a connection with a dark, magnetic 'Supermale', finds herself up against 'Another Woman', and has to solve a 'Buried Ominous Secret', usually in modern Gothic a criminal activity centred on money. The plot generally ends in attempted murder. In *Three Continents* the exotic area is India; the persecuted Harriet is totally passive and after an initial ambivalence towards dark, super-phallic Crishi, becomes his sexual slave, disregarding sinister rumours. (There was, of course, a first wife with a nameless fate.) Rani features as the other woman. (She makes Harriet think of 'stories of intrigue and poison and other hidden deeds taking place in the harem' (199)[16] and has a child who may or may not be Crishi's adulterous offspring.) Harriet's family includes a conventionally vapid mother (in this case also fully occupied with a girlish lesbian affair) and a pathologically spendthrift father, neither of whom is much help to her. The pallid Michael fulfils the textbook role of the Shadow Male, apparently representing the security of childhood, but actually inducting Harriet into the Rawul's 'Sixth World' movement. The Buried Ominous Secret turns out to be an international smuggling ring, masterminded by Crishi who transports jewels and *objets d'art* across borders, under cover of the movement. Throughout the novel the reader is afforded glimpses of the real situation, with recurrent dark hints and a veritable anthology of half-told stories and half-heard conversations in the wings, creating an atmosphere of sustained menace. Elements of historical Gothic are self-consciously introduced. At one point the villain binds Harriet to him, forcing her body to move in unison with his 'as if my body obeyed him more than it did me' (59) until she breaks free and flees. (The context is a three-legged race.) She is later seduced by Crishi in the emblematic locale of the ruined Linton house, through the windows of which the pair have been previously peering. A group of 'bhais', the Rawul's henchmen, rival any eighteenth-century group of *banditti*, and Rani takes to haunting Harriet's bedroom by night, 'her reflection ghostlike in the mirror' (304) like some madwoman in the attic. After a journey through 'uncharted regions' (366) sealed in a small chamber lit by a ghostly blue light (the sleeping coupe of an Indian train) the novel ends with the ascent of a winding stair to a crenellated roof terrace where all is revealed by the villain. The twist upon the tale lies in Harriet's transition from victimhood to complicity. At the close, Harriet joins with her demon-lover to conceal Michael's murder and to forge the suicide note which will ensure that his fortune passes to them.

As a smuggler of art objects Crishi is explicitly connected to the cynical and exploitative transfer of art from one culture to another, in his case via the plundering of the East to the benefit of the West. The questions raised by generic transfer are therefore thematised within the action itself. Artistic transfer is nonetheless a two-way traffic, as Jhabvala's exploitation of European conventions in a postcolonial environment demonstrates. Is this use of Asian Gothic merely a Eurocentric, Orientalist strategy, to adopt Edward Said's terminology?[17] Or does it offer the post-colonial writer opportunities to criticise European textual and ideological practices by strategies unavailable to the realist novel? Does it merely contribute to the already abundant literature of India as horror story? Or can it illuminate the roots of violence in the postcolonial situation?

The answer to these questions depends upon an informed aware-ness of another story within the novel. Jhabvala indicates the relation-ship of the 'unspoken' of Gothic with the activity of 'speaking for' of culture, by firmly connecting the 'unspeakable' nature of events (dark hints, half-told stories) to a story which has already been told so often as to be recognisably a product of Western hegemonic discourse – that of Charles Sobhraj, the Asian serial killer, who is the model for Crishi.

In the 1970s Sobhraj left a trail of bodies across India, Thailand, and Nepal; he specialised in smuggling gems for which he needed a constant supply of fresh passports, bought or stolen from overlanders on the hippy trail. He then graduated to the *modus operandi* of a 'drug and rob' man, first surreptitiously administering laxatives and other drugs, then 'medi-cines' which reduced his victims to helplessness. Many of his targets, like Harriet and Michael, were seeking mystic enlightenment in the East. While planning to rob the jewellery store in Delhi's Imperial Hotel in 1976, Sobhraj was finally caught when he drugged an entire package tour of sixty French graduate engineers, whose instantaneous and simultane-ous collapse in their hotel lobby finally aroused suspicion. Sobhraj was at various points arrested and gaoled in Kabul, Teheran, Greece, and Paris, and made several daring escapes, notably following an unnecessary ap-pendectomy, from which he bore identifying scars. A man of considerable charisma, he often gained the sympathy of his victims and accomplices by tales of his awful youth (as Crishi does with Harriet). His main female accomplice, a young Canadian, appears to have been kept in total sexual thrall to him. Other parallels with the fictitious Crishi are legion. Both men spend part of their youth in Bombay (110), live by jewel smuggling, and participate in murder. The hotel jewellery shop is the locus of mystery in *Three Continents*. Crishi goes in for martial exercises (for Sobhraj it was karate), has abdominal scars (139), prison sentences in Teheran and elsewhere (139), and has carried out gaolbreaks (176). Both Sobhraj and Crishi relish media exposure, the former after his arrest, the latter in connection with the 'Sixth World' movement. At the close, when Harriet is looking for Michael, she encounters Paul, one of the Westerners, who is clearly very unwell. Like others in the group (353), he has given Crishi his passport and is begging for its return. It is an exact replication of the means by which Sobhraj surrounded himself with couriers, targets, and accomplices.

Despite the fact that Charles Sobhraj is still in gaol in India and that there are therefore legal impediments to the enterprise, his story has already been told several times, in two works of 'faction', one since revised and updated, in a TV mini-series, and in various newspapers and magazines, quite sufficient to suggest that the Sobhraj case is one of those 'Orientalist' horror stories which the West likes to repeat.[18] From the first the story served ideological purposes. In India it broke at an opportune moment during the Emergency Rule powers of Indira Gandhi, when the Maintenance of Internal Security Act meant that anyone suspected of 'subversion' could be gaoled indefinitely. In India the international dimension of the story was insisted upon:

> India's newspapers, subdued and fearful under Indira Gandhi's dictatorial powers, relished a story that had no political overtones. The 'notorious gang' and 'international killers' were profiled endlessly, mug shots decorating Sunday feature pages.[19]

In the West the evolution of the story was classically hegemonic, its political complexities steadily watered down in favour of a stereotypically Orientalist tale. One of the first in the field, Thomas Thompson, in his faction, *Serpentine*, drew explicit parallels between the events of Sobhraj's life and the dismantling of the French colonial Empire. As the illegitimate offspring of a Vietnamese mother and an Indian father, born in Saigon when it was under Japanese ocupation, but Vichy French administration, Sobhraj's early experiences included kidnap by the Viet Minh, rescue by the British, abandonment by his mother who married a French army officer, and life on the streets of Saigon. Reclaimed, he moved to

Dhakar, French West Africa, then France, whence he ran away by ship to Saigon, only to be promptly sent to Bombay by his father in a vain attempt to gain Indian citizenship. Stateless, institutionalised at several points, Sobhraj shuttled between countries until adulthood. Thompson's portrayal of him as a casualty of Empire, lacking roots, security, and identity, ends on a note that appears to have offered Jhabvala the cue for the American opening of her novel. In gaol in India Sobhraj was apparently considering his future:

> He required a country in which he was neither known nor wanted by police, one in which riches abounded, one whose boundaries were easy to traverse illegally, one whose residents were generous with attention and applause. At last report, the serpentine roads of destiny – he believed – would lead him to the United States.[20]

Other treatments of the story, however, tended to minimise the post-colonial background. In *Bad Blood* Richard Neville and Julie Clarke read Sobhraj in terms of a paradigm of early rejection and deprivation. Neville, a veteran of the *Oz* 'Schoolkids Edition' obscenity trial had no great reverence for authority, and went to Delhi to interview Sobhraj with a theory 'of Charles as a child of colonialism, revenging himself on the counter-culture'.[21] He concluded, however, that Sobhraj's claims to anti-Imperialist motivation were groundless, and that the story was that of an individual of great potential, whose life resembled the form of Shakespearean tragedy. Updating the book ten years later as a TV tie-in, Neville revealed that his relationship with his co-author had been severely threatened by their involvement in the case, and that they had come close to being polarised into victim and accomplice. Julie Clarke's sympathies had remained with the victims; Neville however admitted that when interviewing Sobhraj he came to feel 'like a conspirator'.[22] The TV mini-series (*Shadow of the Cobra*) developed the hint, focusing its plot on the threat to one romantic relationship (two young journalists) and transforming Sobhraj from child of colonialism to diabolical villain. In an artistic trajectory which says much for the extent to which the rage for the Raj has been transformed into the redemonisation of the East, the role of Sobhraj was taken by Art Malik, veteran of *The Jewel in the Crown*, *The Far Pavilions*, and *Passage to India*. The blurb to the reissued tie-in said it all: 'An audience with psychopathic mass murderer Charles Sobhraj. It was like having supper with the devil.' Reviewers concurred that Sobhraj was a 'plausible, Bruce Lee style, Asian fiend'[23] operating in, the 'dangerous jungle'[24] of Asia. There, this 'diabolically charismatic'[25] villain took his victim on a 'descent into hell'.[26] The evolution of the various accounts shows the West writing and rewriting Sobhraj into the norms of the snakey Oriental villain, with socio-economic readings excised in favour of (at best) popular psycho-analysis, and (at worst) elements of *Vathek*, Milton's Satan, and Fu Man Chu.

In contrast, Jhabvala's understanding of the socio-economic dimension of the story is already evident in her first attempt at the theme. In her short story 'Expiation', the plot centres upon a *nouveau riche* Indian family who have made a fortune in textiles, and their son's fatal involvement with Sachu, a criminal from a deprived background. Sachu's target for kidnap, ransom, and murder is the child of an Indian military family, described as light-skinned educated gentry who speak Hindi with an accent 'like Sahibs'.[27] Arrested, Sachu boasts of his philosophy to the press, much as Sobhraj did. Commentators on the Sobhraj case have frequently expressed bewilderment at the lack of motivation for many of the crimes. In 'Expiation', however, the crime is less the product of a fiendish Oriental torturer than a revenge across both class and race, against the preceding Imperial norms (the Sahibs) and their replication in a newly industrialised India.

The account chimes with recent research on the serial killer, which contextualises his motivation in socio-economic terms. Anthropologist Elliott Layton has argued that serial killers are intensely class conscious and obsessed with status. The majority are adopted, illegitimate, or institutionalised in youth, and seek a sense of identity in international celebrity. Typically their victims are drawn from a social category which is some social bands above the killer, and the prime mission is to wreak revenge on the established order. (Ted Bundy, for example, took the most valuable 'possessions' of the American middle class, their beautiful and talented University women.) In 'Expiation' the fictitious Sachu wreaks revenge simultaneously on the Eurocentric army officers *and* the new entrepreneurial class via the deaths of both their offspring. For Layton, as for Jhabvala, serial killers are the dark consequences of the social and economic formations that pattern our lives. Killings of this nature are a protest against a perceived exclusion from society, and constitute a form of utterance on the part of those who have looked at their lives and pronounced them unliveable.

> The killings are thus also a form of suicide note (literally so with most mass murderers, who expect to die before the day or week is out; metaphorically so for most serial murderers, who sacrifice the remainder of their lives to the 'cause'), in which the killer states clearly which social category has excluded him.[28]

The act itself is therefore the 'note', an unspeakable crime which is nonetheless a message that society must learn to read. Unlike mass murderers, serial killers tend to want to live to tell their stories and bask in fame. Once society has read the message the story will be retold by press and media, and become a means to identity. Two other factors cited by Layton in the formation of the serial killer have a bearing on *Three Continents*: first, he must be inculcated with a dream or ambition which society betrays; secondly, is the necessary existence of cultural forms that can mediate killer and victim in a special sense, ridding victims of humanity and killer of responsibility. (Layton cites the social validation of violent identity in modern films, television, and fiction.)

In retelling the story Jhabvala's daring strategy is to recast it in Gothic mould – apparently redundantly. As Thompson remarked, the case already 'contained enough sex and betrayal and intrigue to fill the darkest scenario'.[29] By exploiting the silences of Gothic, however, Jhabvala avoids contributing to the social validation of the killer. In addition, she is able to repoliticise the story, revealing its horrors without stereotypical demonisation by insisting on the interrelationship of the Gothic 'unspeakable' and the 'spoken for' of culture, the discourse from which the postcolonial is excluded, and into which he feels that he can break only by violence.

Where the Sobhraj case was used in India as a diversion from the increasingly dictatorial nature of the political settlement, Jhabvala supplies a public political dimension by the introduction of the Rawul's militaristic 'Sixth World' movement, which dehumanises its followers and legitimises brutality on the basis of a vaguely transcendental cult. Ostensibly devoted to the unification of the globe by 'Transcendental Internationalism', the Rawul plans its transformation into a 'stateless, casteless, countryless' (201) world by transcending not so much spiritual as national and political bounds, and with them 'the tiny concepts, geographical or other, of an earlier humanity' (241). Linda Bayer-Berenbaum has connected the resurgence of twentieth-century Gothic with the waning of sixties cults, arguing that both movements were motivated by the search for an expanded and intensified consciousness. She therefore likened the Gothic revival to

> a variety of religious cults that have grown in popularity, be they Christian fundamentalist, Hari Krishna, the Sufis, or most recently, the Moonies. Unlike these movements though, Gothicism asserts that transcendence is primarily evil.[30]

In *Three Continents* the Gothic 'secret' provides an ironic revelation of the real import of the Rawul's transcendental activities, in the political world, and the extent to which they operate as a legitimising cover for Crishi, the excluded. Natural and political boundaries *are* crossed, but for criminal reasons. The movement towards being citizens of the world depends heavily for its day to day activities upon stolen passports. The plan to unite the best of all civilisations translates into the pillaging of material artefacts. Harriet and Michael throw off Western materialism, only for it to come back to haunt them from the Third World. Mobility is the mark of both the Western truthseeker – and the serial killer. Just as the latter links the culturally spoken and the unspeakable, so Crishi reveals in his actions the revenge of the excluded. Sobhraj, the stateless exile, killed those whose wilful deracination parodied his own state, just as Crishi, who has had disinheritance forced upon him, sees to it that his condition is shared.

In addition to reflecting the Rawul's project in a dark mirror, so the Gothic structure dramatises Harriet's surreptitious slippage from a countercultural to a collusive position, from victim to accomplice, and implicitly from a readerly to a writerly role. At the beginning of the novel Harriet's stunned silence, as the Rawul takes over, is such as to make her almost a voyeur, watching her story unfold and guessing its outcome from the same hints available to the reader. Again and again the text tells us that Harriet can get no explanations from the men: 'What was it all about? Who were they, and why had they come? I waited for Michael to tell me, but he had no time to tell me anything. "You'll find out," was all he said' (15). The reader is thus brought into close affective proximity to events, while being simultaneously warned off from any uncritical suspension of disbelief. (Rani and Crishi present themselves as mother and son in an 'indifferent, believe-it-or-not way', 23.) Originally Harriet and Michael communicate wordlessly, the one often completing the other's thoughts (14). Crishi, however, appropriates their private language (specifically the term 'neti' meaning 'phoney') and deprives them of it. Though each is enjoying Crishi's sexual favours neither feels able to discuss the matter, converting their former spiritual communion into a shared secret, separately held. They welcome the noise of the swimming hole, because there 'conversation was impossible' (72). Later when Harriet shares her bed with Rani as well, she feels Michael 'willing me not to speak', so that the act remains 'unmentioned, rather than unmentionable' (215). The prohibition on speech even extends to Crishi's marriage proposal. He manages to propose by proxy, through Rani, so that Harriet becomes 'spoken for' without ever being spoken to.

The secret engagement and muffling of events is in strong contrast to the ever more publicity conscious Movement, which develops to the point at which 'interviews became the central activity of the house' (133). The Rawul has a tendency to convert all his utterances into speeches for public consumption, even to his small daughters (268). Linguistic and political structures evolve together. A chat with the Rawul becomes 'more in the nature of an audience. Everything around the Rawul was taking on more formality' (119). The movement to transcend all boundaries begins to use security guards and checkpoints and to beat up intruders. Even Michael's speech patterns change, so that instead of groping for thoughts he becomes brisk and unreflective: 'he no longer had to think . . . It was all there, all formulated' (223). Where Gothic mystery preserves the possibility of unvoiced stories, the Sixth World movement accretes everything to one public formulation, assisted by Anna Sultan, a journalist who provides their first 'major media exposure' (182). Harriet's difficulty in getting at her story contrasts with Anna's ease. Harriet notes that 'Everything I had only guessed at Anna seemed to know for sure' (138). Anna's account nonetheless includes a highly fanciful tale of the Rawul's initial encounter with Crishi, first in his dreams, then promptly discovered asleep in a poet's tomb. Over the others' protests Rani and Crishi endorse the story: ' "it's what the common reader wants," Crishi said. "Ask Harriet . . . Harriet liked it and she's a very common reader. You have to give them these sort of stories" ' (184). The incident provides an explicit comment on the way in which cultural formations function to legitimise exploitation. Anna Sultan herself turns the personal into the public, making her name with a daring profile of a Lebanese leader: 'daring because she had recorded his private along with his public activities, and had not drawn back from chronicling her own affair with him' (133). For Anna any assignment involves a love affair, which is speedily terminated when her story is finished. In Crishi, however, she meets her match as the post-colonial subject refuses textualisation except on his own terms. Crishi's only interest is the book which will publicise, authenticate, and create his identity, whereas Anna becomes personally attached and exploited in her turn – the fate which threatened Richard Neville at Sobhraj's hands. It is a telling image of the revenge of the excluded subject, who turns his own exploitation against his exploiters, to write his own social message.

It is not for nothing that the group are compared to a movie company (40); their lives are being swallowed up by public performance. The Rawul even stages appropriate public ceremonies to authenticate the movement. Harriet's wedding is briskly converted into a symbol of the synthesis of East and West, so symbolic indeed that Crishi spends the wedding night with Rani. The Rawul's idea that the new movement must find a mode of expression 'emancipated from all outworn forms' (143) backfires into irony however, as the couple symbolise their trans-cendent unity by sharing a loving-cup of a more sinister Gothic nature: 'This vessel had crossed deserts and dried-up riverbeds, had been secretly buried, lost for a generation or two, murdered for by sword and poison – it had a lot of history and legend behind it' (148). Appropriately the wine turns out to be spoiled, but Harriet swallows it almost as willingly as the legends. From perceiving herself with Michael as 'blank pages no one had ever written on' (259) Harriet is being steadily scripted into a public role.

A second ceremony which involves the public weighing of the Rawul against a pile of books, supposedly representing the wisdom of the ages, reveals both the totalising project of the movement, and its amorality. Like Crishi, the Rawul intends to textualise himself on his own terms. Michael had wanted to buy bound sets of volumes, but Crishi exercises a financial veto so that the Rawul is actually outweighed by a motley collection of tattered secondhand copies of the Bible, Plato, *The Tibetan Book of the Dead*, Carlos Castaneda, and Kierkegaard. The form of this attempt to appropriate all cultures to one universal meaning is ludicrously parodic; several volumes have to be removed from the scales to balance the Rawul. Significantly 'it was at Kierkegaard that the Rawul started to swing up' (279), appropriately given Kierkegaard's separation of the religious and the ethical spheres. The twins, however, react uncritically. For Michael the event is a summation of 'everything he had thought and read and experienced . . . It was all summed up for him in the pile of books on the one hand . . . and the Rawul on the other' (279). Meanwhile Harriet uses the mythologising process in order to put a high gloss on Crishi's activities, reflecting that 'it doesn't seem to matter that sometimes these gods don't behave too well, Venus running off with Mars, Krishna cheating on Radha – they still remain gods' (277–8).

Once on Indian soil, however, Crishi lives up to Krishna, his trickily elusive namesake, and naked power emerges from behind the myths and legends as the Rawul's movement swiftly modulates into a conventional political party. Far from transporting his followers into a boundless world, he moves the party into an airconditioned hotel, completely cut off from the outside world. Harriet and Michael are once more linguistically isolated – they speak no Indian languages. Michael's death is the direct result of the clash between the spoken and the unspoken. Impatiently he demands that the Rawul make a religious oration, rather than merely entertaining influential politicos: 'When's he going to speak?' 'He's got to speak,' he insists (331). Michael is slow to realise that (to quote Christine Brooke Rose):

> everyone knows that real power, whether political, economic, social, psychological or even mystical, functions silently and has no need of the semblance of speech, even though it never ceases to use that semblance to persuade that we participate.[31]

Secure in his power base, the Rawul dispenses with the mediating forms which had previously legitimised him. Instead his wife speaks, giving secret instructions in her own language to her henchmen who promptly remove Michael. The power to which Michael contributed by his rhetorical formulations is unleashed to silence him, and to consign him to the unspoken of Gothic.

In contrast, Harriet's movement into collusion with crime is rendered as a progression from the unspoken to the fully discursive, as Jhabvala demonstrates that the final horror is equally located in the process of 'speaking for'. When Michael implores Harriet to leave she replies that the Rawul's behaviour is only a temporary means to transcendent ends. '"He's *told* you. Do you think he likes all this any better than you do? No, he doesn't!" I at once answered myself, not giving Michael a chance to say yes' (334). Harriet is taken aback by the sudden silence which meets all her enquiries – the English of the hotel staff evaporates, the Rawul is so concerned with the universal that he cannot stoop to the particular to answer a personal question (348), the jeweller provides only partial and guarded replies. Yet she continues the process of speaking for Michael, pretending to her grandmother that he is on the other end of a phone line, and doing some very fast talking of her own.

Harriet's collusion with both the unspeakable and the textual is ambiguously dramatised at the close in the suicide note which she co-authors with the presumed killer. Harriet knows very well that Crishi's account of Michael's suicide is a lie. (The supposed suicide note is too badly spelled to be his.) She collaborates nonetheless in rewriting the note in more convincing fashion, revising a visibly false story to make it more believable. Revision becomes replication-as-falsity. Harriet would have been truer to the facts of murder if she had allowed the gaps and absences in the original to speak for themselves. No longer a common reader, Harriet has progressed to writing, writing as complicity and betrayal. She writes 'with ease' (383), almost with enjoyment, as if becoming Michael, speaking for him, constructing a fiction of defeated dreams as his motive.

> I said that I – that is, I, Michael – was going away because there was nothing in this world that was good enough for me . . . I said that if once you have these expectations – that is, of Beauty, Truth, and Justice – then you feel cheated by everything that falls short of them; and everything here – that is, here, in this world – does fall short of them. It is all neti, neti. (383)

As that last word indicates, Harriet uses their private language to authenticate a public document. Spiritual communion becomes the unspeakable. Framed to meet legal requirements, the note is multiply authored – ostensibly by Michael, actually by Harriet, partly at Crishi's dictation

– and is the product of multiple silencing, that of the postcolonial subject, that of the woman excluded from knowledge, and – fatally – of
the representative of the society which excluded them. At the close Crishi
has carried out the action which communicates a social message of
defeated hopes, while Harriet, writing as a male and at the same time
writing off a male, has produced a socially legitimising text. The note
therefore conceals – and sanctions – an act of violence.

This essay began with a question – whether the Gothic novel is an
accomplice in the process of Eurocentric textualisation of the East, or
whether it may serve to reveal the sources of violence in the colonial
encounter. In countercultural Harriet, who slips into the position of
accomplice, Jhabvala provides a searching investigation of the psycho-
pathology of power, the process of domination and its relation to mediating cultural forms. The complicity of the writer in generic manipulation
and transfer may indeed amount to collusion in violence and exploitation,
but may also reveal the bases of such violence in silencing and exclusion.
The duplicity of Gothic – its propensity for crossing boundaries, violating
taboos, transgressing limits, together with its sense of blockage, privation
and prohibition against utterance – makes it the perfect means to dramatise the horrors of the relationship between the social group which sanctions its actions by cultural forms, and the excluded from discourse, who
speak by deeds. The Gothic undermines the Rawul's pretensions to one-
ness and totalisation at the same time as it preserves the unspeakable
quality of the killer's actions. By its intertextual nature, its ability to translate from one text to another and back, it prevents the univocal from
holding sway. At the close, therefore, Jhabvala offers a multiple text, a
piece of writing which conceals a secret and reveals a silenced story,
which demonstrates the writer's complicity and (by highlighting issues
of fictionality) separates the reader from affective collusion. As the original suicide note showed, truth for the postcolonial writer may be
measured as much by its failure to represent itself as by its social production. What the Gothic does not say, its half-told stories, constitutes
the evidence of a contrary project undermining public formulations. By
preserving the unspoken within the text Jhabvala remains true to the
events of both political and social history.

Notes

This essay first appeared under the same title in *Modern Fiction Studies* 40, 1
(spring 1994).

1 Examples include Jean Rhys, *Wide Sargasso Sea* (London: Deutsch, 1966); Bessie
   Head, *A Question of Power* (London: Heinemann, 1973); Ruth Prawer Jhabvala,

Heat and Dust (London: John Murray, 1975); Margaret Atwood, *Lady Oracle* (Toronto: McLeland and Stewart, 1976); Anne Hébert, *Héloïse* (Paris: Seuil, 1980); Bharati Mukherjee, *Jasmine* (London: Virago, 1990); Alice Munro, *Lives of Girls and Women* (Toronto: McGraw Hill Ryerson, 1971); Isak Dinesen (Karen Blixen), *Seven Gothic Tales* (London: Putnam, 1934); V. S. Naipaul, *Guerrillas* (London: Deutsch, 1975); Paul Scott, *The Raj Quartet* (London: Heinemann, 1966–75); J. G. Farrell, *Troubles* (London: Cape, 1970); Toni Morrison, *Beloved* (New York: Knopf, 1987).

2 K. Blixen, *Out of Africa* (New York: Random House, 1938), p. 64. See Eric O. Johannesson, *The World of Isak Dinesen* (Seattle: University of Washington Press, 1961), p. 129.

3 *Out of Africa*, p. 65.

4 V. S. Naipaul, *Guerrillas* (London: Penguin Books, 1976), p. 9.

5 A point made by Neil Cornwell, *The Literary Fantastic* (London: Harvester-Wheatsheaf, 1990), Chapter 4.

6 The phrase is Susan Gubar's, quoted in Elizabeth Abel, Marianne Hirsch, and Elizabeth Langland (eds.), *The Voyage In* (Hanover and London: University Press of New England, 1983), p. 335.

7 C. Brontë, *Jane Eyre* (Oxford University Press, 1963), p. 341.

8 R. Terdiman, *Discourse/Counter-Discourse: The Theory and Practice of Symbolic Resistance in Nineteenth Century France* (Ithaca, New York: Cornell University Press, 1985), p. 65.

9 R. Kidd, *The Quiet Stranger* (Edinburgh: Mainstream, 1991).

10 P. Brantlinger, *Rule of Darkness: British Literature and Imperialism, 1830–1914* (Ithaca, New York: Cornell University Press, 1988), Chapter 8. Brantlinger notes that late Victorian and Edwardian spiritualist literature is filled with metaphors of exploration, immigration, conquest, and colonisation, tending to describe the passage to the 'other side' as a voyage of emigration. For a sympathetic and illuminating discussion of *Lady Oracle* as Gothic novel see Molly Hite, *The Other Side of the Story* (Ithaca, New York: Cornell University Press, 1989), Chapter 4.

11 I am indebted for this observation to Mary Gordon, 'Where Women Come In: Whose Realism Is It Anyway?', Belgian–Luxembourg American Studies Association Conference on Neo-Realism in Contemporary American Fiction, Ghent, 1991.

12 E. Kosofsky Sedgwick, *The Coherence of Gothic Conventions* (London: Methuen, 1986), p. 13.

13 L. Sucher, *The Fiction of Ruth Prawer Jhabvala: The Politics of Passion* (London: Macmillan, 1989).

14 R. Prawer, 'The Short-Story in England: 1700–1753', London University MA thesis, 1950, p. 42. (I am grateful to Ruth Prawer Jhabvala for permission to quote this passage.)

15 J. Russ, 'Somebody's Trying To Kill Me And I Think It's My Husband: The Modern Gothic', in Juliann E. Fleenor (ed.), *The Female Gothic* (Montreal: Eden Press, 1983), pp. 31–56.

16 R. P. Jhabvala, *Three Continents* (London: Penguin, 1988, first published 1987). Page references which follow quotations in parentheses are to the Penguin edition.

17 E. Said, *Orientalism* (New York: Pantheon, 1978).

18 One is reminded here of the 1830s revelations about *thuggee*, the murder of unsuspecting travellers by Hindu religious assassins, which provided a sensationalist focus for British reformist writing, and the first best-selling Anglo-Indian novel, Philip Meadows Taylor's *Confessions of a Thug* (1839). See Brantlinger, *Rule of Darkness*, Chapter 3.

19 T. Thompson, *Serpentine* (London: Macdonald, 1980), pp. 565–6.

20 *Serpentine*, p. 659.

21 R. Neville and J. Clarke, *Bad Blood: The Life and Crimes of Charles Sobhraj* (London: Pan, 1979), p. 350.

22 R. Neville and J. Clarke, *Shadow of the Cobra: The Life and Crimes of Charles Sobhraj* (London: Penguin Books, 1989), p. 343. For an account of the miniseries see *Radio Times*, 15–21 July 1989, pp. 4–5 and *The Listener*, 13 July 1989, p. 33.

23 *Books and Bookmen*, February 1980, p. 11.

24 *Far Eastern Economic Review*, 13 August 1976, p. 10.

25 *Books and Bookmen*, February 1980, p. 11.

26 *Bestsellers*, January 1980, p. 383.

27 R. P. Jhabvala, 'Expiation,' *New Yorker*, 10 October 1982, p. 49.

28 E. Layton, *Hunting Humans: The Rise of the Modern Multiple Murderer* (London: Penguin Books, 1989), pp. 26–7. First published as *Compulsive Killers* (New York University Press, 1986). I am grateful to Bruce Babington of the University of Newcastle upon Tyne for drawing this book to my attention, despite the sleepless night it occasioned.

29 *Serpentine*, p. xi.

30 L. Bayer-Berenbaum, *The Gothic Imagination* (London and Toronto: Associated University Presses, 1982), pp. 12–13.

31 C. Brooke-Rose, *A Rhetoric of the Unreal: Studies in Narrative and Structure, Especially of the Fantastic* (Cambridge University Press, 1983), p. 389.

Gothic convention and modernity
in John Ramsay Campbell's short fiction

John Ramsay Campbell, whose literary career started in 1964, is a very prolific writer who has recently achieved popular success together with a certain amount of critical recognition. His literary itinerary is worth studying since he wrote his first stories in the imitative vein with *The Inhabitants of the Lake* and *Less Welcome Tenants* where he borrows from H. P. Lovecraft's myth cycle of alien outer space entities. He then gradually got rid of Lovecraftian themes and began developing a more personal fictional universe, remarkably coherent and cohesive both in terms of subject matter and style. He has written over the last two decades several scores of short stories published in various collections. Among the most famous are *Demons by Daylight* (1973), *The Height of the Scream* (1976), *Dark Companions*, and, more recently *Scared Stiff* (1987)[1] – short stories with an explicit erotic content – and *Dark Feasts* (1987), a selection of old and new stories. While continuing to produce short stories, he has also increasingly shifted to novel writing with provocative works titled *The Doll Who Ate His Mother* (1976), *The Face That Must Die* (1979),[2] *The Nameless* (1981), *The Hungry Moon* (1986), and *Ancient Images* (1988) in which he partly reverts to the Lovecraftian vein, though not to Lovecraftian style.

My analysis is centred on the short stories, though I may refer to some novels when necessary. My starting point is a discussion of the label that has been given Ramsay Campbell's fiction by some critics, in particular Gary William Crawford who refers to it as 'urban Gothic'.[3] This statement is worth studying on various grounds. First, it raises a problem of definition because it uses a word that may have several meanings and concerns a more or less extended semantic field. French criticism, for instance, will tend to consider its historical acceptation as referring to a specific moment of literary production codified into a genre illustrated by such celebrated figures as Ann Radcliffe, Mathew Gregory Lewis, Charles Robert Maturin among others. On the other hand, many critics tend to label 'Gothic' any literature dealing with terror, horror, macabre related themes,[4] which leads them to include writers or works that have little in common with what Rosemary Jackson defines in her book as 'fantastic' or what the French critics call *littérature fantastique*.[5] If one chooses the restricted historical meaning of the word, which I consider more adequate, the association of 'urban' and 'Gothic' implies a relation between past and present, literary tradition and modernity which has to be defined.

Indeed, the very concept of 'urban Gothic' is paradoxical. Gothic literature in the tradition of Ann Radcliffe, furthered by Sheridan Le Fanu in *Uncle Silas* (1864) and by more modern writers such as Mervyn Peake, implies the predominant role of a certain topography whose specific features are dramatised. Indeed, as everbody knows, the setting of these stories is a castle, or its religious equivalent, an abbey, or a modernised version, the old aristocratic mansion. These places are generally in a state of decay and degradation and are characterised by rather complex architectural patterns: towers, staircases, winding passages, caves and labyrinths which constitute, by foregrounding darkness, mystery and potential threat, an ideal locus for the development of the narrative patterns inherent to the Gothic quest. This type of setting supposes also archaic, medieval social structures, strongly hierarchic modes of organisation and sets of values which are, in theory, incompatible with what the word 'urban' suggests – all the more so as 'Gothic' is usually connected with the notion of remoteness, isolation (a place set apart from the world), whereas 'urban' implies an integration in a complex framework of buildings and houses and streets; but also the notion of collectivity, community, and the cohabitation of diversified social groups. It thus supposes proximity and even promiscuity, the necessity or the urge to communicate with other people and, at times, the inability to do so, as is illustrated in Campbell's stories.

I attempt to explore this apparent contradiction and see to what extent these two notions are enlightening for an approach to Campbell's original contribution to the fantastic genre. Campbell relies on the Gothic tradition and consciously uses Gothic settings and trappings, Gothic motifs and characters. However, he manages to transform these elements by foregrounding a specific locus of terror (borrowing the main features from Liverpool, his native town), by developing character ambivalence and by subverting conventional narrative patterns. What thus prevails is a very disquieting mood, and a world outlook sustained by specific strategies and stylistic choices, which carries us far away from the conventional Gothic.

Campbell shares with Gothic novelists the idea that the *setting* has a predominant role and almost assumes the status of a character. He consciously uses Gothic settings almost in the same way as Ann Radcliffe (or Shirley Jackson) would use them. Let me mention briefly a few examples. Apart from the Lovecraftian locus in 'The Room in the Castle', we can note the role played by the mansion in 'Napier Court' where a ghost is supposed to possess an old Victorian house, pregnant with signs that testify to the overwhelming authority of the mother. The house in 'The Chimney' plays a similar part. We could also mention the haunted house of 'Call First' with its conventional creakings. There may be substitutes for this Gothic locus: for example in 'Lilith's' the shop where books and accessories on black magic and the occult are sold is steeped in darkness, suggestive of hidden forces. The abandoned church in 'The Hands', a shelter for an occult sect, leads into a network of corridors and passages where the protagonist gets trapped. In *The Doll Who Ate His Mother*, Campbell attributes Gothic features to the various houses through which the monstrous Chris Kelley is chased. He uses also other Gothic places: indeed, underground spaces play an important part in various stories as testified by such titles as 'The Cellars', and 'The Man in the Underpass'. The labyrinth motif is exploited and becomes a metaphor of the loss of landmarks linked with an impending identity crisis in 'The End of A Summer's Day' where a young woman visiting a cave steeped in darkness with her boyfriend, realises that the person whose hand she is grasping has turned into a frightened, groping blind man, clinging to her. The underground realm is here a metaphor for the potential dissolution of their relationship, adumbrating future degradation. However in many stories, as in 'The Cellars', it becomes a sheer locus of terror, a setting of darkness and isolation where nightmarish visions and monstrous creatures may become real.

As well as these Gothic settings, Campbell uses Gothic *characters* and *motifs*. The Gothic heroine, the young, pure, innocent (usually virgin) girl victimised in the Gothic novels is represented by such characters as Alma in 'Napier Court' who is characterised as a well-bred petit bourgeois girl, submissive to her parents' authority and reading her French class books. One of those is ironically called *Victimes du devoir*. Other feminine characters are given similar attributes. Indeed, Rose in *The Parasite* is a typical Gothic heroine who becomes gradually isolated, estranged and finally pursued by the evil characters, (including her husband) acting on behalf of Peter Grace the sorcerer. In the same way Clare in *The Doll Who Ate His Mother*, shares some features of the Gothic heroine: she is idealistic, innocent, romantic (she almost falls in love with her brother's monstrous murderer) and is also pursued at the end through the dark passages of the ultimate house where she finally realises that her potential lover is the criminal maniac himself. The other conventional Gothic figure present in Campbell's works is the all-powerful evil character represented by Peter Grace in *The Parasite* or John Strong in *The Doll Who Ate His Mother*, among others. Chris Kelley himself is an almost Dracula-like figure, the difference being that he is also a victim, an instrument in the hands of a powerful sorcerer. As I suggested, Campbell's stories also exploit Gothic narrative *structures*: the pattern of the quest or pursuit and the pattern of revenge and retribution. Many stories concern an isolated individual confronting danger. They emphasise a certain progressive development of the plot, punctuated by climactic moments, usually linked with the revelation of the supernatural element and the subsequent tragic fate of the protagonist. At times, however, instead of this gradual intrusion of the phenomenon, Campbell plunges the reader, from the outset, into an atmosphere of terror which he steadily intensifies up to the end.

This strategy implies a difference from the traditional Gothic ending. There is no rational explanation given of the supernatural phenomena (as happens in Ann Radcliffe's novels), neither is there a cathartic release. Characters as well as readers remain in the grip of supernatural phenomena to the end and ambiguity is sustained as to the origin of these phenomena. Are they mere projections of a diseased mind, or actual manifestations of supernature, or both? Anyhow, the stories are open-ended and tension remains. No order or balance is re-established and this is, of course, a major distinction linked with the transformation and modernisation of Gothic motifs and of the Gothic world outlook.

For the relative timelessness of the Gothic, Campbell substitutes the regulated routine of life in an urban environment which in his case borrows its features from present day Liverpool. Campbell, as Lovecraft did with Arkham, creates Brichester, a fictional and mythical double of Liverpool, which becomes a backcloth for many of his stories. One feature of this setting is its anchoring in a drab, gloomy reality, which is again very different from the stylisation of the Gothic. Campbell describes suburban areas with a lot of accurate details concerning topography, itineraries, buildings, objects, people encountered, all of these sustaining referential illusion. We don't need the 'suspension of disbelief' to adhere to his stories because they present familiar elements: the tedium of daily life, the alienation caused by too much noise, too much light, too much promiscuity, the dirt and squalor inherent to city life.

Hence the development of modernised *loci* for horror and terror such as the street which is of paramount importance because it is a path enabling the protagonist to go beyond familiar boundaries and also because its anonymity is fraught with potentialities (another key word for

Campbell as in the story titled 'Potential'), usually associated with evil, supernatural encounters. There are more specific places: warehouses and waste-grounds but also, more interestingly, telephone booths, cinemas, fairgrounds, highways, underground markets; all the staples of modern activity including offices and hotels. In *Down Under*, a secretary is assaulted by entities reminiscent of Lovecraft but which seem to be generated by the squalid and routine-like activities of the office where she works. We could also note the emphasis on means of transport (scenes often taking place on buses or trains), illustrating one of the writer's major ideas, that the fantastic is not necessarily associated with night and isolation (as testifies the title of one of his collection of essays, *Demons by Daylight*). In fact Campbell manages to trace the uncanny in the familiar and his device of using a lot of 'realist operators' is all the more efficient because the reader believes it could happen anywhere – and why not to himself? – since he also uses telephone booths, rides on buses, frequents book shops and cinemas and works in offices, factories, and warehouses.

This anchoring in 'modernity' in terms of setting is reinforced by the introduction of situations, activities, habits that characterise actual life in urban environments. Characters in Campbell's stories are not isolated or idle. They have a job, either outside or at home, or at least social activities. Some are writers, artists, the children go to school and to the playground. People go shopping, drink in pubs, meet friends. They often walk a lot, explore the urban network of streets, sometimes beyond known boundaries. They are not, in general ('Napier Court' may be an exception) restricted to purely mental activity even though there is an obvious interaction between mental processes and external happenings as in *Ash* where the protagonist is gradually driven to insanity by the recurring and inexplicable falling of ashes.

To these familiar elements are often added the specific features of the counter-culture of the seventies in England. Many stories are set in the youth milieu and refer to the youth culture based on rock music and drugs, films and comic strips, and concerned with the occult, extrasensory perceptions, and altered states of consciousness, but also attracted towards community life and spiritual experiences. Together with this comes also an emphasis on sex, either explicitly, as in *Scared Stiff*, where such problems as sexual perversion or impotence are clearly illustrated; or, in numerous stories more implicitly, homosexuality in 'The Telephones' for example, or sexual repression and frustration in 'Napier Court'.

Another important contribution of modernity is the omnipresence of the mass media. One cannot overestimate the role played by news headlines (sometimes used as a device of narrative dislocation or fragmentation) referring to bloody crimes, fits of insanity, satanic rites, suicide, etc. –

which reinforces the latent paranoid leanings of the characters – but also by book or magazine covers, cinema posters, fragments of radio broadcasts, television images, all conveying an overpowering sense of threat and disruption. The underlying idea is that violence is now commonplace, part of the prevailing mood, and that it is always present in front of our eyes or in our minds. Simply, Campbell's stories actualise what is already there, potentially in our life. Instead of being an exceptional circumstance, it has become the norm. This approach marks also a very important departure from the Gothic outlook based on the idea of transgression and subsequent retribution. Contrary to this, Campbell's world is basically amoral. Quoting Angela Carter who suggests that the horror story becomes a 'holiday from morality', Campbell himself admits that the idea of supernatural evil can be used as an alibi for horrors human beings could perpetrate themselves.[6] Some stories are even endowed with a subversive quality that Rosemary Jackson would appreciate as she considers it as a necessary feature of the genre.

This change in world outlook is also testified to by the transformation of the characters who cease to represent a Manichean view of the universe. There is often no clear cut distinction between 'good' and 'evil' characters. Chris Kelley is both a monster and a victimised adolescent. The tramp in *Baby* is the ruthless murderer of an old, helpless (and possibly pregnant) woman but also a victim of this same woman or rather her 'familiar' since she proves eventually to be a witch (the witch motif is the only conventional motif that is often used by Campbell for example also in 'The Trick'). Most characters, Campbell seems to say, (and this is a fundamentally pessimistic creed) have a potential for evil that they will tend to develop. Even children can be murderers in fancy or act. This is illustrated in 'Macintosh Willy' and more terrifyingly in 'Potential' where a young student is led under the influence of drugs to become a criminal, and thus to benefit from the worship of the group and be recognised as a potential leader. This ambivalence is also expressed in the motif of the double used in 'The Scar', where a peaceful shopkeeper happily married with two children, proves to have a maniacal murderous double, a projection of his own repressed sadistic tendencies. Moreover, the wife's brother, who has discovered the truth, also develops a potentially evil double at the end, inititiating a kind of unending cycle. Thus Gothic heroines are no longer pure nor innocent and heroes can quickly turn into villains, or housewives develop criminal impulses as in 'Horror House of Blood' where the shooting of some fictitious but impressive 'gore' scenes in a flat used as film set, triggers actual and irrepressible violent instincts.

The same ambiguity is sustained in terms of discourse since we never precisely know what is real and what is unreal. There is, for instance, no strict demarcation between the dream sequences and the so-called reality. Within a single paragraph, one jumps from one level to another, as for instance in 'Napier Court', or 'The Depths', the story of a writer harassed and traumatised by the fictional images generated by his own imagination. The real is derealised by various devices and the oneiric world tends to acquire more substance than the everyday reality. Campbell thus builds up a fictional universe where the relationships between parents and children are consistently degraded, where the couple disintegrates under the pressure of external phenomena which can also be interpreted as projections of internal conflicts. The relatively high proportion of child characters, either victimised or victimising, may appear a provocative choice, but it can also be related to the writer's own predicament as suggested in the preface to *The Face That Must Die*. The originality of Campbell's approach to the fantastic lies also in the way he emphasises characters' altered and distorted perceptions. The attitude of the protagonists is gradually affected by the environment or by their own subconscious drives and they are led to compulsive, phobic behaviour patterns, while they lose touch with concrete, human reality. This obsessional quality (reminiscent of Poe) which can be found in most of his tales is also perfectly conveyed by certain devices at the level of style.

The external environment is consistently seen as hostile, potentially agressive and dangerous. Natural elements partake of this as well as man-made ones, often residues of the consumer society. We could give numerous examples: 'grass blades whipped the air like razors' . . . 'the sunlight seemed violent and pitiless, vampirising the landscape' . . . 'Trees beside the road were giant scarecrows brandishing tattered foliage . . .'[7] Among other devices, Campbell has indeed recourse to a rather conventional pathetic fallacy as in: 'buildings glared like blocks of salt'. But he does use also more original and provocative images to suggest modern paranoia: 'children were heaped in the back seats scrambling over each other like a nest of spiders'.[8] At times, he uses unexpected and forceful associations as in the portrait of the witch character in 'The Trick': 'the mouth was a thin bloodless slit full of teeth . . . the eyes seemed to have congealed around hatred'.[9] Here, the dominant feeling determines physical appearence and becomes a material, almost palpable element. In 'The Depths' he also inverts the two elements of a comparison, suggesting the primacy of the fantastic feature: 'on the roof of a pub extension gargoyles began barking for they were dogs'.[10] Far from being verbose like King's or baroque like Lovecraft's, Ramsay Campbell's style is remarkably terse and economic, as for example in: 'birds swooped, shrieking knives with wings', where analogy suggests exaggerated, distorted perceptions. The use of metonymy also illustrates this feature of his style in a sentence where a knife is reduced to the glint of the blade: 'the glints in their hands were sharp'.[11]

All these devices contribute to emphasise what we may call a paranoid rather than schizoid vision of the world. One of the best illustrations of this is most certainly 'Litter' which develops a very convincing metaphor of modern alienation. The following passages suggest the monstrous metamorphosis of trivial elements as seen through a possibly (though nothing is asserted) unbalanced mind: that of the I narrator who is passing through a new underground market made of plastic, tiles, and glass which replaces the old street market. Down there, in the windswept halls, mere plastic bags become 'small white shapes scurrying, somersaulting and hopping agressively'. A conglomerate of rubbish turns into a multi-coloured mass that shifts and crawls, but more frighteningly is seen as a limbless, mindless embryo, then a hulking creature, a composite and anthropomorphised monster whose lungs are paperbags, and for which cash receipts serve as tendrils:

> A few empty milk cartons clattered into sight, pale water dripping from their torn mouths. Some sodden newspapers flapped dismally at the corners of the pillars, detaching themselves at last and falling to the tiles to flutter feebly like dying birds. A couple of magazines lay face down in dirty pools, trying to raise themselves . . . Then cardboard boxes began to lumber into view, tumbling and rolling on their distorted edges, and a wind buffeted me from all four sides; an odd wind. All of a sudden I found myself cut off on three fronts, and the litter waiting, flapping and clattering nervously.[12]

We could give numerous other examples of this paranoid view which leads to the alteration of perceptions and to the distortion of commonplace elements, and which is conveyed by descriptive devices far more suggestive to my mind than the mere traditional evocation of 'monsters' with claws or tentacles. Sometimes also, horror stems from deeper recesses of man's psyche, as in 'The Depths' where, as the title suggests, is emphasised the dangerous quality of the imaginative function when it plays with the boundaries of rationality. This motif of the writer as 'witch apprentice' is developed in several stories where the protagonist is a writer or an artist unleashing uncontrollable forces, those that are generated by his own creative ability, and we can see here a notion of reflexivity (the writer reflecting on his own status and predicament) which could be associated with a postmodern approach in literature. This is strikingly illustrated in 'The Change' where the main protagonist, a writer of horror stories, sees his own familiar environment turn into a nightmare while he also suffers from a crisis of inspiration. The catalysing element

is a new street lamp shedding a bluish light over everything. The setting and the people undergo a gradual and subtle transformation: the
neighbouring streets have 'an unnatural stillness', the pavement is seen
as 'oppressively close' while human beings look increasingly deformed,
with discoloured, plastic, or puttylike faces: 'Their heads were out of
proportion, or their faces lopsided; their dangling hands looked swollen
and clumsy.'[13] At first, the writer manages to provide a rational explanation: 'the clinical light simply emphasised imperfections, or his eyes were
tired', but soon, the irrational takes over. Transformation then affects his
own house, which is steeped in deadly bluish light. The writer becomes
estranged from his wife, refuses to communicate with her and more and
more loses touch with the external world. He ends up fighting with a
creature who looks like a 'luminous dead mask' which leaps at him with
its claws. The end of the story implies that the creature could be his wife
as perceived through his diseased perceptions and consciousness while he
himself loses all sense of identity: 'As he looked, he became less and less
sure of what he was seeing. As to who was seeing it, he had no idea at
all.'[14] The bluish light radiating from the street lamp can here be seen as
the concrete agent of the transformation, but it can also be interpreted as
a metaphor representing the imaginative force which animates the writer
and which may lead him to insanity if it is not kept under control. In this
story, the writer fails to express himself through his art while familiar
reality becomes uncanny and nightmarish. Writing can then be seen as
a cathartic operation which enables the writer to channel the imaginary
as it encroaches upon everyday reality and threatens to destroy the individual's mental balance.

The concept of 'urban Gothic' as applied to Ramsay Campbell is
thus more interesting if we restrict the word 'Gothic' to its historical
acceptation. If we choose a broader meaning, it may apply to any work
dealing with supernatural elements in a city environment, which is far
from exceptional in fantastic literature. Reference to the Victorian Gothic
helps us seek a filiation between Campbell and a certain literary tradition
which is not limited to the eighteenth- or early-nineteenth-century Gothic
since Campbell uses strategies reminiscent of M. R. James, Sheridan Le
Fanu, and more contemporary writers such as Robert Aickman and Shirley
Jackson.

The relative originality of Campbell lies first in the transformation
of conventions, then in the interaction between the various features of
the narrative (setting, action, psychology, dreams, phantasms) and more
precisely in the subtle blending of interiority and exteriority. More specifically, Campbell's works lead us to reconsider a distinction that has
been made[15] between a disjunctive 'schizophrenic' literature that would be

labelled fantastic, implying a dislocation of the psyche: split personality but also de-realisation, disconnectedness, allusive and elusive meanings; and a conjunctive 'paranoid' literature, aiming at a totalising, all-interpreting approach that tends to be more associated with science fiction, especially when written by Philip K. Dick or J. G. Ballard. By being *both* schizophrenic and paranoid, Campbell's fiction shows that fantastic literature is not limited to some aspects of the human psyche, that it can encompass and transpose at an imaginative level the whole spectrum of reality while reflecting the diseases of the modern world. We could deplore, with Gary William Crawford, the inability of Campbell to conjure up a sense of the sublime, as classic Gothic writers could do in their best achievements, but maybe this endeavour would be vain and irrelevant in the context of an alienated society where such emotions and aesthetic values have become meaningless.

Notes

1 *Scared Stiff* (Macdonalds: London, 1987), includes 'Lillith's' and 'Napier Court', discussed in this Chapter.
2 *The Doll Who Ate His Mother* (New York, 1976); *The Face That Must Die* (New York, 1979).
3 G. W. Crawford, *Ramsay Campbell* (Starmont Reader's Guide 48, 1988).
4 Maurice Levy discusses these issues in his article 'Heurs et malheurs d'un mot: "Gothique", critiques et sémantique', in *Du vebe au geste: mélanges en l'honneur de Pierre Danchin* (P. U. Nancy, 1986).
5 R. Jackson, *Fantasy: The Literature of Subversion* (New Accents, Methuen: London, 1981).
6 See his Introduction to *Dark Feasts* (Robinson Publishing: London, 1987). *Dark Feasts* reprints 'Macintosh Willy', 'The Man in the Underpass', 'The Room in the Castle', 'Horror House of Blood', 'Call First', 'The Chimney', 'The Hands', 'The Scar', 'The End of a Summer's Day', amongst others.
7 'The Depths' in *Dark Companions* (Fontana Paper Backs: London, 1982), pp. 87, 88.
8 'The Telephones' in *The Height of the Scream* (Star Editions: London, 1981), p. 177.
9 'The Trick' in *Dark Companions*, p. 142.
10 'The Depths' in *Dark Companions*, p. 74.
11 *Ibid.*, p. 93.
12 'Litter' in *Dark Companions*, p. 132.
13 'The Change' in *Dark Companions*, p. 175.
14 *Ibid.*, p. 183.
15 J. Raynaud, *Fantastique et Science-Fiction: essai de différenciation*, in *Cahiers du CERLI* (1982).

INDEX

Page numbers in **bold** indicate the main reference to a subject.